DISCARDED

D1252812

IRELAND

from the

Flight of the Earls

to

Grattan's Parliament

beaṫa an sṫaraiḋe ḟirinne

"Truth is the Life of History"

From the drawing by Sir Frederick Burton in "Leabhar na gCeart" ("The Book of Rights"), a Tenth Century Gaelic manuscript, first printed in 1847.

Preface

THIS volume is one of a series of three Documentary Records illustrating Irish history as seen and described by contemporary witnesses and participants. I have endeavoured from an immense mass of undigested material to arrange a consecutive narrative. The aim has been to provide a book, not only useful to the student of history, but interesting to the general reader—and also, it is to be hoped, reasonably fair to the conflicting parties which have contributed to the troubled but fascinating story of Ireland.

Together with eye-witnesses' accounts of parliaments, speeches, conferences and military campaigns, there are numerous surveys of Ireland as it was seen by " old " and " new " Irishmen, by Catholics and Protestants, by foreign travellers—neutral, friendly or hostile—by planters, surveyors, or special correspondents. Some of the observers quoted wrote with detached curiosity, some with angry prejudice, heightened by envy and greed, others, like the exile who saw Ireland only in his dreams, through eyes dazzled with love. Selections have been given from the statements of prominent political figures, from Government proclamations and rebel proclamations, from the reports of official Commissioners, from the fabrications of rogues and forgers, and from the dying speeches of heroes and martyrs.

Many important phases of Irish history are very briefly illustrated in these volumes. The economic and technical difficulties attending the publication of a work so ambitious as this in recent years may reasonably be invoked to excuse some of its imperfections. I have had to reject or to abbreviate many passages rich in human and historical interest. It is hoped, however, that the series does give a varied, lively and continuous picture of Irish history. J. J. O'Leary, Chairman of C. J. Fallons, has met my suggestions generously, and indeed, I do not think that any writer could have worked under more friendly and helpful auspices. With his encouragement I have sought out and included a great number and variety of illustrations, many of which have not appeared in book form before now.

I have endeavoured to arrange these records of a tangled story in such a way that they may be readily followed by readers who have not access to specialised studies of Irish history. The notes are intended to be purely explanatory, but I have occasionally attempted to summarise events during periods of exceptional disintegration and change. " Irish history," as Lecky says, " is marked by obscure agrarian and social changes, and sometimes very perplexing alterations in the popular sentiment which can only be elucidated by copious illustrations."

JAMES CARTY.

Victoire Remportée par Le Roy Guillaume III
Designé aprés la Nature et paint

Portion of a contemporary drawing which shows in one lar
prepared from the sketches and descriptions of eye-witnesses.

Irlandoise a la Riuiere de Boyne en Irlande le 1er Iuillet 169...
...y, et Gravé par Theodor Maas.

...he entire battlefield of the Boyne.   It is said to have been
...Cooper at ye 3 Pidgeons in Bedford St."

Acknowledgments

THANKS are due to the following for permission to quote passages or to reproduce illustrations used in this volume:

To the Talbot Press, Dublin, for Padraic Pearse's version of *Mo Bheannacht leat, a Scríbhinn* and Thomas MacDonagh's of *Eamon an Chnuic*; to Dr. George O'Brien and the Librarian, Trinity College, Dublin, for the quotation from *Advertisements of Ireland* (1623); to Mr. Frank O'Connor and Messrs. Macmillan and Co., for the lines from *Kilcash* and *Valentine Brown*; to the late Dr. Robin Flower and to Messrs. Constable and Co., for the lament on the Flight of the Earls (*Anocht is uaigneach Eire*); to the Catholic Record Society, Maynooth College, for the late Dr. Paul Walsh's translation of Tadhg Ó Cianáin's account of the Earls' arrival in Rome; to the Earl of Belmore, for the selection from his father's Social Notes on the Ulster Plantation, published in the *Ulster Archæological Journal*, 1894; to the Rev. Father Guardian, Franciscan Friary, Merchant's Quay, Dublin, for the facsimile of a page from the *Annals of the Four Masters* in the handwriting of Brother Michael O'Cleirigh; to Rev. Father Dargan, S.J., Rector, Clongowes Wood College, for the quotations from a manuscript *History of the War in Ireland, 1641–1653 by a British Officer*, in the College Library; to Dr. W. C. Abbott and the President of Harvard University for the note to Cromwell's campaign in Ireland; to the Trustees of the National Library of Ireland for Cromwell's proclamation against looting; for the reproductions of Irish devotional works printed in Louvain and Paris; and for the extract from the manuscript known as *A Light to the Blind*; to Dr. D. A. Chart, ex-Deputy-Keeper of the Record Office, Northern Ireland, and the Representative Body of the Church of Ireland, for the lines from the *History of the Church of Ireland*, Vol. II; to Mr. Arland Ussher for the quotation from his translation of Merriman's *Cúirt an Mheadhon Oidhche*; to Mr. Padraic Colum for his poem, "The Old College of the Irish, Paris"; to Messrs. Longmans Green, for the extract from W. E. H. Lecky; to the Editor of the *Journal of the Royal United Services Institute*, for the paragraphs from an article by the late Sir Charles Oman; to Messrs. McCaw, Stevenson & Orr for permission to use extract from the Rev. G. Hill's *Plantation of Ulster*.

Every care has been taken to seek and obtain permission for the use of literary passages and pictorial representations which may be copyright. The publishers are grateful for the cordial co-operation with which their requests for such permission have been met. If, however, any copyright material has been included inadvertently, they ask the indulgence of the authors, publishers, or institutions concerned.

Contents

	PAGE
PUBLISHER'S NOTE	V
PREFACE	VII
ACKNOWLEDGMENTS	X
INTRODUCTION	XIII
CHRONICLE OF EVENTS	XIV
COUNTRY AND PEOPLE IN THE XVII CENTURY	1
THE FLIGHT OF THE EARLS	28
THE ULSTER PLANTATION	38
THE CONFEDERATION OF KILKENNY	54
THE CROMWELLIAN SETTLEMENT	67
THE BOYNE AND LIMERICK	79
COUNTRY AND PEOPLE IN THE XVIII CENTURY	101
THE PENAL TIMES	133
STATE AND PARLIAMENT	149
THE IRISH OVERSEAS	172
INDEX	190

ST. PATRICK'S PURGATORY IN IRELAND

This is the frontispiece to " Vie et purgatorie du St. Patrice," published at Brussels in 1659. Originally written in Spanish, it was afterwards translated into French and reprinted several times in both languages.

Introduction

MODERN Ireland begins with the Seventeenth Century. The older Ireland suffered a decisive defeat in 1601. Spain, then the greatest imperial power in the world, had sent a small expedition to Munster to aid the Irish resistance movement against the English conquest. The expedition was of little more than token value, and it landed in the South, where the Irish forces were disorganised, and not in the North, where they were strong. O'Neill, O'Donnell, and their Spanish ally, Don Juan del Aquila, were defeated by Queen Elizabeth's Deputy, Lord Mountjoy, at the Battle of Kinsale (1601).

When King James VI of Scotland became King of England in 1603, Scotland and Ireland, although still separate kingdoms—Scotland until 1707 and Ireland until 1800—lost much of their independent character. For the first time, all Ireland came under the effective rule of the British crown. Ulster, hitherto the most completely Gaelic of the Irish provinces, the most obstinate in its resistance to English rule, was left defenceless by the flight to the Continent of its two great princes. The modern Ulster problem began.

This volume, IRELAND FROM THE FLIGHT OF THE EARLS TO GRATTAN'S PARLIAMENT (1607–1782), begins with the mysterious and tragic Flight of the Earls, and goes on to the sequel to that episode—the Ulster Plantation; then to "The War of the Three Kingdoms" (Ireland, England and Scotland); the Confederation of Kilkenny; the Cromwellian Settlement; the Wars of William and James; the Penal Times; the progress of the Irish Parliament from complete subservience to legislative independence. A chapter has been added on the Irish exiles overseas. The illustrations include early maps and plans of provinces and towns and of the new settlements in Ulster; facsimiles of Gaelic books of devotion printed abroad; contemporary prints of the battles of the Boyne and Limerick; early pictures of the Irish Parliament; portraits and proclamations.

IRELAND FROM GRATTAN'S PARLIAMENT TO THE GREAT FAMINE (1783–1850), the next volume in the series of Documentary Records, takes up the story where this volume leaves off, and continues it to the middle of the 19th Century.

IRELAND FROM THE GREAT FAMINE TO THE TREATY (1851–1921), brings the series down to a time within living memory.

Chronicle of Events

1601 - Battle of Kinsale. Defeat of Irish and Spanish by Queen Elizabeth's Deputy, Lord Mountjoy.

1603 - Submission of Hugh O'Neill to Mountjoy. End of the Nine Years' War.

1607 - Flight of the Earls.

1611 - Beginning of the Ulster Plantation.

1613–5 - Irish Parliament of James I.

1632–6 - Annals of the Kingdom of Ireland (" The Four Masters ").

1633–40 - Wentworth (Earl of Strafford's) rule of " Thorough."

1641 - The Rising in Ulster begins the " War of the Three Kingdoms."

1642–52 - The Confederation of Kilkenny.

1645 - Rinuccini, Archbishop of Fermo, arrives as Papal Nuncio to the Confederation.

1646 - Eoghan Ruadh O'Neill's victory at Benburb.

1649 - Ormond defeated at Rathmines, " that fatal rout that lost all Ireland."

1649 - Cromwell in Ireland. Sack of Drogheda and Wexford.

- Death of Eoghan Ruadh O'Neill.

1653 - The Cromwellian Settlement.

1664 - Act of Explanation—Cromwellian Settlement upheld.

1672 - Sir William Petty estimates the population of Ireland at 1,100,000.

1681 Execution of Blessed Oliver Plunket at Tyburn.

1689 - King James II's Irish Parliament.

- Siege and Relief of Derry.

1690 - Battle of the Boyne.

1691 - Battle of Aughrim.

- Treaty of Limerick.

1695   -   Penal Laws : First set passed by the Irish Parliament of William III. No Irish Catholic in Parliament until 1829.

1698   -   The Williamite Parliament refuses to ratify the Treaty of Limerick.

       -   English Act of Parliament destroys the Irish Woollen trade.

1704-15 -   Further group of Penal Laws against Catholics.

1719   -   " Sixth of George I." English Parliament enacts that Irish Parliament is subordinate to and dependent upon England.

1724   -   Swift's *Drapier Letters*.

1726   -   Death of Aodhagan O Rathaille.

1735   -   Bishop Berkeley's *Querist*.

1739-40 -   First great Potato Famine. Number of deaths estimated at 400,000.

1757   -   Catholic Committee for relief against Penal Laws formed.

1761-2 -   Agrarian disturbances general. Whiteboys very active in Munster and Oakboys in Ulster.

1771   -   Irish emigration to America (especially from Ulster) at its height.

1777   -   Irish Volunteers—established to defend the country against French invasion—soon become a powerful weapon for Irish interests.

1778   -   First Catholic Relief Bill. (Catholics enabled to hold leases.)

1780   -   Restrictions on Irish trade removed.

1782   -   Second Catholic Relief Bill. (Catholics enabled to buy freeholds and teach schools.)

       -   The Dungannon Convention of Irish Volunteers demands legislative Independence and rejoices at the relaxation of the Penal Laws " against our Roman Catholic fellow-subjects."

       -   Legislative independence demanded by Irish Parliament and accepted by British Parliament, which repeals the " Sixth of George I."

Mo ḃeannaċt leat, a sċríḃinn

Mo ḃeannaċt leat, a sċríḃinn
Go hInis aoiḃinn Ealga
Truaġ naċ léir ḋam a beanna
Ġiḋ gnáṫ a ceanna ḋearga.

Slán ḋá huaisle is ḋá hoireaċt,
Slán go roi-ḃeaċt ḋá cléirċiḃ,
Slán ḋá ḃantraċtaiḃ caoine,
Slán ḋá saoiṫiḃ re héigse.

Mo ṡlán ḋá máġaiḃ míne,
Slán ḟá míle ḋá cnocaiḃ;
Moċean ḋon tí tá innti
Slán ḋá linntiḃ 's ḋá loċaiḃ.

Slán ḋá coilltiḃ ḟá ċorċaiḃ,
Slán ḟós ḋá corċaiḃ iascaiġ,
Slán ḋá móintiḃ 's ḋá ḃántaiḃ,
Slán ḋá ráṫaiḃ 's ḋá riascaiḃ.

—Seaṫrún Céitinn.

* * * *

MY BLESSING WITH THEE, WRITING

My blessing with thee, writing,
To the delightful isle of Erin.
Alas, that I see not her hill-tops,
Tho' frequent blaze their beacons !

Farewell to her princes and people,
A fond farewell to her clerics,
Farewell to her gentle women,
Farewell to her learned in letters !

Farewell to her level plains,
A thousand farewells to her hills,
All hail to him that dwelleth there,
Farewell to her pools and lakes !

Farewell to her fruit-bearing forests,
Farewell to her fishing weirs,
Farewell to her bogs and leas,
Farewell to her raths and moors !

—*Translated by* Padraic Pearse.

2

JUSTICE LUKE GERNON (1620)

IRELAND is at all poynts like a young wench that hath a green sicknes ... She is very fayre of visage, and hath a smooth skinn of tender grasse. Indeed she is somewhat freckled (as the Irish are) some partes darker than others. Her flesh is of a softe and delicate mould of earth, and her blew vaynes trayling through every part of her like rivulets. She hath one master vayne called the Shannon, which passeth quite through her, and if it were not for one knot (one mayne rock) it were navigable from head to foot. She hath three other vaynes called the sisters—the Suir, the Nore and the Barrow which, rising at one spring, trayle through her middle parts and joyne together in their going out.

Her bones are of polished marble, the grey marble, the black, the redd and the speckled, so fayre for building that their houses shew like colledges, and being polished, is most rarely embelished. Her breasts are round hillockes of milk-yielding grasse, and that so fertile, that they contend with the vallyes . . . Of complexion she is very temperate, never too hott, nor too could, and hath a sweet breath of favonian winde.

She is of a gentle nature. If the anger of heaven be agaynst her, she will not bluster and storme, but she will weep many days together, and (alas) this last summer she did so water her plants, that the grass and blade was so bedewed, that it became unprofitable, and threatens a scarcity. Neyther is she frosenharted, the last frost was not so extreame here as it was reported to be in England. . . .

How shall I describe her towns, her people, her flocks? . . . Dublin is the most frequented, more for conveniency than for majesty. There resides the Deputy and the Council. . . . The buildings are of timber and of the English form, and it is resembled to Bristol, but falleth short. The circuit of the Castle is a huge and mighty wall four-square, and of incredible thickness, built by King John, within it are many fayre buildings, and there the Deputy keeps his court. There are two cathedrals under one Archbishop, St. Patrick's and Christchurch. St. Patrick's is more vast and ancient, the other is in better repayre.

You will expect to know the state of our State. It is not very magnificent, nor to be disregarded. There is a presence where they stand at all times uncovered, and a cloth of State under which the Deputy sitteth. When that he sitteth at meat, there sit of men of quality as many as the table will contayne. When he goeth abroad in solemn manner, all whom it concerns do attend him. Before him go the gentlemen, captynes, knights, and officers, all on foot. Then cometh the Deputy riding in state, and before him a knight bareheaded carrying the sword. After the Deputy, the nobles, the Council, and the Judges all in foot-clothes. His guard consists of fifty tall men, they wear not red coates, but soldier's cassocks, and halberts in theyr hands. On principal festivals, the herald goes before him in a coat of arms. So much of Dublin I may call it her Whyte hall. Let us take our journey to Waterford.

3

Waterford is situated upon the best harbour, and in a pleasant and temperate ayre. The buildings are of English form and well compact. There is a fayre cathedral, but her beauty is in the quay, for the wall of the towne extending for near half a mile along the water, between that and the water, there is a broad quay maynly fortifyed with stone and strong piles of timber, where a ship of the burden of 1,000 tons may ride at anchor. It was famous for merchandise, but her high stomack in disobeying the State deprived her of her Magistrate, and now she is in the government of a soldier.

Lymericke divides itself into two parts, the high town, which is compassed with the Shannon, and the base town, and in form it doth perforth resemble an hour glass, being bound together by that bridge which divides the two parts. A philosopher that saw a little town with wide open gate, gave warning to the citizens to shut up their gate lest the town should run out. The founders of this city were more considerate, for they have fenced the base town with such a huge strong wall that travellers affirm they have not seen the like in Europe. It is a mile in compass, and three men abreast may walk the round.

But that which is most notorious to my judgment is the quay wall. This wall is extended from the town wall into the middle of the river, and was made for a defence and harbor for the shipping. It is in length about 200 paces, and it is a double wall. In the bottom it is a mayne thickness, and so continueth until it be raysed above high water. Then there is within it a long gallery arched over head, and with windows most pleasant to walk in, and above that a terrace to walk upon with fayre battlements, at the end of it there is a round tower with two or three chambers, one above the other, and a battlement above.

Kilkenny is an inland town situate in a pleasant valley, and upon a fresh river. It is praised for the wholsome air, and delightful orchards and gardens, which are somewhat rare in Ireland. The houses are of grey marble fayrely built, the fronts of theyr houses are supported (most of them) with pillars, or arches under which there is an open pavement to walk on. At one end of the town is a large cathedral, at the other end, a high mounted Castle appertaining to the Earls of Ormond, but now it is allotted to the portion of the Countesse of Desmond.

The Derry, and Colrane are of the new plantation in the North, they are reported to be fayrely built, but they are like new palaces. They are not slated nor the flowers laid yet; let them alone till they be finished. . . .

In this peregrination you have viewed the country in passing, the villages are distant each from other about two miles. In every village is a castle and a church, but bothe in ruin. The baser cottages are built of underwood, called wattle, and covered, some with thatch and some with green sedge, of a round form and without chimneys, and to my imagination resemble so many hives of bees, about a country farm. In the end of harvest the villages seem as big again as in the spring, their corn being brought into their haggards, and laid up in round cocks, in form of their houses. And, by the way, there is no meat so daynty as a haggard pig, a pig that hath been fed at the reek, take him at a quarter old, and use him like a roasting pig; because his bigness should not be offensive, they serve him up by quarters.

Here I would conclude with our buildings, but when I look about I cannot but bewail the desolation which civil rebellion hath procured. It looks like the later end of a feast. Here lieth an old ruined castle like the remainder of a venison pasty, there a broken fort like a minced pie half subjected, and in another place an old abbey with some turrets standing like a carcase of a goose broken up. It makes me remember the old proverb—It is better to come to the end of a feast, than the beginning of a fray. But I have held you too long among this rubbish.

Let us converse with the people. Lord, what makes you so squeamish? Be not afraid. The Irishman is no Cannibal to eat you up, nor no lowsy Jack to offend you.

The man of Ireland is of a strong constitution, tall and big-limbed, but seldom fat, patient of heat and cold, but impatient of labour. Of nature he is prompt and ingenious, but servile, crafty and inquisitive after news, the symptoms of a conquered nation. Their speech hath been accused to be a whining language, but that is among the beggars. I take it to be a smooth language well comixt of vowels and of consonants and hath a pleasing cadence.

This is the earliest printed map of Dublin. It was first published in John Speed's " Theatre of the Empire of Great Britain" (London, 1611). Speed wrote of Dublin: " This the is royall seat of Ireland, strong in her munition, beautifull in her buildings, and (for the quantitie) matchable to many other Cities, frequent for traficke and intercourse of merchants."

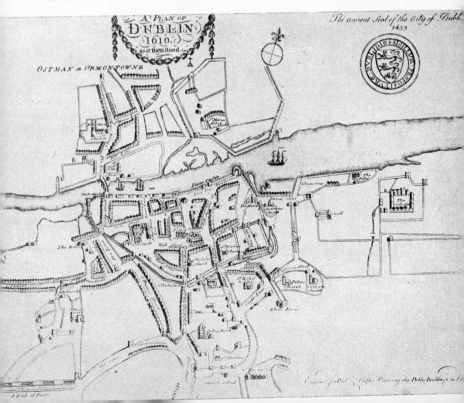

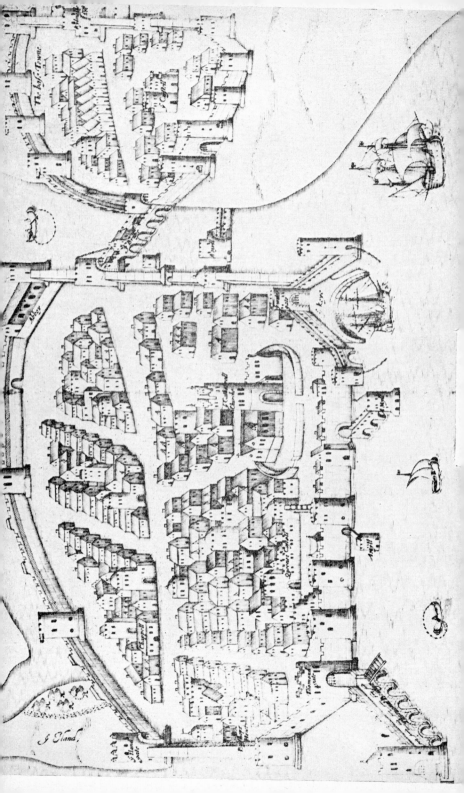

The better sort are apparelled at all points like the English only they retain their mantle, which is a garment not indecent. It differs nothing from a long cloak, but in the fringe at the upper end, which in could weather they wear over their heads for warmth. Because they are commanded at publick assemblyes to come in English habit, they have a trick agaynst those times, to take off the fringe and to put on a' cape, and after the assembly past, to resume it agayne. His brogues are single-soled, more rudely sewed than a shoo but more strong, sharp at the toe, and a flap of leather left at the heels to pull them on. His hat is a frieze cap close to the head with two lappetts, to button under his chinne. And for his weapon he wears a skeyne which is a knife of three fingers broad, of the length of a dagger and sharpening towards the point with a rude wooden handle. The ordinary kerne seldom wears a sword. They are also wedded to theyr mantle, they plow, they ditch, they thresh with theyr mantles on. But you look after the wenches.

The women of Ireland are very comely creatures, tall, slender and upright. Of complexion very fayre and cleare-skinned (but freckled) with tresses of bright yellow hayre, which they chain up in curious knots and devises. They are not strait-laced nor plated in their youth, but suffered to grow at liberty so that you shall hardly see one crooked or deformed. . . . I never saw fayrer wenches nor fowler calliots, so we call the old women. Of nature they are very kind and tractable.

Luke Gernon, from whose lively "Discourse" this account of Irish geography, cities and people is taken, was second Justice of Munster, residing at Limerick in 1620. The full text is preserved among the Stowe Papers in the British Museum.

The Civill Irish Woman   *The Civill Irish man*

FROM SPEED'S MAP OF IRELAND (1610)

Seatrún Céitinn (1632)

Cibé duine 'san mbiat cuireas roime Seancus no Sinnsearóact críce ar biot do leanmain no do lorgaireact, is eaó óligeas cinneaó ar an slige is soiléire noctas fírinne stáirde na críce, agus dáil na fóirne áitigeas í, do cur go soléir síos: agus do bríg gur gabas réim' ais foras feasa ar Éirinn d'faisnéis, do measas ar dtúis cuid dá leattrom agus d'á h-eugcomlann d'eugnac; agus go h-áirite an t-eugcomtrom atá ag a óéanam ar a h-áitigteoirib, mar atáid na Sean-Gaill atá 'na seilb tuilleaó agus ceitre céad bliaóan ó gabáltas Gall i leit, mar aon le Gaeóealaib atá 'na seilb (beagnac) re trí míle bliaóan. Óir ní fuil stáairde o soin i leit dá scríobann uirre nác ag iarraió locta agus toibéime do tabairt do Sean-Gallaib agus do Gaeóealaib bíb.

Bíoó a fiaónaise sin ar an dteist dobeir Cambrens, Spenser, Stanihurst, Hanmer, Camden, Barclaí, Morison, Davis, Campion, agus gac Nua-Gall eile dá scríobann uirre ó soin amac, ionnus gur b'é nós, beagnac, an priompiollán doghnib, ag scríobaó ar Éireanncaib. Is eaó, iomorro, is nós do'n priompiollán, an tan tógbas a ceann i san samraó, beit ar foluamain ag imteact, agus gan cromaó ar mion-scoit, d'á mbi san macaire, nó ar blát dá mbi i lubgort, gémaó rós no líle uile iad, act beit ar fuaidreaó go dteagmann bualtrac bó nó otrac capaill ris, go dtéid d'á unfairt féin ionnta.

Mar sin do'n droing tuas; ni cromaó ar súailcib nó ar soibeusaib na n-uasal do Sean-Gallaib agus do Gaeóealaib do bí ag áitiúgaó Éirinn re na linn do rinneadar, mar atá scríobaó ar a gcróóact agus ar a gcrabaó, ar ar togadar do mainistreacaib, agus ar a dtugadar d'fearann agus d'fódaib re h-altóir óóib; ar ar bronnadar do tearmannaib d'ollamnaib Éireann, agus ar gac cábas dá dtugsaó do pearsannaib agus do preulároib eaglaise: ar gac comall síota dá dtugsaois d'á n-ollamnaib, agus ar gac cotugaó do boctaib agus dó óilleactaib; ar gac bronntanas dá dtugdaois d'éigsib agus do lutc iarratais, agus ar méid a n-einig d'aoióeaóaib, ionnus nac féadar go fírinneac a ráó go raibe lutc a sár-uigte i bféile 'san Coraip riam do réir a gcumas féin i gcomaimsir óóib,

GLEN

*Geoffrey Keating (1570–1650 ?) was
time in hiding in the Glen of Aherlow,*

Ʒṙöeaṫ ní h-aoın-níṫ ṫíoḃ so lonʒaınceaṙ le cnoınıcıḃ Nua-Ʒall na
h-aımsıne seo, aċc ıs eaṫ ṫoʒníṫ cnomaṫ an ḃeusaıḃ roṫaoıne aʒus
caılleaċ mḃeaʒ n-uıníseal, an ṫcaḃaınc maıc-ʒníoṁ na n-uasal ı
nṫeanṁaṫ.

—ꝼonus ꝼeasa an Éınınn.

GEOFFREY KEATING (1632)

ANYONE who sets out to trace the history or antiquities of a
country should explain the condition of the country and of its
people. Since I have undertaken to examine the origins of Irish
history I cannot but deplore the prevailing anti-Irish bias—the un-
fairness shown alike to the " old foreigners " [Anglo-Irish], who have been
here for four centuries, and to the Gaels, who held possession for nearly
three thousand years. Modern writers on Ireland have cast reproaches on
both.

This is illustrated by the works of Cambrensis, Spencer, Stanihurst,
Hanmer, Camden, Barckley, Moryson, Davies, Campion and other
British writers [since the Norman invasion]. All these are like beetles,
for it is the nature of the beetle, raising its head in summer, to move to
and fro without alighting on flower of field or garden, roses or lilies, but
rolling itself in the dung of horses and cows.

So with the foreign beetles. These
writers say nothing of the nobility of
Ireland—of their valour and piety, of
the abbeys they founded and endowed, of
their respect for monks, prelates and men
of learning, of their provision for widows,
orphans, the poor and needy. They pass
over Irish generosity and hospitality—un-
surpassed in Europe, judged by the means
of the bestowers . . . Nothing of all this
is mentioned in the chronicles of the
foreigners ; they dwell entirely on the
habits and customs of the baser sort,
ignoring the more worthy.—*Groundwork
of the Knowledge of Ireland.*

*Above is a summary in English of the famous
passage in Keating's history (page 8) in which he
defends Ireland against the unjust aspersions of foreign
critics or, as they might in modern times have been
called, propagandists. In the piece quoted and
translated on page 10, he explains his own standpoint. The anti-Irish stories of Giraldus Cambrensis, written four and a half centuries earlier,
were still credited abroad in Keating's time.*

w

d in Co. Tipperary. He spent some
mory is still cherished by the people.

Seaŧrún Céiṫinn (1632)

Uime sin, aṫá vóiġ aġam cibé léaġṫóir comṫrom léiġfeas ġaċ breuġruġav v'á nveimimaġ Cambrens, aġus ar na Nua-Ġallaib seo leanas a lorġ, ġurab mó creivfeas an breuġnuġav vo ġním ar a mbreuġaib ioná vo'n innisin sceul vo ġnío cáċ, óir aṫáim aosta, aġus vronġ víob san óġ; vo ċonnaic mé aġus ṫuiġim prím-leaḃair an ṫseanċusa, aġus ní facavar-san iav aġus vá ḃfaicvís, ní ṫuiġfíve leo iav.

Ní ar fuaṫ ná ar ġráv vroinġe ar bioṫ seaċ a ċéile, ná ar furáileaṁ aonvuine, ná vo súil re soċar v'faġḃáil uaiv cuirim rómam stáir na h-Éireann vo scríoḃav aċa vo ḃríġ ġur ṁeasas ná'r ḃ'oirċeas coṁ-onóraiġe na h-Éireann vo ċríċ, aġus com-uaisle ġaċ fóirne v'ár áitiġ í, vo vul i mbáṫav, ġan luav ná iomráv vo ḃeiṫ orra: aġus measaim ġurab córaive mo ṫeist vo ġaḃáil ar Éireannċaib ar an ṫuarasġḃáil vo ḃeirim vo ḃríġ ġurab ar Ġaevealaib is ro-ṁó ṫráċtaim. Cibé le n-ab mór a n-abraim riu, naċ inṁeasta ġo mbearainn breaṫ le báiv aġ taḃairt iomav molta ṫar mar vo ṫuilleavar orra, aġus mé féin vo Ṡean-ġallaib vo réir bunavasa.—Forus Feasa ar Éirinn.

GEOFFREY KEATING (1632)

I HOPE that every fair-minded reader who sees my criticism of Cambrensis and other foreigners like him will give credit to my refutation of their libels. I am old, and some of them were young. I have seen and understood the great historical books which they never saw, and which, if they had seen, they could not have understood. And I have not been moved by love or hatred for one party or another.

I am not writing Irish history at the behest of anyone or with any hope of profiting by it, but because I thought that a country as worthy of honour as Ireland and people as noble as those who have inhabited it, should not go down into oblivion till their story was told. And I think my estimate of the Irish should be accepted, because it is mainly of the Gaels that I treat. If anyone thinks that I am predisposed in their favour, let him recollect that I am not likely to praise them beyond their deserts because I belong myself to the Anglo-Irish.—*Groundwork of the Knowledge of Ireland.*

Geoffrey Keating's " Forus Feasa," the first general history of Ireland written in the Irish language, was circulated extensively all over Ireland in manuscript copies. " Of all men," says Hardiman, " Keating was best qualified to give a true picture of this country, from a knowledge of its civil affairs, manners, customs, poetry, music, architecture, besides his intimate acquaintance with many ancient manuscripts, extant in his time but since dispersed or destroyed."

H. BOURGCHIER, EARL OF BATH (1623)

AND that which adds much to the speedy flourishing of any land, the natives there are as apt to learn as any nation, as capable, of discipline, as hardy to endure, as able men, as active, and now for the most part as willing to embrace good government, civility and industry, being animated thereto by the example and thrifty precedents of their neighbours, the English and Scots. And that which wastes half the substance of England, riot in apparel and meat, the common sort of that nation know it not. And though the Spaniard and Italian in moderate diet and homely clothes be said to exceed all kingdoms, and thereby to raise themselves to much wealth, yet in this they are far surpassed by the Irish, who live more poorly and in more penurious manner by half than they or any other, I mean the peasantry : but they are to be reformed in their nasty sluggishness and laziness.

There lives not a people more hardy, able, active and painful when once they break off their sluggishness; neither is there any will endure the miseries of war, as are famine, watching, heat, cold, wet, travel and the like, so naturally and with that facility and courage that they do. The Prince of Orange, His Excellency used often publicly to deliver that the Irish are soldiers the first day of their birth ; the famous Henry IV. late king of France, said there would prove no nation so resolute martial men as they, would they be ruly, and not so headstrong ; and Sir John Norris was wont to ascribe this in particular to that nation above others that he never beheld so few of any country as the Irish that were idiots and cowards, which is very notable.

No people is more in awe of their sovereign, or more willing or cordial to obey when justice is duly ministered with equality to them, their wrongs redressed, the oppressors and offenders punished according to their desert. The apparent injuries and heavy oppressions of the inferior ministers and under officers of that realm most commonly occasioned and procured the natives there so often to transgress the bounds of their allegiance and duty. And this being reformed, as now it begins to be, and industry there established by laws, proclamations and edicts in the same degree as they are in other civil countries, His Majesty without doubt will soon repair the losses he hath sustained by that kingdom with increase of interest and will reap the comfort by the country and people which are long expected, that being his own handiwork and as he terms it his masterpiece.—*Advertisements of Ireland.*

This description is from a manuscript in the Library of Trinity College, Dublin, which has been edited by Dr. George O'Brien and published by the Royal Society of Antiquaries, Ireland (1923). Dr. O'Brien considers that the author was probably Henry Bourgchier, 5th Earl of Bath, one of the "new Irish," whose sympathies are nevertheless seen in his reference to Ireland as "our own poor country," and to the great Franciscan scholar, Father Luke Wadding, then in Rome, as "our countryman."

11

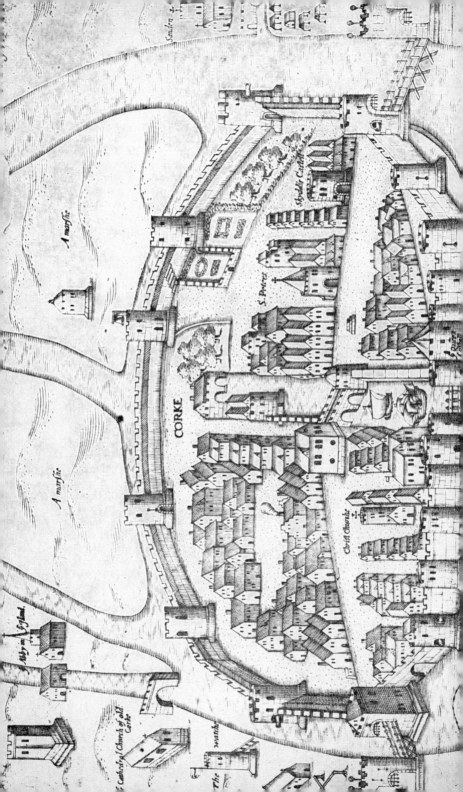

Senden

A marshe

A marshe

A marshe

CORKE

S. Peters

S.horch Castle

Chrst Churche

S. My in Veglad.

The Cathedral Church of old Corke

The watch

LA BOULLAYE LE GOUZ (1646)

THE Irish of the southern and eastern coasts, follow the customs of the English; those of the north, the Scotch. The others are not very polished, and are called by the English, savages. The English colonists were of the English Church, and the Scotch were Calvinists, but at present they are all Puritans. The native Irish are very good Catholics. . . .

The Irish gentlemen eat a great deal of meat and butter and but little bread. They drink milk, and beer into which they put laurel leaves, and eat bread baked in the English manner. The poor grind barley and peas between two stones and make it into bread, which they cook upon a small iron table heated on a tripod; they put into it some oats, and this bread which in the form of cakes they call Haraan, they eat with great draughts of buttermilk. Their beer is very good, and the eau de vie, which they call Brandovin [*Brandy*] excellent. The butter, the beef, and the mutton, are better than in England.

The towns are built in the English fashion, but the houses in the country are in this manner. Two stakes are fixed in the ground, across which is a transverse pole to support two rows of rafters on the two sides, which are covered with leaves and straw. The cabins are of another fashion. There are four walls the height of a man, supporting rafters over which they thatch with straw and leaves. They are without chimneys and make the fire in the middle of the hut, which greatly incommodes those who are not fond of smoke. The castles or houses of the nobility consist of four walls extremely high, thatched with straw; but to tell the truth they are nothing but square towers without windows, or at least having such small apertures as to give no more light than there is in a prison. They have little furniture, and cover their rooms with rushes, of which they make their beds in summer, and of straw in winter. They put the rushes a foot deep on their floors, and on their windows, and many of them ornament the ceiling with branches.

They are fond of the harp, on which nearly all play, as the English do on the fiddle, the French on the lute, the Italians on the guitar, the Spaniards on the castanets, the Scotch on the bagpipe, the Swiss on the fife, the Germans on the trumpet, the Dutch on the tambourine, and the Turks on the flageolet.

The Irish are fond of strangers, and it costs little to travel amongst them. When a traveller of good address enters their houses with assurance, he has but to draw a box of snuff, and offer it to them; then these people receive him with admiration, and give him the best they have to eat. They love the Spaniards as their brothers, the French as their friends, the Italians as their allies . . .
—*De La Boullaye le Gouz.*

"*Les Voyages et Observations du Sieur de la Boullaye le Gouz*" *was published in Paris,* 1653.

François le Gouz Sieur de la Boullaye le Gouz Gentilhomme Angevin

HIBERNIA ANTIQVA

A SYMBOLICAL FIGURE OF IRELAND, 1654

Frontispiece from Sir James Ware's " De Hibernia et Antiquitatibus ejus Disquisitiones" (1654). Ireland is shown as a lady with a leash of greyhounds, standing in a wooded landscape with herds of cattle and deer.

14

THE PAPAL NUNCIO'S SECRETARY (1645)

THE country through which we passed from Kenmare to Kilkenny, though mountainous, is very agreeable, and, since the richest pastures are found everywhere, it abounds in herds of every kind. One also came frequently upon long valleys, studded with groves and woods—not very big or dense—a pleasant rather than a fearsome feature of the landscape. For seventy miles the prospect was of this kind, but, having crossed the mountains, we entered upon a broad plain, varied with hills and valleys, delightful to look at, well cultivated, and rich in an infinite number of herds, especially cows and sheep. From the sheep the people get a very fine wool, known amongst us in Italy as *English* wool.

The men are fine-looking and of incredible strength, swift runners, and ready to bear every kind of hardship with cheerfulness They are all trained in arms, especially now that they are at war. Those who apply themselves to letters are very learned, and well fitted to the professions and sciences.

The women are distinguished by their grace and beauty, and they are as modest as they are lovely. Their manners are marked by extreme simplicity, and they mix freely in conversation on all occasions without suspicion or jealousy. Their dress differs from ours, and is somewhat like the French. They also wear cloaks reaching to their heels and tufted locks of hair, and they go without any head-dress, content with linen bands bound up in the Greek fashion, which display their natural beauty to much advantage. Their families are very large. Some have as many as thirty children, all living; not a few have fifteen or twenty, and all these children are handsome, tall and strong, the majority being fair-haired, white-skinned and red-complexioned.

Food is abundant, and the inhabitants eat and entertain very well. They are constantly pledging healths, the usual drinks being Spanish wines, French claret, very good beer and excellent milk. Butter is used abundantly with all kinds of food. . . . There is also plenty of fruit—apples, pears, plums, artichokes. All eatables are cheap. A fat ox costs sixteen shillings, a sheep fifteen pence, a pair of capons, or fowls, five pence ; eggs a farthing each, and other things in proportion. A good-sized fish costs a penny, and they don't bother about selling game. They kill birds almost with sticks. Both salt and fresh water fish are cheap, abundant, and of excellent flavour. . . . We bought a thousand pilchards and oysters for twenty-five *baiocchi* (twelve and a half pence). The horses are numerous, strong, well-built, and swift. For £5 you can buy a nag which in Italy could not be got for a hundred gold pieces. —DIONYSIUS MASSARI, Dean of Fermo : *A letter from Limerick to Florence.*

Dr. Massari came to Ireland with Archbishop Rinuccini, Papal Nuncio to the Confederation of Kilkenny, in 1645 (see page 59). The letter from which this passage is taken was written in Italian to the Nuncio's brother in Florence.

A. JOUVIN, DE ROCHEFORT (1672)

THE Castle of Dublin is strong, enclosed by thick walls and by many round towers that command the whole town ; on them are mounted a good number of cannon. The court is small, but the lodgings, although very ancient, are very handsome, and worthy of being the dwelling of the Viceroy. The principal gate is in a great street, called Casselstrit [Castle street], that runs from one end to the other of the town ; in the middle of it is an open space in which the principal streets of Dublin meet. That of Aystrit is fine ; in it is the town-hall with a fine clock, which is before Christ Church.

This great church seems to me to have been some abbey ; the cloisters are converted into shops of tradesmen, and the abbey-house serves for the court in which pleadings are held. This same street passes by the open place called Fichstreit [Fishamble street], which is the fish-market, that terminates at one of the ancient city gates between two great towers, where are the two prisons. Beyond this is a great suburb, which is at present both the best and largest part of Dublin.

A little river runs through the largest street, called Tomstrit [Thomas street], wherein dwell several workmen of different trades for the conveniency of this rivulet, of which they make use, and that waters and cleanses all the suburb, the houses of which are fine and straight. I went to see the metropolitan church of St. Patrick, tutelar of all Ireland : it has been much damaged by thunder, and principally its high tower. There is an open spot used for the market-place like that called the Haymarket. Here is a large covered market-house. So that Dublin, with its suburbs, is one of the greatest and best-peopled towns in Europe, and the residence of all the nobility of the kingdom of Ireland.

There is a stone bridge, which joins this small part of the town called Oxmonton to the greater. On that side which lies by the water is a great quay, where are the finest palaces in Dublin. I was there shown the ancient abbey of St. Mary, formerly, after that of Armagh, the richest in the whole island ; at present only the ruins of it are remaining. I lodged in this suburb, from whence I often went to walk in the great meadows by the side of the river, contemplating the country and the situation of this famous town, which seemed to me to be near high mountains on one side, and on the other adjoining to a fine country, with this advantage that it is in the middle of the island of Ireland ; so that the produce of the country may be conveniently brought thither from every part, as well as what comes by sea from foreign countries, with which, by the means of its port, it may traffic.

One may go to the town of Kilkenny, which lies fifty miles from Dublin, to see the fine castle of Monsieur the Duke of Ormont, rich on every side with marble, and ornamented with many things so curious, that those who have seen it say that it surpasses many palaces of Italy. It is only ten leagues from Waterford, which is one of the good sea-ports of this kingdom, as are those of Wexford, Cork, Kinsale, Limerick and

Galway, from whence sail every year many vessels, loaded with leather, butter, cheese, tallow, salt meat and fish; as also with a kind of cloth manufactured in the country, which is very cheap, and is carried to Spain, Italy and often to the American Islands, from whence a return is made of divers merchandises of those countries, as I have observed in several sea-ports of this kingdom, which is the richest of all Europe in things necessary for human life, but the poorest in money.

This causes provisions to be so cheap, that butter and cheese are commonly sold at a penny the pound; a pound of beef, at the butchery, for eight deniers; veal and mutton a penny; a large salmon just out of the sea, threepence; a large fresh cod, twopence; a pair of soles, or quaviver, above a foot broad, a penny; an hundred herrings, threepence; so that one is served with flesh and fish in the best manner for twelvepence a day. In fine, this is the land of plenty. And, moreover, on the road, if you drink two pennyworth of beer at a public-house, they will give you of bread, meat, butter, cheese, fish, as much as you choose; and for all this you only pay your twopence for the beer, it being the custom of the kingdom, as I have experienced wherever I have been.

This island is between the degrees 51 and 56. It may be about 200 French leagues in length, and fifty in breadth. It has several large towns, great castles, and good seaports. They have suffered much in the last civil wars on account of religion, when they were almost all ruined, the inhabitants punished, and the rest banished from the kingdom for having resisted the will of their King, and persisted in following the Catholic religion, which was rooted in the hearts of many. These have been forbidden, upon pain of death, to return, for fear that the religion might in time revive, and little by little increase in the kingdom. In truth the Irish are naturally inclined to the Catholic religion; there are even in Dublin more than twenty houses where Mass is secretly said, and above a thousand places, and subterraneous vaults and retired spots in the woods, where the peasants assemble to hear Mass celebrated by some priests they secretly maintain.—A. JOUVIN, DE ROCHEFORT: *Le Voyage d'Europe.*

A. Jouvin, de Rochefort, a Frenchman, visited England and Ireland about 1668. An account of his visit was published in Paris (1672).

* * * * *

SIR WILLIAM PETTY (1672)

THE housing of 160,000 families, is, as hath often been said, very wretched. But their clothing is far better than that of the French peasants, or the poor of most other countries; which advantage they have from their wool, whereof 12 sheep furnisheth a competency to one of these families. Which wool, and the cloth made of it, doth cost these poor people no less than £50,000 *per ann.* for the dyeing it; a trade exercised by the women of the country. Madder, alum and indigo are imported, but the other dyeing stuffs they find nearer home, a certain mud taken out of the bogs serving them for copperas, the rind of several trees and saw-dust for galls; as for wild and green weeds, they find enough, as also of Rhamnus-berries.

17

ST. PATRICK'S PURGATORY

Throughout the seventeenth and eighteenth centuries, St. Patrick's Purgatory in Lough Derg, Co. Donegal, remained, as it had been during the Middle Ages, a place of pilgrimage for the Irish people. Several official attempts were made to suppress the pilgrimage, but all failed. This engraving of the Station Island is from the "Lyra Hibernica" of Thomas Carve, chaplain to Butler's regiment in the service of the German Emperor.

The diet of these people is milk, sweet and sower, thick and thin, which also is their drink in summer time, in winter small-beer or water, But tobacco taken in short pipes seldom burnt, seems the pleasure of their lives, together with sneezing : insomuch, that two-sevenths of their expense in food is tobacco. Their food is bread in cakes, whereof a penny serves a week for each ; potatoes from August till May, muscles, cockles and oysters near the sea ; eggs and butter made very rancid, by keeping in bogs. As for flesh, they seldom eat it, notwithstanding the great plenty thereof, unless it be of the smaller animals, because it is inconvenient for one of these families to kill a beef, which they have no convenience to save. So as 'tis easier for them to have a hen or rabbit than a piece of beef of equal substance.

Their fuel is turf in most places ; and of late, even where wood is most plentiful, and to be had for nothing, the cutting and carriage of the turf being more easy than that of wood. But to return from whence I digressed : I may say that the trade of Ireland, among 19 in 22 parts of the whole people, is little or nothing, excepting for the tobacco abovementioned, estimated worth about £50,000, forasmuch as they do not need any foreign commodities, nor scarce any thing made out of their own village. Nor is above one-fifth part of their expense other than what their own family produceth, which condition and state of living cannot beget trade.

The clothing is a narrow sort of frieze, of about twenty inches broad, whereof two foot, called a bandle, is worth from 3½d. to 18d. Of this, seventeen bandles make a man's suit, and twelve make a cloak. According to which measures and proportions, and the number of people who wear this stuff, it seems that near thrice as much wool is spent in Ireland as exported ; whereas others have thought quite contrary, that is, that the exported wool is triple in quantity to what is spent at home.

As for the manners of the Irish, I deduce them from their original constitutions of body, and from the air ; next from their ordinary food ; next from their condition of estate and liberty, and from the influence of their governors and teachers, and lastly from their ancient customs, which affect as well their consciences as their nature. For their shape, stature, colour and complexion, I see nothing in them inferior to any other people, nor any enormous predominancy of any humour.

Their lazing seems to me to proceed rather from want of employment and encouragement to work, than from the natural abundance of flegm in their bowels and blood. For what need they to work, who can content themselves with potatoes, whereof the labour of one man can feed forty ; and with milk, whereof one cow will, in summer time, give meat and drink enough for three men, when they can every where gather cockles, oysters, muscles, crabs, &c., with boats, nets, angles or the art of fishing ; and can build an house in three days ? And why should they desire to fare better, though with more labour, when they are taught, that this way of living is more like the patriarchs of old, and the saints of later times, by whose prayer and merits they are to be relieved, and whose example they are therefore to follow ? And why should they breed more cattle, since 'tis penal to import them into England? Why should they raise more commodities, since there are not merchants sufficiently stocked to take them of them, nor provided with other more pleasing foreign commodities, to give in exchange for them? and how should merchants have stock, since trade is prohibited and fettered by the statutes of England? And why should men endeavour to get estates, where the legislative power is not agreed upon; and where tricks and words destroy natural right and property?

They are accused of much treachery, falseness and thievery, none of all which, I conceive, is natural to them; for as to treachery, they are made believe, that they all shall flourish again, after some time; wherefore they will not really submit to those whom they hope to have their servants; nor will they declare so much, but say the contrary, for their present ease, which is all the treachery I have observed; for they have in their hearts not only a grudging to see their old properties enjoyed by foreigners, but a persuasion they shall be shortly restored.

As for thievery, it is affixt to all thin-peopled countries, such as Ireland is, where there cannot be many eyes to prevent such crimes; and where what is stolen, is easily hidden and eaten, and where 'tis easy to burn the house, or violate the persons of those who prosecute these crimes, and where thin-peopled countries are governed by the laws that were made and first fitted to thick-peopled countries; and where matter of small moment and value must be tried with all the formalities which belong to the highest causes. In this case there must be thieving, where is withal neither encouragement, nor method, nor means for labouring, nor provision for impotents.—*The Political Anatomy of Ireland.*

Sir William Petty (1623-87), economist, surveyor, physician, inventor, carried out the famous Down Survey of Ireland under Cromwell, and himself secured extensive Irish estates.

* * * * * *

THOMAS DINELEY (1680)

IRISH nurses are very tender and good to the children of others of higher degree, and most commonly their love is more to them than to their own, this begets a relation and kindred without end, and they become followers of their foster brothers and sisters.... Earl Desmond, a FitzGerald in Queen Elizabeth's time, a traytor, was discovered by his own foster brother who follow'd him to the gallows. The descendant in a direct line from the said Earl of Desmond is said now to be a brogue maker, or maker of Irish shoes, in the county of Kerry, which, had they not forfeited their estates, as it is now worth, it is thought it would be the largest in this kingdom by 3 parts, for any particular, and at least by modest computation £200,000 per annum ...

The common people of both sexes wear no shoos after the English fashion, but a sort of pumps called brogues. The vulgar Irish women's garments are loose body'd, without any manner of stiffening, they never wear bodys to check or direct the course of nature; having like a night

20

cap made of a napkin about their heads instead of night geer; never at any time using hats after the manner of the vulgar English, but covering and defending their heads from rain with a mantle, as also from the heat of the sunne; to which Spanish lazy use the Irish men apply their cloaks.

Dyet generally of the vulgar Irish are potatoes, milk, new milk, which they call sweet milk, bonny clobber, mallabaune, whey curds, large brown oatcakes of a foot and half broad bak't before the fire, bread made of bare, a sort of barley, pease, beans and oatmeale, wheat or rye for great days.

A CARLOW VILLAGE, 1680—T. DINELEY

Besides potatoes roasted in the embers, they feed on parsnips, carrots and watercresses. Butter, laid up in wicker basketts, buried for some time in a bog, to make a provision of an high taste for Lent. Near the shores they eat sea-weeds—as dilisk, slugane. At fairs their eating is very barbarous, each proffering his friend a chop of mutton, or beef, which they call a spoule, out of the pot, without salt [or] sauce; or salmon without vinegar.

For food, among people of condition, a sort of swine's flesh they eat, which differs from the custom of England. It is neither sucking pig,

21

pork or bacon ; it is called pigging rigging, a sort of pig between it and a pork, this they slit in the middle, head and all, and so roast it by the name above.

The vulgar are inclin'd to drink beer and usquebath in excess, and both men, women, and children are addicted to tobacco in an abundant manner which, in a pipe of two inches long, they shagh round (and which is a terme signifying " here," that they deliver with).

Several English themselves are degenerated into such meer Irish that they have not only suffered themselves and their posterity, by the neglect and scorn of the use of their own proper language, English, to forget it, but to be ashamed of the names of their ancestours, because English, though noble and of great antiquity, and converted them into Irish surnames.—*Tour in Ireland.*

Thomas Dineley (d. 1695), well-known English traveller and antiquary, visited in Ireland in 1680. The account which he wrote of his tour was published by the Royal Society of Antiquaries, Ireland (1870). The manuscript is preserved in the National Library of Ireland.

* * * * * *

SIR HENRY PIERS, 1682

THERE are from the highest to the lowest classes of them that are very ingenious and docile : in this only unhappy, that they will not breed their youth in our universities, neither in this kingdom nor in England, because of the religion therein professed, but choose rather, being not permitted to have public schools of their own, to educate their children under private professors, or else send them abroad into France or Spain for their breeding. Neither is a priest now among them of any repute, if he has not spent some years abroad.

They are much given to Hospitality from the highest to the lowest, even the meanest will receive into his house a stranger, and impart the best of his fare unto him : in this generosity they seem rather to exceed on occasions than fall short, especially when they make any public treats, for at such times it is usual with them not to suffer their guest to part until their whole stock of provision be spent. Their women are generally beautiful, and love highly to set themselves out in the most fashionable dress they can attain.

The landlords of old were, and still are, great oppressors of their tenants and followers, and very much given to cosher upon them, that is, to come for sometimes with their family and live on them ; nevertheless they are very industrious to preserve them from the wrongs and oppressions of others ; and if this were the utmost of their kindness to their tenants it were truly commendable, but in this they too often exceed, for many of them will not spare to protect their tenants against the payment of their just debts ; insomuch as after you have been at cost and charges in the law, and come with your execution, you happen well if you find not all your debtor's goods seized on by the landlord for his rent, and so mear a matter it is with an Irishman to be protected by his landlord from the injuries of others, that it is a common saying in the mouths of most of them : *What boots it me to have a landlord, if he defend me not,* both in just and unjust causes ; and another saying they have as rife as this : *Defend me and spend me,* insomuch that it seems they give themselves up to their landlord's pleasure, as to what he willeth for himself, in case he will suffer none else to do the like. These things, tho' true as to the main, admit of many exceptions ; for I know several that are truly just and conscientious in their ways, both superiors and inferiors ; and this matter of exception holds not only in this instance but in most of what I have written, or shall write of all degrees of this people.

As to the inferior rank of husbandmen called Scoulloges, which may be Englishised, farmer or husbandman, or yet more properly boors, they are generally very crafty and subtile in all manner of bargaining, full of equivocations and mental reservations, especially in their dealings in fairs and markets ; whereas if lying and cheating were no sin, they make it their work to over reach any they deal with, and if by any slight or fetch they can hook in the least advantage, they are mighty tenacious thereof, and will not forget the same unless over-powered by the landlord, who is the party addressed to for justice.

I will crave the reader's patience to suffer me a while to give an instance of the dealing of this sort of men, and their customs in the manage of their husbandry one with another. Every townland held by them is grazed in common, that is, every man's stock goes indifferently over all the pastures of the town. The difference lies here, he who holds the greatest number of acres in the arable, is supposed the more able farmer, and consequently is allowed to have more cattle on the pastures of the town than he who holds fewer acres, or a lesser holding as they call it. The great evil hereof generally is overstocking their ground, by means whereof it is too often seen once in three or four years, that they hazard the loss of their stock ; as they graze in common, so one who is not acquainted with them would think, that they plow in common. too. For it is usual with them to have ten or twelve plows at once going in one small field ; nevertheless every one here hath tillage distinct, tho' all appear fenced up in one mear or ditch. They divide usually one field into acres, half-acres, stangs, that is roods ; and of these they make so many lots or equal shares, as there are plows in the town ; so as a man whose share may amount to three acres, shall not have perhaps half an acre together, but scattered up and down in all quarters of the field. This ariseth thro' that great care and concern every man hath lest he should be over-reached by his neighbour ; and they will take upon them to be judges to an extreme nicety of the quality and quantity of each rood of ground ; and to make sure work, will bring their ropes to measure, as formally as a surveyor his chains. . . .

In countries that are rocky, as some part of Thomond, where corn is not to be had in so great plenty . . . they have a custom every May-day, which they count their first of summer, to have to their meal one formal dish, whatever else they have, which some call stirabout or hasty-pudding, that is flour and milk boiled thick ; and this is holden as an argument

23

of the good wives good huswifery, that made her corn hold out so well, as to have such a dish to begin summer fare with; for if they can hold out so long with bread, they count they can do well enough for what remains of the year 'till harvest; for then milk becomes plenty, and butter, new cheese, and curds and shamrocks are the food of the meaner sort all this season; nevertheless in this mess, on this day, they are as formal that even in the plentifullest and greatest houses where bread is in abundance all the year long, they will not fail of this dish, nor yet they that for a month before wanted bread. . . .

In their marriages, especially in those countries where cattle abound, the parents and friends on each side meet on the side of an hill or, if the weather be cold, in some place of shelter, about midway between both dwellings. If agreement ensue, they drink the agreement bottle, as they call it, which is a bottle of good usquebagh and this goes merrily round; for payment of the portion, which generally is a determinate number of cows, little care is taken; only the father or next of kin to the bride, sends to his neighbours and friends *sub mutuae vicissitudinis obtentu*, and everyone gives his cow or heifer, which is all one in this case, and thus the portion is quickly paid; nevertheless caution is taken from the bridegroom on the day of delivery for restitution of the cattle, in case the bride die childless within a certain day limited by agreement, and in this case every man's own beast is restored. Thus care is taken, that no man shall grow rich by often marriages. On the day of bringing home, the bridegroom and friends ride out, and meet the bride and her friends at the place of treaty, being come near each other, the custom was of old to cast short darts at the company that attended the bride, but at such distance that seldom any hurt ensued; yet it is not out of the memory of man, that the lord of Howth on such an occasion lost an eye: this custom of casting darts is now obsolete.

On the patron-day in most parishes, as also on the feasts of Easter and Whitsuntide, the more ordinary sort of people meet near the ale-house in the afternoon, on some convenient spot of ground and dance for the cake; here, to be sure, the piper fails not of diligent attendance; the cake to be danced for is provided at the charge of the ale-wife, and is advanced on a board on the top of a pike about

ten feet high; this board is round, and from it riseth a kind of a garland, beset and tied round with meadow flowers, if it be early in the summer; if later the garland has the addition of apples set round on pegs fastened unto it.—*Description of Westmeath.*

Sir Henry Piers (1623–91), a Westmeath landowner, residing at Tristernagh Abbey, wrote his description at the suggestion of the Protestant Bishop of Meath. He remarks: "I find little or nothing that can be said of this county, that may not be said indifferently of all."

★　　★　　★　　★　　★　　★

CONNAUGHT, 1610—JOHN SPEED

25

KILCASH

What shall we do for timber?
  The last of the woods is down,
Kilcash and the house of its glory
  And the bell of the house are gone;
The spot where her lady waited
  That shamed all women for grace,
When earls came sailing to greet her
  And Mass was said in that place. . . .

Nor sound of duck or of geese there,
  Hawk's cry or eagle's call,
Nor humming of the bees there
  That brought honey and wax for all,
Nor the sweet gentle song of the birds there
  When the sun has gone down to the West,
Nor a cuckoo atop of the boughs there
  Singing the world to rest.

There's a mist there tumbling from branches
  Unstirred by night and by day,
And a darkness falling from heaven,
  And our fortunes have ebbed away;
There's no holly nor hazel nor ash there
  But pastures of rock and stone,
The crown of the forest is withered
  And the last of its game is gone.

I beseech of Mary and Jesus,
  When the great come home again,
With long dances danced in the garden,
  Fiddle music and mirth among men,
That Kilcash, the home of our fathers
  Be lifted on high again,
And from that to the deluge of waters
  In bounty and peace remain.

                    —*Frank O'Connor.*

CILL ĊAIS

Caḋ a ḋéanfaimíḋ feasta gan aḋmaḋ,
Tá deireaḋ na gcoillte ar lár
Níl tráċt ar Ċill Ċais ná a teaġlaċ
'S ní cluinfear a cling go bráṫ.
An áit úḋ 'na gcoṁnuiġeaḋ an deiġ-ḃean
Fuair graḋam is meiḋir tar ṁnáiḃ
Ḃíoḋ iarlaí ag tarraingt tar tuinn ann
'S an t-Aifreann binn dá ráḋ. . . .

Ní ċluinim fuaim laċan ná gé ann,
Ná fiolar ag déanaḋ aeir cois cuain,
Ná fiú na mbeaċa cun saoṫair
Taḃarfaḋ mil agus céir don tsluaiġ.
Níl ceol binn milis na n-éan ann
Le h-aṁarc an lae dul uainn,
Ná an cuaiċín ar ḃarra na ngéag ann,
Ó is í ċuirfeaḋ an saoġal cun suain.

Tá ceo ag tuitim ar ċraoḃa ann
Ná glanann le grian ná lá.
Tá smúit ag tuitim ó'n spéir ann
'S a cuid uisge go léir ag tráġaḋ.
Níl coll, níl cuileann, níl caor ann
Aċt cloċa is maol-ċloċáin,
Páirc an ḟorġaois gan craoḃ ann,
Is d'imṫiġ an géim cun fáin.

Aiṫċim ar Ṁuire is ar Íosa
Go dtagaiḋ sí arís ċugainn slán,
Go mbeiḋ rinncí fada 'gaḃáil timċeall
Ceol beiḋlín is teinte cnáṁ,
Go dóċtar an baile seo ár sinnsear,
Cill Ċais ḃreaġ, arís go hárd
'S go bráṫ nó go dtiocfaḋ an díleann
Ná feicfear é arís ar lár.

Kilcash, the famous castle of the Butlers, long since in ruins, six miles from Clonmel, gave its name to one of the most popular Gaelic songs. " Her lady " was Lady Margaret Bourke, daughter of the Earl of Clanrickarde, widely celebrated for her beauty, charm, and goodness of heart. Reckless destruction of Irish woods was a feature of the 17th century. The French traveller de Beaumont said of the country later: " It is now almost destitute of trees ; and when, on a fine day in spring, it appears though bare, full of sap and youth, it seems like a lovely girl deprived of her hair."

CHAPTER II.

The Flight of the Earls

TO-NIGHT IRELAND IS DESOLATE

This night sees Eire desolate !
  Her chiefs are cast out of their state,
  Her men, her maidens weep to see
  Her desolate that should peopled be.

How desolate is Connla's plain
  Though aliens swarm in her domain ;
  Her rich bright soil had joy in these
  That now are scattered overseas.

Man after man, day after day,
  Her noblest princes pass away
  And leave to all the rabble rest
  A land dispeopled of her best.

Men smile at childhood's play no more,
  Music and song, their day is o'er ;
  At wine, at Mass the kingdom's heirs
  Are seen no more ; changed hearts are theirs

Her chiefs are gone. There's none to bear
  Her cross, or lift her long despair ;
  The grieving lords take ship. With these
  Our very souls pass overseas.

                Translated by Robin Flower

ᚪnoᚅᚈ ıs uᚐıᚷneᚐᚉ éıre

Anoᚅᚈ ıs uᚐıᚷneᚐᚉ Éıre,
  Do beır póᚷrᚐ ᚐ fír-fréıṁe
  Ᵹruᚐıde ᚐ feᚐr 's ᚐ fıonn-bᚐn flıoᚉ,
  Ꞇreᚐd ıs ıonᚷnᚐd ᚷo h-uᚐıᚷnıoᚉ.

THE FLIGHT OF THE EARLS

Uaigneaċ anoċt Clár Connla
 Ʒé lán d'foirinn allṁarḃa,
 Sáit an ċláir fionnaċraiʒ féin
Do'n Spáin ionnarḃtair iaroséin.

Aʒ triall ʒan locaḋ tar lear
 Uainn do roiʒniḃ mac Mileaḋ,
 Ʒé daoineaċ aon ḟáoḃuiʒ finn
Fáʒburd ʒan aonneaċ Éirinn.

Ʒan ʒáire fá ʒníoṁraḋ leinḃ
 Cosʒ ar ċeol, ʒlas ar Ʒaoiḋeilʒ,
 Mic ríoʒ, mar nár ḋual do'n ḋreim,
Ʒan luaḋ ar fíon ná ar aifrinn.

Ní fuil díoḃ fear a hiomċair
 D'éis ar imtiʒ d'Éirionnċaiḃ;
 Ríoʒraḋ Ḃanba fá ḃroid troim
Aʒ ʒoid ar n-anma asoinn.

—Aindrias Mac Marcuis.

mullan, *Lough Swilly, from whence the Earls, O'Neill and O'Donnell, sailed for the Continent,* 1607.

THE FOUR MASTERS (1632)

THE AGE OF CHRIST, 1607.—Maguire (Cuconnaught) and Donough the son of Mahon, son of the Bishop O'Brien, brought a ship with them to Ireland, and put in at the harbour of Swilly. They took with them from Ireland the Earl O'Neill (Hugh, the son of Ferdorcha), and the Earl O'Donnell (Rury, the son of Hugh, son of Manus), with a great number of the chieftains of the province of Ulster.

These were they who went with O'Neill—namely, the Countess Catherina, the daughter of Magennis, and her three sons, Hugh, the Baron, John and Brian ; Art Oge, the son of Cormac, son of the Baron ; Ferdorcha, son of Con, son of O'Neill; Hugh Oge, the son of Brian, son of Art O'Neill; and many others of his faithful friends. These were they who went with the Earl O'Donnell : Caffar, his brother, and his sister Nuala ; Hugh, the Earl's son, wanting one week of being one year old ; Rose, the daughter of O'Doherty, and wife of Caffar, with her son, Hugh, aged two years and three months ; the son of his brother, Donnell Oge, son of Donnell ; Naghton, the son of Calvagh, son of Donough Cairbreach O'Donnell, together with many of his faithful friends. They entered the ship on the festival of the Holy Cross, in Autumn.

This was a distinguished crew for one ship ; for it is indeed certain that the sea had not supported, and the winds had not wafted from Ireland, in modern times, a party of one ship who would have been more illustrious, or noble in point of genealogy, or more renowned for deeds, valour, prowess, or high achievements than they, if God had permitted them to remain in their patrimonies until their children should have reached the age of manhood. Woe to the heart that meditated, woe to the mind that conceived, woe to the counsel that decided on, the project of their setting out on this voyage, without knowing whether they should ever return to their native principalities or patrimonies to the end of the world.

—*Annals of the Kingdom of Ireland (the Four Masters).*

For a note on the Four Masters, with facsimile in the handwriting of Brother Michael O Clerigh, see pages 52–3.

*   *   *   *   *   *

SIR JOHN DAVIES (1607)

MY most honourable good lord,—Your lordship hath received advertisement at large from the Lord Deputy and council of the departure of the Earls of Tyrone and Tyrconnell out of this kingdom, which, being an accident extraordinary, I conceive your lordship will accept in good part divers relations thereof, and sundry men's notes and observations thereupon ; and I for my part do the rather trouble your lordship with my letters at this time, because this occurrence, if all the circumstances thereof be true, which upon the first report are brought into the state, doth cross my coming over this next term, by interrupting the business wherein I should have been employed.

For the accident, doubtless, it is true that they are embarked and gone, with the most part of that company of men, women, and children, which are named in the proclamation; it is true they took shipping the fourteenth of this present September; that the Saturday before, the Earl of Tyrone was with my Lord Deputy at Slane, where he had speech with his lordship of his journey into England, told him he would be there about the beginning of Michaelmas term, according to his Majesty's directions; that he took his leave of my Lord Deputy in a more sad and passionate manner than he used at other times; that from thence he went to Mellifont, Sir Garret Moore's house, where he wept abundantly when he took his leave, giving a solemn farewell to every child and every servant in the house, which made them all marvel, because it was not his manner to use such compliments.

From thence, on Sunday, he went to Dundalk; on Monday he went to Dungannon, where he rested two whole days; on Wednesday night, they say, he travelled all night with his impediments, I mean his women and children; and it is likewise reported that the countess, his wife being exceeding weary, slipped down from her horse, and, weeping, said she could go no farther; whereupon the earl drew his sword, and swore a great oath that he would kill her in the place, if she would not pass on with him, and put on a more cheerful countenance withal.

Yet the next day, when he came near Lough Foyle, his passage that way was not so secret but the governor there had notice thereof, and invited him and his son to dinner; but their haste was such as they accepted not that courtesy, but they went on, and came that Thursday night to Rathmullan, a town on the west side of Lough Swilly, where the Earl of Tyrconnell and his company met him.

There they took some beeves from one Francis Whyte, an Englishman, and killed them for their provision. There the Earl of Tyrconnell sent for the foster-father of his brother Caffar O'Donel's son, willing him to bring the child with him. He presently repaired with the child towards the place where the earls lodged; but being met by the way by the Baron of Dungannon and Caffar O'Donel himself, they took the infant violently from him, which terrified the foster-father, so as he escaped by the swiftness of his horse, their horses being tired with travelling.

As for us that are here, we are glad to see the day wherein the countenance and majesty of the law and civil government hath banished Tyrone out of Ireland, which the best army in Europe and the expense of two millions of sterling pounds did not bring to pass. And we hope his Majesty's happy government will work a greater miracle in this kingdom than ever St. Patrick did; for St. Patrick did only banish the poisonous worms, but suffered the men full of poison to inhabit the land still; but his Majesty's blessed genius will banish all those generations of vipers out of it, and make it, ere it be long, a right fortunate island. . . .

—*Sir John Davies to the Earl of Salisbury.*

Sir John Davies (1569–1623), Attorney General of Ireland 1606–19, was the author of several famous tracts justifying the English conquest. He was Speaker of the Irish House of Commons 1609–11.

PORTION OF LAST PAGE OF THE LETTER, DROPPED AT THE DOOR OF THE COUNCIL CHAMBER, DUBLIN CASTLE, WHICH LED TO THE FLIGHT OF THE EARLS

SUMMARY OF STATE PAPERS (1607)

THE most probable cause of their flight seems to be that, the fact of Lord Howth's being in communication with the Privy Council in England and with Sir Arthur Chichester at Dublin becoming known to Tyrconnell, he apprized Tyrone of it, and assured him that, he might not have been included in Howth and Delvin's catalogue, he would be certainly arrested when he should appear in London for the hearing of the cause between him and O'Cahan before the Privy Council. About that time John Bath was sent into Spain to ask the King of Spain for an asylum, as they feared it was intended to arrest them ; but the King of Spain was unwilling to receive them, for he would give no offence to the King of England, being now in league with him. But soon afterwards, news coming that Tyrone was sent for into England, and that Tyrconnell was to be taken and committed in Ireland, a messenger was sent to bid them be in readiness to attend the coming of a ship, which should be sent for soon after.

The events that followed upon the flight of the Earls showed that Lord Howth's tale of a general (or of any) insurrection was untrue . . . Sir John Davies's judgment of their flight was the true one, that they fled for fear ; and Salisbury repeatedly assured Chichester afterwards that all his intelligence from abroad proved there was no design on the part of the King of Spain to aid them. Tyrone's own statement is consistent with this. He concludes the collection of his grievances (addressed to His Majesty after his flight) with complaints of the watch kept upon him in Ulster, and the intention displayed by Sir Arthur Chichester in examining Maguire in order to obtain evidence against him, and placing Captain Leigh, that ' whispering companion,' as Sheriff of Tyrone, as a spy upon him, and seeing that the Lord Deputy sought his destruction, he esteemed it a strife against the stream for him to live secure in Ireland. He added that the insults he received from inferior officers were sufficient to drive any human creature not only to forego a country, were it ever so dear to him, but also the whole world, in order to eschew such a government.

—*Calendar of State Papers, Ireland, James I, 1608-10.*

An anonymous letter, left in Dublin Castle on May 18, 1607, alleged a plot by O'Neill and O'Donnell, with the support of the Pope and the King of Spain, to seize all Ireland. The writer of the letter was a nobleman of discredited character, Christopher St. Lawrence, Baron of Howth. The Earls, having reason to fear for their lives, fled the country. Lord Deputy Chichester, who knew that St. Lawrence's story was an invention, wrote : " I like not his look and gesture when he talks with me of this business."

The third page of this momentous document is reproduced on page 32, with the signatures of the Lord Deputy and members of the Council. Chichester adds : " This is the originall ytselfe."

SIR ARTHUR CHICHESTER (1607)

WHEREAS the Earls of Tirone and Tirconnell, Hugh, Baron of Dungannon, Caffer Oge O'Donnell, brother to the said Erle of Tirconnell, and Arte Oge O'Neale, nephew to the said Erle of Tirone, having taken with them the Countess of Tirone and two of the youngest sonnes of the said Erle of Tirone, and the son and heir apparent of the said Erle of Tirconnell, being an infant of the age of one year or thereabouts, with divers others of his servants and followers, have lately embarqued themselves at Lough Swilly in Tirconnell, and are secretly and suddenly departed out of this relme, without licence or notice given to us or any other of his Majesty's ministers of their departure . . . forasmuch as the manner of their departure, considering the quality of their persons, may raise manie doubtes in the mynds of his Majesty's loving subjects in those parts, and especially because it may be conceived by the common sort of people inhabitinge the several counties of Tirone and Tirconnell, that they are in danger to suffer prejudice in their lands and goods for the contempt of offence of the said erles . . . we doe therefore, in his Majestie's name, declare, proclaim, and publishe that all and everie his Majestie's good and loyal subjects inhabitinge the said several countries of Tirone and Tirconnell, shall and may quietly possess and enjoy all and singular their lands and goods, without the trouble or molestation of any of his Majestie's officers or ministers, or any other

SIR ARTHUR CHICHESTER

person or persons whatsoever, as long as they disturb not his Majestie's peace, but live as dutiful and obedient subjects.

And forasmuch as the said Erles, to whom his Majestie, reposing special trust in their loyaltie, had committed the government of the said several countries, are now undutifully departed ; therefore his Majestie doth gratiously receive all and everie his said loyal subjects into his own immediate safeguard and protection, giving them full assurance to defend them and every of them, by his kingly power, from all violence are wrong which any loose persons among themselves, or any other forraine force, shall attempt against them. . . .
—*Proclamation, 20th September, 1607.*

Sir Arthur Chichester, Baron of Belfast (1563-1625), was Lord Deputy of Ireland, 1605-16. He urged the suppression of Gaelic institutions, " abolishing their ceremonies and customs in religion and lordlike Irish government." In spite of his assurances to the people of Ulster in the above Proclamation, he superintended the great Plantation.

34

HUGH O'NEILL, EARL OF TYRONE (1607)

IT was by public authority proclaimed in his manor of Dungannon that none should hear Mass upon pain of losing his goods and imprisonment, and that no curate or ecclesiastical person should enjoy any cure or dignity without swearing the oath of supremacy, and entering to the chapters or congregations of those that professed the contrary religion ; and that those that refused to do so, were actually deprived of their benefices and dignities, as by the Lord Deputy's answer given upon a petition exhibited by the Earl in that behalf may appear, as also by the Lord Primate of Ireland, that put the same in execution in the Earl's country daily. . . .

Where it pleased his Majesty to allow the Earl to be Lieutenant of his country, yet had he no more command there than his boy, since the worst man that did belong to the sheriff would command more than he, and that as well within the Earl's own house as abroad in the country ; for if any one that they had had anything to say unto were within the Earl's house, they would not attend his coming out, but even burst open the doors of his house to bring him out, and never do the Earl so much honour in any respect as once to acquaint him therewith, or send to himself for the party, though he had been within the house when they would attempt these things. And if any of the Earl's officers would, by his direction, order or execute any matter betwixt his own tenants, with their own mutual consents, they would be driven to restore the same again, also be amerced by the sheriff, indicted as felons, and so brought to their trial for their lives for the same ; so as the earl, in the end, could scarce get any of his servants that would undertake to levy his rents. . . .

The Earl did further perceive the Lord Deputy earnest to aggravate and search out matters against him, touching the staining of his honour and dignity, and specially did very distinctly examine Maguire, and did use many persuasions unto him, to signify if he might lay any matters to his charge all which were fetches . . . to come upon the Earl with some forged treason, and thereby to bereave him both of his life and living.

" *Articles exhibited to the King's most excellent Majesty, declaring certain causes of discontent offered the Earl, by which he took occasion to depart his country.*" *The above is from a long Statement forwarded on behalf of Hugh O'Neill to King James I in* 1607 *from Louvain, and now in the Public Record Office, London.*

* * * * * *

TADHG Ó CIANÁIN (1607)

XXXI. The next day, the thirtieth of October, Ó Neill's son, the Colonel of the Irish [regiment], came with them to a large well-equipped company of captains and of noblemen, Spanish and Irish and of every other nation. On the following Saturday the Marquis Spinola, the commander-in-chief of the King of Spain's army in Flanders, came to them from Brussels with a large number of important people and welcomed them. He received them with honour and gave them an invitation to dinner on the next day in Brussels.

TOMB OF THE EARLS IN ROME

ABOVE IS A PORTRAIT OF HUGH O'NEILL, EARL OF TYRONE, OLD AND BLIND

XXXII. On Sunday, the fourth of November, after having heard Mass, the lords set out in coaches, their nobles and retinue attending them on horseback. They came that day to Nyvel, a distance of five leagues. It was a nice town, well fortified with a garrison of the King. The governor was a Spaniard. He came with his soldiers to meet them and welcomed them. When they dismounted he offered to give up the keys of the city to Ó Neill, but he refused to accept them. The governor invited them to supper that night, but they did not consent to go. The governor stayed with Ó Neill that evening, and brought musicians and dancers with him. As they were about to retire he sent a sergeant-major to Ó Neill to ask him to give the watch-word. Ó Neill thanked him, but requested himself to give it as he was accustomed to do every other night.

The following day they went to Prima Porta, a distance of three leagues. They stopped there that night. They sent on some persons before them to Rome. After that they went two leagues to Ponte Molle. Peter Lombard, the archbishop of Armagh and primate of Ireland, came with a noble young man in his company, having a large number of coaches sent by cardinals, to meet them to that place. The steward of each of a certain number of the cardinals came to them to welcome them and to receive them with honour in the cardinal's name. Then they proceeded in coaches. They went on until they came to Rome. Porta del Populo was the name of the gate by which they entered the city. They went on after that through the principal streets of Rome in great splendour. They did not rest until they reched the great church of San Petro in Vaticano. They put up their horses there, and entered the church. They worshipped, and went around, as if on a pilgrimage, the seven privileged altars in the church. Afterwards they proceeded to a splendid palace which His Holiness the Pope had set apart for them in the Borgo Vecchio [and in the Borgo] Santo Spirito.

XCVIII. On the fourth of May, the day of the week being Sunday, and the year of the Lord being then one thousand six hundred and eight, his Holiness the Pope consented to their coming in person into his presence at three o'clock in the afternoon. The cardinals sent a number of good coaches and some of the most excellent and most beautiful horses in the world, to them, to conduct them to the palace where the Pope was. They went to the splendid palace which is called Monte Cavallo. The Holy Father, Paul V, was awaiting them there. When they appeared before him, he received them with respect, with kindness, with honour, and with welcome. Then they themselves and their followers, one after another, kissed with humility and reverence his holy foot. They were about one hour of the day in his presence, and he was courteous, glad, and kind to them during that time, asking them of what occurred to them and how they had fared. They took their leave after having received holy benediction. They gave thanks to God and the Holy Father for the respect and the reverence wherewith he had exhibited his great, merciful kindness to them.—*Tadhg O Cianáin.*

O Cianáin accompanied the Earls in the ship from Rathmullen and in their journey across the Continent to Rome. He belonged to a family of hereditary chroniclers, attached to the Maguires of Fermanagh. The above passages are from a manuscript preserved by the Irish Franciscans in Rome and later brought to Ireland.

CHAPTER III.

The Ulster Plantation

" For the plain shall be broke
By the share of the stranger,
    And the stone-mason's stroke
Tells the woods of their danger ;

The green hills and shore
Be with white keeps disfigured,
    And the Mote of Rathmore
Be the Saxon churl's haggard !

The Gael cannot tell,
In the uprooted wildwood
    And red ridgy dell,
The old nurse of his childhood . . .

We starve by the board,
And we thirst amid wassail—
    For the guest is the lord,
And the host is the vassal.

Through the woods let us roam,
Through the wastes wild and barren ;
    We are strangers at home !
We are exiles in Erin ! "

—SIR SAMUEL FERGUSON (from the Irish of Ó Gnímh).

*   *   *   *   *   *

WHATEVER god or demon may have led the first of them to these shores, the Anglo-Irish and Scottish Ulstermen have now far too old a title to be questioned. They were a hardy race, and fought stoutly for the pleasant valleys they dwell in. And are not Derry and Enniskillen *Ireland's*, as well as Benburb and the Yellow Ford ?—and have not those men and their fathers lived, and loved, and worshipped God, and died there ?—are not their green graves heaped up there—more generations of them than they have genealogical skill to count ? A deep enough root those planters have struck into the soil of Ulster, and it would now be ill striving to unplant them.—JOHN MITCHEL : Preface to *The Life ord Times of Aodh O'Neill.*

38

Bishop Rothe (1617)

THE Viceroy should have considered more carefully before he put forward a title, flimsy and imperfect, to these lands (in Co. Wexford), on behalf of the King, and expelled from their ancient possessions harmless poor people who have many children and no friends to take their part. They have nothing but flocks and herds, no trade but agriculture, no learning. They are unarmed, but so active in mind and body that it is dangerous to drive them from the homes of their ancestors, making the desperate seek revenge and even the more moderate think of taking to arms. Their weapons have been taken from them, but they are in a mood to fight with fists and feet and to tear their oppressors with their teeth. Despair is a sharp spur. These Leinstermen and others like them now see no hope of restitution or compensation. It is their nature that they would rather live on husks at home than feast richly anywhere else, and they will fight for their altars and hearths, and seek a bloody death near the graves of their fathers rather than be buried as exiles in foreign earth and alien sands.—*David Rothe, Bishop of Ossory.*

The vivid portrait reproduced here appears to be the work of a contemporary artist.

DAVID ROTHE, BISHOP OF OSSORY.

The passages in verse and prose quoted on this and the preceding page introduce the great drama of the Ulster Plantation. The smaller plantations of Longford, Wexford, etc., were inspired by the same school of Stuart " statecraft " and explain the profound uneasiness of the Irish people at that period: (1) The verses from Fearflatha O Gnimh, a contemporary Ulster poet, were translated by Sir Samuel Ferguson (1810-86), poet and Deputy Keeper of the Record Office, Ireland, a Belfast man, whose ancestors came to Ireland about 1640. (2) John Mitchel, the great Protestant Irish patriot. (3) The quotation from the "Analecta Sacra" of David Rothe, Bishop of Ossory (1573-1650) is the more effective, coming as it did from a Catholic prelate of great learning, moderate political views, and Anglo-Irish descent.

AMONG the descendants of the settlers it has been a cherished faith that our worthy ancestors came here to find homes only in a howling wilderness, or rather, perhaps, in a dreary and terrible region of muirland and morass. We very generally overlook the fact that the shrewd and needy people whom we call our forefathers, and who dwelt north and south of the Tweed, would have had neither time nor inclination to look towards the shores of Ulster at all, had there been here no objects sufficiently attractive, such as green fields, rich straths, beauteous valleys, and herds of Irish cattle adorning the hillsides. But such was indeed the simple truth.

The glowing account of Fermanagh, for example, from the facile and graphic pen of Sir John Davys, would have been at least equally, if not more appropriate as a description of Ulster in general ; for although few of our northern counties are so picturesque as the one thus selected by him for special admiration, there are several more fertile and productive. "We have now," said he, when writing to Salisbury, " finished [their work as plantation commissioners] in Fermanagh, which is so pleasant and fruitful a country, that if I should make a full description thereof it would rather be taken for a poetical fiction than for a true and serious narrative."

We are generally accustomed to believe that the Irish of Ulster, in the seventeenth century, were ignorant of all agricultural pursuits, including, of course, the management of domesticated animals. Our plantation records, however, show us clearly enough that we have been mistaken to a very considerable extent in this conclusion also. Their knowledge and management in such matters would fall far short, to be sure, of our present requirements ; but, as compared with their neighbours, whether English or Scottish, it is pretty evident that the Irish of Ulster only wanted peace to enable them to excel both, as agriculturists.

During the seven years' war already referred to, the native inhabitants of this province were reduced to the lowest depths of misery by the systematic destruction of their cattle and growing crops ; but even in the brief lull or interval of peace that succeeded, from the spring of 1602 until the autumn of 1607, the recuperative process appears to have been of a very remarkable character indeed.

On the flight of the Earls at the latter date, Sir Thomas Phillips made a journey from Coleraine to Dungannon, through the wooded country of Loch-inis O'Lynn, or Loughinsholin, and thereupon wrote to Salisbury, expressing among other matters, his unfeigned astonishment at the sight of so many cattle and such abundance of grain as he had observed all along his route from the one town to the other. . . . The hillsides were literally covered with cattle, where creaghting went on, no doubt, in its most attractive forms; the valleys were clothed in the rich garniture of ripening barley and oats; whilst the woods swarmed with swine—20,000 of these animals being easily fattened yearly (as Phillips himself afterwards affirmed) in the forest of Glenconkeyne alone. As an evidence of the agricultural tastes and achievements of the natives in that " pleasant and fruitful country of the O'Cahans," Phillips stated, in his *Project* for planting it, that " the Irishmen have been so addicted to tillage that a Bristowe ban barrel of barley was sold but for 18d. in the market of Coleraine " . . . Sir Oliver St. John, who was intimately acquainted with the capabilities of the Ulster Irish as farmers, recommended that the escheated lands should be let directly from the crown to the natives who had been in possession, and who, in turn, would have given the king large rents. Preface to *An historical account of the plantation of Ulster*, 1608-20 (Belfast, 1877).

Rev. George Hill (1810-1900) was Librarian at Queen's College, Belfast, 1850-80. His long and elaborate book on the Ulster Plantation, illustrated with many extracts from contemporary documents, is still the standard work on the subject.

SIR JOHN DAVIES (1606)

AFTER the end of the last term my Lord Deputy took a resolution to visit three counties in Ulster, namely Monaghan, Fermanagh, and Cavan, which, being the most unsettled and unreformed parts of that province, did most of all need his lordship's visitation at this time. . . On Monday night (July 21st) his Lordship camped in the field upon the borders of Ferney . . . and albeit we were to pass through the wildest and wastest parts of the north, yet had we only for our guard six or seven score foot and fifty or three score horse, which is an argument of a good time and a confident Deputy; for in former times, when the State enjoyed the best peace and security, no Lord Deputy did ever venture himself into those parts without an army of eight hundred or one thousand men. . . .

Touching Maguire's mensal lands, which were free from all common charges and contributions of the country, because they yielded a large proportion of butter and meal and other provisions for Maguire's table; albeit the jury and other inhabitants did set forth these mensal lands in certainty, which, lying in several baronies, did not in quantity exceed four ballibetaghs, the greatest thereof being in the possession of one MacManus and his sept, yet touching the certainty of the duties or provisions yielded unto Maguire out of these mensal lands, they referred themselves unto an old parchment roll, which they called an indenture, remaining in the hands of one O'Bristan, a chronicler and principal brehon of that country. Whereupon O'Bristan was sent for, but was so aged and decrepit as he was scarce able to repair to us. When he was come we demanded of him the sight of that ancient roll, wherein, not only the certainty of Maguire's mensal duties did appear, but also the particular rents and other services which were answered to Maguire out of every part of the country.

The old man, seeming to be much troubled with this demand, made answer that he had such a roll in his keeping before the war, but that in the late rebellion it was burned among other of his papers and books by certain English soldiers. We were told by some that were present that they had seen the roll in his hands since the war. Thereupon my Lord Chancellor being then present with us did minister an oath unto him, and gave him a very serious charge to inform us truly what was become of the roll. The poor old man confessed that he knew where the roll was, but that it was dearer to him than his life, and therefore he would never deliver it out of his hands unless my Lord Chancellor would take his like oath that the roll should be restored unto him again.

My Lord Chancellor, smiling, gave him his word and his hand that he should have the roll redelivered unto him if he would suffer us to take a view and a copy thereof. And thereupon the old brehon drew the roll out of his bosom, where he did continually bear it about with him. It was not very large, but it was written upon both sides in a fair Irish character; howbeit, some parts were worn and defaced with time and ill-keeping.

—*A Letter from Sir John Davies, Attorney-General of Ireland* (1606).

ROYAL PROCLAMATION (1607)

COMMISSION to inquire into the KING'S Title to the several escheated and forfeited Lands in *Ulster,* in the several Countys of *Armagh, Tyrone, Colerain, Donegall, Fermanagh* and *Cavan,* in Order to the Plantation there ; with Articles and Instructions annexed.

Whereas great scopes and extent of Land in the several Counties of *Armagh, Tirone, Coleraine, Donegall, Fermanagh,* and *Cavan,* within our Province of *Ulster,* are escheated and come to our Hands by the attainder of sundry Traitors and Rebells, and by other just and lawfull Titles, whereof we have caused heretofore several Inquisitions to be taken, and Surveys to be made, which being transmitted and presented unto us, we considered with our Privy Councell attending our Person, how much it would advance the Welfare of that Kingdom, if the said Land were planted with Colonies of civil Men, and well affected in Religion ; where-upon there was a Project conceived for the Division of the said Lands into Proportions, and for the Distribution of the same unto Undertakers, together with certain Articles of Instruction for such as should be appointed Commissioners for the said Plantation ; which Project and Articles signed with our own Hand we have lately transmitted unto you our Deputy.

* * * * * *

WILLIAM MONTGOMERY (1696)

I HAVE heard honest old men say that in June, July and August, 1606, people came from Stranraer, four miles, and left their horses at the port, hired horses at Donaghadee, came with their wares and provisions to Newtown, and sold them, dined there, stayed two or three hours, and returned to their houses the same day by bedtime. . . . Then you might see streets and tenements regularly set out, and houses rising (like Cadmus's colony) on a sudden, so that these dwellings became towns immediately.

Yet among all this care and indefatigable industry for their families, a place of God's honour to dwell in was not forgotten or neglected, for indeed our forefathers were more pious than ourselves, and as soon . . . as the old castle was so repaired (as it was in spring-time 1606), as might be shelter for that year's summer and harvest, for Sir Hugh and for his servants that winter, his piety made some good store of provisions in those fair seasons, towards roofing and fitting the chancel of that church, for the worship of God ; and therein he needed not withdraw his own planters from working for themselves, because there were Irish Gibeonets and garrons enough in his woods to hew and draw timber for the sanctuary. . . .

—Montgomery Papers.

The Montgomery Papers were written by William Montgomery of Rosemount, Co. Down, in his old age, 1696-1706. He recalls the incursion of Scots into Antrim in 1606, the dispossession of the Irish, and extinction of the great house of O'Neill of Clannaboy. These events set a headline for the Plantation of Ulster five years later. The Montgomery Papers, selections from which had been published in the "Belfast Newsletter," have been edited by Rev. G. Hill (Belfast, 1869).

CASTLE AND BAWN OF CARRICKMACROSS

ENTRANCE TO BAWN AT BELLAHILL, NEAR CARRICKFERGUS

Rev. Andrew Stewart (1620)

KING James had prepared a place and liberty in Ireland for them [the Scots], and having given some lands to some men whom he had nobilitated, these men sought tenants for their lands; and from Scotland came many, and from England not a few, yet all of them generally the scum of both nations, who, for debt, or breaking and fleeing from justice, or seeking shelter, came thither, hoping to be without fear of man's justice in a land where there was nothing, or but little, as yet, of the fear of God. And in a few years there flocked such a multitude of people from Scotland that these northern counties of Down, Antrim, Londonderry, &c., were in a good measure planted, which had been waste before; yet most of the people, as I said before, made up a body (and, it's strange, of different names, dialects, tempers, breeding, and, in a word, all void of godliness), who seemed rather to flee from God in this enterprise than to follow their own mercy. Yet God followed them when they fled from Him—albeit, at first it must be remembered that they cared little for any church.—REV. ANDREW STEWART (Minister of Donaghadee): *History of the Church of Ireland after the Scots were naturalized.*

This contemporary account has been published in P. Adair: A true narrative of the rise and progress of the Presbyterian Church in Ireland (1866).

★   ★   ★   ★   ★   ★

Earl of Belmore (1894)

THE grants made to the Patentees or Adventurers under the Plantation of Ulster were usually of the nominal extent of either 2,000, 1,500, or 1,000 acres. This extent was only nominal, because generally only "profitable acres" were counted, and a good deal of more or less reclaimable land was thrown in. On each "proportion" or estate the grantee would be expected to build a "castle" or fortified house. This would appear, from the report of Pynnar's survey of Ulster made in 1619-20, to have usually varied from sixty to eighty feet in length, and to have consisted of a house of two or three stories, surrounded, in most instances, by a "bawne," or rampart of lime and stone. As the houses appear to have been in some cases of the same length as the "bawne," which was usually, but not always, square, each house had probably a small courtyard in front and rear . . .

The ruins of several of these plantation castles in Fermanagh still exist. The accommodation for the families inhabiting them must have been limited. Near them, or at any rate somewhere on the estate, were often villages of a few houses, which are sometimes described as being built of "cage work." There is what I should suppose to be a very fair specimen of one of the smaller of these castles in the grounds of the Buncrana Castle demesne, County Donegal. It is situated near the river and the present dwelling-house. It has no bawne, and would seem to

45

have had an outside flight of stone steps from the ground to the first floor, and to have had another floor above, with gabled ends. This house, of which I have only seen the outside, is so short, that I am doubtful whether it could have had more than one or at most two rooms on each floor.—*Some social notes of the Ulster Plantation.*

★   ★   ★   ★   ★   ★

Fríoċ an uain-se ar Inis Fáil,
   buime mac Mileaḋ Easpáin;
Ruġaḋ a neart, fríoċ a faill,
   ġaċ críoċ aġ teaċt fá a tuairim.

Tuġaḋ slán ġaċ fir impe,
   iomḋa a huile 's a héiġcinnte ;
A neaṁ ġlóir is saoḃ re seal,
   Sean-Róiṁ na naoṁ 's na neiṁeaḋ.

Ní tuit cara tar a ceann,
   Ní faġtar troid 'n-a timceall;
Mo truaiġe mar tarla i-nnioġ
   Laḃra uaiḋe ní héistior.

Do ḋíoġlaḋ cneaḋa cat nġall;
   Fuaraḋ ar óġḃaḋ eaċtrann
A n-algas don eirġ re heaḋ,
   Tanġas re ġreim na nġaoiḋeal.

Dá mbiaḋ compán nó cara,
   Do ċlainn Néill anallana,
Do ċröfeaḋ mar tarla an tír,
   Do ċaoifeaḋ daṁna a ḋimbriġ.

—Eoċaiḋ Ó hEoġusa.

These verses, voice of an older Ulster which the " new foreigners " were seeking to destroy, are from a long poem by O'Hussey, poet of the Maguires of Fermanagh, whose Ode to Hugh Maguire (1600) is well known to modern readers in the fine English version by James Clarence Mangan. O'Hussey, who died about 1613, deplores the decline and fall of the ancient Gaelic aristocracy and traditional civilisation with these also the passing of the bardic order, of which he himself was a brilliant representative. Inisfail, he says, is taken at a disadvantage, strangers are crowding in and claiming her as their own ; her sons will no longer fight for her as a prize ; no voice speaks for her ; the foreigners can wreak their wicked will. One of the O'Neills of old, were he to see the country now, would shed tears at its weakness. The race of the Gael are still proud and strong, but catastrophe was in store for them

46

because of their lawlessness in times past. Standish O'Grady, who published a large part of the text of this poem in his Catalogue of the Irish Manuscripts in the British Museum, considered that O'Hussey's tone justifies the assumption that the Plantation of Ulster was in progress when he was writing.

MAPS AND MAP-MAKERS (1603–41)

This map of the lands granted in Derry (1613) by James I in the Great Plantation to the city of London is from the Survey made by Sir Thomas Phillips, now with other maps of the plantation in the Archbishop of Canterbury's Library, Lambeth. The lettering describes it as " A general platt of the lands belonginge to the City of London, as they are divided and set out to the 12 Companies as they doe butt and bound each upon the particular platts whereof doe followe more at large described."

Sir Thomas Phillips, who made the survey, had been a captain in the Nine Years' War against O'Neill and O'Donnell (1594-1603) and one of the British Commissioners for the government of Ulster after the Flight of the Earls. He himself acquired much land, as well as valuable patents and monopolies, including one for the manufacture of Irish whiskey. He urged the plantation of Derry as " a perpetual strength to the King and an everlasting memory to the City of London."

Before Phillips, mapmakers in Ulster paving the way to confiscation, had a perilous passage. " Our geographers do not forget," says Sir John Davies, " what entertainment the Irish of Tyrone gave to a mapmaker about the end of the late rebellion ; for, one Barkeley being appointed by the late Earl of Devonshire to draw a true and perfect map of the north part of Ulster (the old map of Tyrone being false and defective), when he came into Tyrone the inhabitants took off his head because they would not have their lands discovered."

LONDON COMPANIES' LANDS

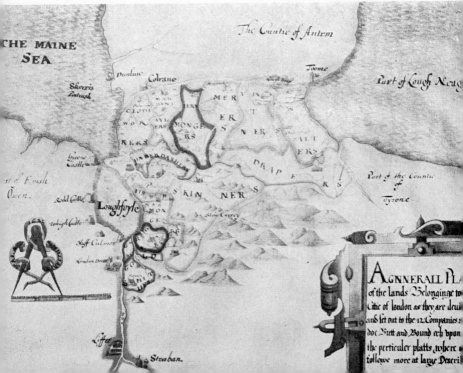

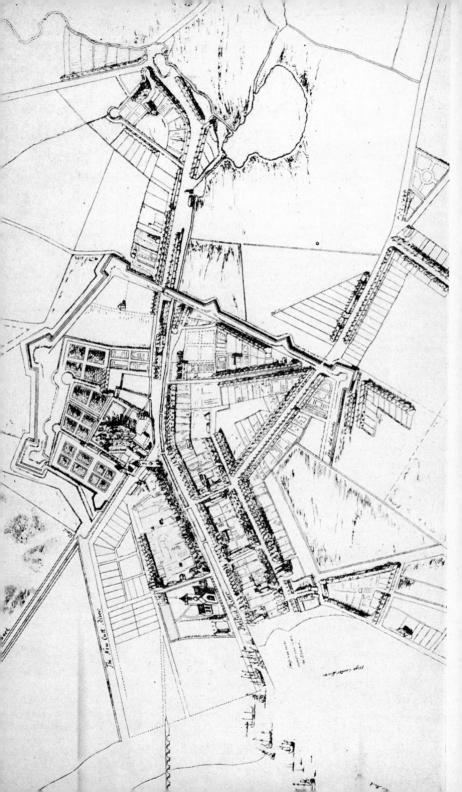

PLANTATION COMMISSIONERS (1611)

WE came to Belfast where we found many masons, bricklayers, and other labourers awork who had taken down the ruins of the decayed Castle there almost to the vault of the cellars, and had likewise laid the foundation of a brick house 50 foot long which is to be adjoined to the said Castle by a staircase of brick which is to be 14 foot square. . . .

The Castle will defend the passage over the ford at Belfast between the Upper and Lower Clandeboye, and likewise the bridge over the Owynvarra between Malon and Belfast. This work is in so good forwardness that it is like to be finished by the middle of next summer.

The town of Belfast is plotted out in a good form, wherein are many families of English, Scotch, and some Manxmen already inhabiting, of which some are artificers who have built good timber houses with chimneys after the fashion of the English Pale, and one inn with very good lodging which is a great comfort to the travellers in those parts. Near which town Sir Arthur Chichester hath ready made above twelve hundred thousand of good bricks, whereof after finishing of the said Castle, house, and Bawn, there will be a good proportion left for the building of other tenements within the said town.

Not far from Belfast the said Sir Arthur Chichester hath impalled a park of three mile compass where he intendeth to build a house of lime and stone, but a timber house with chimneys is already built therein, which is compassed about with a rampier of earth and sods and a deep ditch standing full of water. . . . A mile and somewhat more from Knock-fergus we saw a farm house of the Lord Deputy built of timber after the English fashion enclosed round with a Bawn ditched about and a strong hedge thereupon, the walls of which house are lately made up with stone. Upon divers other portions of the Lord Deputy's lands there are many English families, some Scots and divers civil Irish planted, and there are three mills already built upon several parts of the said lands ; and timber and other materials are also provided for the building of another mill near unto Belfast.—*Report of the Plantation Commissioners of the work done by servitors on lands in Down, Antrim and Monaghan* [1611].

*   *   *   *   *   *

NICHOLAS PYNNAR (1619)

I HAVE in the Book before written set down all the particulars I find of the State of the Plantation of his Majesty's escheated Lands in *Ulster* now to stand.

And, *First*, it appears by the Particulars, that in the *British* Families within mentioned, there are 6215 Bodies of Men ; but I may presume further to certify partly by observing the Habitation of these Lands, and partly by conferring with some of Knowledge among them, that upon Occasion, there may be found in those Lands at least 8000 Men of *British* Birth and Discent, to do his Majesty Service for defence thereof, though the fourth Part of the Land is not fully inhabited.

Secondly, It appears by the Particulars, that there are now built within the Counties of *Ardmagh, Tyrone, Donegall, Fermanagh, Cavan,* and *London-Derry,* 107 Castles with Bawnes, 19 Castles without Bawnes, 42 Bawnes without Castles or Houses, 1897 Dwelling Houses of Stone and Timber, after the *English* manner at Townreeds, besides very many such Houses in several parts which I saw not ; and yet there is great want of Buildings upon the Lands, both for Townreeds and otherwise ; and I may say that the abode and continuance of those Inhabitants upon the Lands is not yet made certain, although I have seen the Deeds made unto them. My Reason is, that many of the *English* Tenants do not yet plough upon the Lands, neither use Husbandrie ; because, I conceive

ULSTER IN THE 18TH CENTURY—A BLEACH GREEN IN CO. DOWN

they are fearful to stock themselves with Cattle or Servants for those Labours. Neither do the *Irish* use Tillage ; for they are also uncertain of their stay upon the Lands ; so that, by this means, the *Irish* ploughing nothing, do use greasing, the *English* very little, and were it not for the *Scottish* Tenants, which do plough in many places of the Country, those Parts may starve, by Reason whereof, the *British,* who are forced to take their Lands at great Rates, do lie at the greater Rents, paid unto them by the *Irish* Tenants, who do grease their Land ; and if the *Irish* be put away with their Cattle, the *British* must either forsake their Dwellings, or, endure great Distress on the suddain. Yet the Combination of the *Irish* is dangerous to them, by robbing them, and otherwise.

I observe the greatest number of *Irish* do dwell upon the Lands granted to the City of London ; which happeneth, as I take it, two ways, *First*, There are five of the Proportions assigned to the several Companies, which are not yet estated to any Man, but are in the Hands of Agents ; who finding the *Irish* more profitable than the *British* Tenants, are unwilling to draw on the *British*, perswading the Company, that the Lands are Mountainous and unprofitable, not regarding the future Security of the whole : *Secondly*, The other seven of the Proportions are leased to several Persons for 61 Years, and the Lessees do affirm, that they are not bound to plant English, but may plant with what People they please : neither is the City of London bound to do it by their Patents from his Majesty, as they say ; and by these two Actions, the *British* that now are there, who have many of them built Houses at their own Charges have no Estates made unto them, which is such Discouragement unto them, as they are minded to depart the Land ; and without better Settlement will seek elsewhere, wherein it is very fit, the City have Direction to take a present Course, that they may receive their assurances ; and this being the Inconveniency, which in this Survey I have observed, further than what was set down formerly by Sir Josias Bodley's last Survey, I have thought good to make the same known to your Lordships, submitting the further Consideration thereof to your Lordships' deep Judgment.—NICHOLAS PYNNAR'S *Survey* (1619).

Nicholas Pynnar was directed " to survey and make a return of the proceedings and performance of conditions of the undertakers, servitors, and natives planted."

*   *   *   *   *   *

COUNCIL OF IRELAND (1641)

WE humbly presume, with all confidence, to say that the plantations here prudently begun by Queen Elizabeth, and piously proceeded in by his Majesty's most blessed father, as by the blessing of God they have prospered well, to the great advantage of the Crown and benefit of the inhabitants planted, so they have been the very original and preservation of the peace and happiness which of late years this Kingdom has enjoyed. That by them several English towns, castles, houses of strength, and churches have been built in many remote and desolate parts of the Kingdom, more societies of Protestants settled than are in all the Kingdom besides, religion, civility, schools, manufacture and trades in a good measure from the time introduced ; a clergy well enabled by glebes of his Majesty's bounty and otherwise, and the lands by habitation generally raised to values far above former times. That in the plantations great parts of the lands have been so assured to the British by provisoes in the grants, and otherwise, as they must for ever remain English, and cannot in point of interest come into the hands of the Irish, which adds much to the strength of the Government and service of the Crown. That by them the great Irish lords, who for so many ages so grievously infested this Kingdom, are either taken away or so levelled with others in point of subjection as all now submit to the rule of the law.

A PORTION OF THE DEDICATION AND INTRODUCTION OF THE ANNALS OF THE FOUR MASTERS IN THE HANDWRITING OF BROTHER MICHAEL O'CLERIGH.

The Annals of the Four Masters (1632–6)

WHILE the Plantation of Ulster, according to official reports, was being successfully completed, a group of poor scholars of the Order of St. Francis were gathering up the threads of Ulster history as far back as writing or tradition could reach, and compiling the " Annals of the Kingdom of Ireland," better known as the " Annals of the Four Masters." The collection of the material occupied many years ; the work is said to have been written in the neighbourhood of the ruined Franciscan monastery of Donegal.

The chief compiler was Brother Michael O'Clerigh, member of a family which for generations had been professional historians to the princely house of O'Donnell. A lay brother in the Irish Franciscan monastery at Louvain, he was sent by his superiors to Ireland at a time of comparative peace, when the persecution of Catholics was not intense, to collect, transcribe, and synchronise the annals of Ireland, with special reference to the province of Ulster. " In all Irish history," says his modern biographer, Father Brendan Jennings, O.F.M., " there is no more wonderful and touching figure than the humble and learned Brother, wandering through the length and breadth of our land, gathering up and transcribing the precious fragments of Ireland's sacred and profane history, that the glories of her past might live."

Brother Michael's three colleagues, according to Father John Colgan (1645), were Fearfeasa O Mulconry, Peregrine O Clerigh, and Peregrine O Duigenan. Maurice O Mulconry and Conaire O Clerigh also gave some help.

In the passage shown in facsimile on the opposite page, he begins by beseeching God to bestow every happiness that may redound to the welfare of his body and soul upon Farrell O'Gara, Lord of one of the two Members of Parliament for the County of Sligo in the year 1634. He goes on to say :

" It is self-evident, wherever nobility and honour flourish, that nothing is more glorious or more worthy of praise than to revive the knowledge of ancient authors and of the illustrious personages and nobles of former times, so that succeeding generations might cherish the memory of their ancestors.

" I, Michael O Clerigh, a poor brother of the Order of St. Francis, have come before you, o noble Farrell O'Gara, knowing what grief and sorrow it was to you (for the glory of God and the honour of Ireland) that the race of the Gael has passed under a cloud of darkness, and that no memorial remains of our saints and virgins, our bishops, abbots, and church dignatories, our kings and princes, lords, chieftains, and men of learning. I explained to you that I thought I could get the assistance of the chroniclers whom I most esteemed to compile a book of annals, in which the aforesaid matters might be put on record ; and that, should they not be written down now, they would not again be discovered to be put on record until the end of the world."

CHAPTER IV.

Confederation of Kilkenny

CONFISCATIONS based on legal quibbles, religious disabilities, the fear that the government might yield to the fanatical party in England and Scotland which clamoured for the extirpation of Catholicism, the example of the successful rebellion of the Scottish Covenanters, all led up to the great upheaval of 1641. The revolt, at first confined to the old Irish in Ulster, rapidly spread until it covered the whole island.—W. F. BUTLER: *The Cromwellian Confiscation.*

* * * * * *

"Parties on the back of parties, at war with the world and with one another."—THOMAS CARLYLE *on the Confederation of Kilkenny.*

* * * * * *

Kilkenny Castle, where the Confederation held some of its meetings

[I.T.A

STATEMENT BY THE CATHOLICS OF IRELAND (1641)

HEADS of the causes which moved the Northern Irish, and Catholicks of Ireland, to take arms (1641).

1. IT was plotted and resolved by the Puritans of England, Scotland, and Ireland, to extinguish quite the Catholick religion, and the professors and maintainers thereof, out of all those kingdoms ; and to put all Catholicks of this realm to the sword, that would not conform themselves to the Protestant religion.

2. THE State of Ireland did publickly declare, that they would root out of this realm all the natives, and make a total second conquest of the land, alledging, that they were not safe with them.

3. ALL the natives here were deprived of the benefit of the ancient fundamental laws, liberties, and privileges, due by all laws and justice to a free people and nation, and more particularly due by the municipal laws of Ireland.

4. THAT the subjects of Ireland, especially the Irish, were thrust out forcibly from their ancient possessions, against law, without colour or right ; and could not have propriety or security in their estates, goods or other rights, but were wholly subject to an arbitrary power, and tyrannical government, these forty years past, without hope of relief or redress.

5. THEIR native youth here, debarred by the practice of state, from all learning and education, in that the one only university here, excludes all Catholicks thence ; neither are they suffered to acquire learning or breeding beyond seas, of purpose to make them rude and ignorant of all letters.

6. THE Catholicks of this realm are not admitted to any dignity, place, or office, either military or civil, spiritual or temporal, but the same conferred upon unworthy persons, and men of no quality, who purchase it for money, or favour, and not by merit.

7. ALL the trading, traffick, shipping, and riches of this whole isle by the corruption of the State, are engrossed by the Dutch, Scottish, and English, not residing here, who exclude the natives wholly from the same ; and who return the product, and all their flock and coin back unto their native countries.

8. ALL the staple and rich commodities of the realm are turned to monopolies, and heavy impositions against law laid on all merchandize.

9. THE principal native wares of the land exported into foreign parts, unwrought and unmanufactured, thereby depriving the kingdom of all manual trades and occupations ; and driving the natives to furnish themselves from head to foot, with manufactures from abroad, at very dear rates.

55

10. ALL their heavy and insufferable pressures prosecuted and laboured by the natives of this kingdom, with much suit, expense, and importunity, both in parliament here, and in England before his Majesty, to be redressed, yet could never be brought to any happy conclusion, or as much as hope of contentment, but always eluded with delays.

11. COMMON justice, and the rights and privileges of parliament, denied to all the natives of the realm; and the antient course of parliamentary proceeding wholly declined.

12. HIS majesty's royal power, honour, prerogative, estate, revenue, and rights, invaded upon, by the puritan faction in England. . . .

17. ALL the natives in the English plantations of this realm, were disarmed by proclamation, and the protestant plantators armed, and tied by the conditions of their plantations, to have arms, and to keep certain numbers of horse and foot continually upon their lands, by which advantage, many thousands of the natives were expulsed out of their possessions, and as many hanged by martial law, without cause, and against the laws of this realm; and many of them otherwise destroyed, and made away, by sinister means and practices.

18. HALF this realm was found to belong unto his majesty, as his ancient demesne and inheritance, upon old feigned titles of three hundred years past, by juries, against law, their evidence and conscience, who were corrupted to find the said titles, upon promise of part of those lands so found for the king, or other reward, or else were drawn thereunto by threats of the judges in the circuits, or by heavy fines, mulcts, and censures of pillory, stigmatizings, and other like cruel and unusual punishments.

—E. LODGE: *Desiderata Curiosa Hibernica* (1772).

* * * * * *

THE EARL OF CASTLEHAVEN (1683)

ON my arrival at Kilkenny, I found the town very full, and many of my acquaintance, all preparing for war. To this end they had chosen amongst themselves, out of the most eminent persons, a Council, to which they gave the title of The Supreme Council of the Confederate Catholics of Ireland, and formed an oath of association, by which all were bound to obey them. They had made four generals for the respective provinces of the kingdom; Preston, of Leinster; Barry, of

56

Mounster; Owen Roe O Neil, of Ulster; and one Bourke, of Conaught; and being to give commissions, they caused a seal to be made, which they called the seal of the council.

I was sent for to this Council to tell my story, where I gave them a particular account of my adventures; and being asked what I intended to do? I answered, to get into France, and from thence into England. Hereupon they told me their condition, and what they were doing for their preservation and natural defence, seeing no distinction made, or safety but in arms; persuading me to stay with them, being I was beloved in the country, had three sisters married amongst them, was persecuted on the same score they were, and ruined so, that we had no more to lose but our lives. I took two or three days to think of this proposition, and to examine the model of government they had prepared against the meeting

LEINSTER, 1610—JOHN SPEED

of the General Assembly, and most particularly their oath of association.

Having spent some time on these thoughts, and at last taken my resolution, I returned to the Supreme Council, thanked them for their good opinion of me, and engaged myself to run a fortune with them. Whether anger and revenge did not incline me to it, as much as any thing else, I cannot certainly resolve. This I well remember, that I considered how I had been used, and seen my house burning as I passed by; besides that I was a light man, with no charge, and without any hopes of redress from the king, who was then engaged in an intestine war. Now being thus a confederate, and having taken the oath of association, they made me one of the council, and general of the horse under Preston.

The first assembly met the 24th of October, 1642. It differed little from a Parliament, but that the lords and commons sat together. They approved, without delay, all the Council had done, and settled a model of government, viz:—That at the end of every general assembly, the Supreme Council should be confirmed or changed, as they thought fit. That it should consist of twenty-five, six out of each province, three of the six still resident; the twenty-fifth was myself, with no relation to any province, but to the Kingdom in general. Every province had a provincial assembly, which met on occasions: and each county had commissioners for applotting money within themselves, as it came to their shares, on the general applotment of the province. Many other things there were as to government, but these are the most remarkable.

The General Assembly being ended, the Supreme Council sent envoys to the king of France, Mr. Rotchford, and after him Mr. Geoffrey Barron; To the king of Spain, F. James Talbot, an Augustine Fryar; to the Pope, first, Mr. Richard Belling, after him the bishop of Ferns, and Mr. Nicholas Plunket. Besides these they had residents with all these princes, but they were generally

THE SEAL OF THE CONFEDERATION

churchmen. The King of France first sent them in return M. Monarie, to whom succeeded M. Du Moulin, and after him M. Talloon. The King of Spain first sent M. Fuysot, a Burgundian, to whom succeeded the Count of Berehaven, after him Don Diego de' los Torres. The Pope sent one Scarampo, priest of the Oratorian Order, who remained till the coming of Rinuccini, Archbishop and Prince of Fermo, in quality of Nuncio.

THE PAPAL NUNCIO (1645)

TOWARDS evening Ireland came in sight, and we approached a bay which, from a little river that flows into it is called the Bay of Kenmare. That night we cast anchor in a secure place. Next day with little wind and very slow sailing, we reached land. . . . My first lodging was in a shepherd's hut in which animals also took shelter. There we stayed two days, to rest from our fatigues and return thanks for our preservation.

The Secretary [of the Confederation] and others greatly regretted that we were unable to land at Waterford, where, they say, I should have been received with prepared demonstrations, and firing of cannon. But I felt glad that fortune had led me to a lonely and unknown part of the country, where no Apostolic minister had ever been before. . . . I travelled slowly towards Kilkenny, halting because of my indisposition at the villages belonging to Catholic nobles well affected to the Holy See. People now began to join me from all quarters, hastening to offer welcome.

The members of the Supreme Council, hearing from Secretary Belling of my arrival, sent three representatives with two companies of horse to congratulate me on my safe arrival and to escort me, while danger might be apprehended from the vicinity of the enemy. These officers were Richard Butler, brother to the Marquis of Ormond but a Catholic, Lord Netterville, and Nicholas di Tegnier, a priest, who met me at Dromsecane, twelve miles from Macroom. The evening before my arrival at Kilkenny I stopped at a villa three miles from the town, to give time for all the preparations for my reception. Here four noblemen of the Council waited on me, accompanied by Mr. Belling who came to welcome me again. One of them, a man of letters, delivered a short oration.

When I was in my litter we set out, and in a space of three miles I was met by all the nobility and all the young men of Kilkenny, besides crowds of other persons in different detachments the leaders of each dismounting to compliment me. First came a troop of fifty scholars, all, nevertheless, armed with pistols. Having careered around me, they conveyed their compliments through a youth crowned with laurel in a richer habit than the rest, who recited some verses to me . . .

The Catholics of Ireland have from time immemorial been divided into two adverse factions. One under the name of the old Irish, although dispersed over the four provinces of the Kingdom, are yet more numerous in that of Ulster, which seems to be in a manner their head-quarters, since it was there the Earl of Tyrone (Hugh O'Neill) placed himself at their head and carried on a long war on their behalf against Queen Elizabeth. The other faction may be called the old English, a race introduced into Ireland at the time of Henry II, and so called to distinguish them from the new English who came over with the Protestant heresy. . . .

The discord between these two factions may be attributed to the following causes : the old Irish averse to heresy are also averse to the dominion of England, and refused to accept of the ecclesiastical property offered to

THE MARKET CROSS, KILKENNY, AND PART OF HIGH STREET, FROM A
WATER COLOUR IN THE NATIONAL MUSEUM

*Many pamphlets
about the events in
Ireland were publish-
ed in London from
1641 onwards. Most
of these, like the
specimen shown here,
were extremely sen-
sational and untrust-
worthy.*

Approved, Good, and Ioyfull Newes
From IRELAND:

Relating how the Castle of Artaine was taken from the Rebels, two
of their Captaines kild, and one taken prisoners by the protestants.
With the arrivall of 2000 foot, and 300 horse from *England*.

Also a great skirmish betweene the Protestants and the Rebels at a
place neere *Felstou*, wherein the English obtained great renowne and victory.

Whereunto is added,
A true relation of the great overthrow which the English gave the
Rebels before *Drogheda* sent in a Letter bearing date the 27 of *February*,
to Sir *Robert King* Knight at Cecill house in the Strand.
Printed by Order of Parliament.

LONDON,
Printed for *Iohn Wright*, 1641.

them when the Kings of England apostatized from the Church. The new Irish on the contrary enriched with the monastic possessions, and bound to the King no less by obligation than interest, desire nothing better than the increase of the royal prerogative ; acknowledge no laws save those of that Kingdom, are completely English in their prejudices, and in consequence of their connection with the heretics, less jealous of the difference of religion. Nature even seems to widen the breach by difference of character and qualities, the new party being for the most part of low stature, quick-witted and of subtle understanding, while the old Irish are tall, simple-minded, unrefined in their manner of living, generally slow of comprehension and quite unskilled in negotiation. They regard each other with mutual distrust. . . .

At the time of my arrival the greater part of the Catholic troops were under the command of two generals, Owen O'Neill and Thomas Preston, the latter of the new Irish, the former of the old, who were not only rivals by nature, and from party spirit, but embittered by jealousy from having both served in the Flemish wars, and from having even then shown signs of mutual aversion. . . . These two chiefs, so different in their aims, so opposite in their management of affairs, were still more different in their nature. The O'Neill, a man of few words, cautious and phlegmatic in his operations, a great adept in concealing his feelings ; the other very subject to fits of anger in which he was so rash and outspoken.

JEAN BAPTISTE RINUCCINI, *Archbishop of Fermo.*

On the opposite page is a picture of old Kilkenny. " This beautiful and interesting drawing," not only shows the Cross (where the Papal Nuncio was solemnly received in 1645), but supplies " a curious glimpse of the quaint old houses of the Highstreet as they appeared before the removal of the Cross and some of them as they stood within my own recollection, preserving in detail the surrounding high-peaked gables, projecting penthouses and picturesque bay windows "— J. G. PRIM in " Transactions Kilkenny Archaeological Soc.", 1853).

* * * * * *

LORD MAGUIRE (1645)

ON Thursday, February the 20th, he was drawn on a sledge from the Tower through London, and so to Tyburn ; where being removed into a cart, he kneeled and prayed awhile, after which Sheriff Gibbs spake to him, representing the heinousness of his crimes. . . .

SHERIFF GIBBS : Do you believe you did well in those wicked actions ?
MAGUIRE : I have but a short time, do not trouble me.
SHERIFF : Sir, it is but just that I should trouble you, that you may not be troubled forever.
MAGUIRE : I beseech you, sir, trouble me not, I have but a little time to spend.
SHERIFF GIBBS : I shall give you as much time after as you shall spend to give satisfaction to the people. I do require you, as an instrument set

in God's stead here, to make an acknowledgement to the people, whether you are sorry for what you have done, or no, whether it be good or no ?

MAGUIRE : I beseech you do not trouble me ; I am not disposed to give you an account. Pray give me leave to pray.

DOCTOR SIBBALD : Give glory to God that your soul may not be presented to God with the blood of so many thousand people.

SHERIFF GIBBS : You are either to go to Heaven or Hell ; if you make not an ingenuous confession your case is desperate. Had you any commission or no ?

MAGUIRE : I tell you there was no Commission that ever I saw.

SHERIFF GIBBS : Who were actors or plotters with you or gave you any Commission ?

MAGUIRE : For God's sake, give me leave to depart in peace.

Then they asked him if he had some Pardon or Bull from the Pope for what he did. To which he only answered, " I am not of the same religion with you." And being further urged about a Bull or Pardon, said " I saw none of it. All that I knew I delivered in my examinations ; all that I said in my examinations are true ; All that I said is right. I beseech you let me depart in peace." And so not returning them any answer to their questions, he continued mumbling over a paper which he had in his hand, as he had done from his first coming.

The Sheriff commanded his pockets to be searched, whether he had no Bull or Pardon about him, but they found in his pockets only some beads and a crucifix, which were taken from him. And then Dr. Sibbald said to him, " Come, my Lord, leave those and acknowledge your offence to God and the world. One drop of the blood of Jesus Christ is able to purge away all the heavy load of blood that is on you. It is not your Ave Marias nor these things will do you any good, but it is Agnus Dei, qui tollit peccata Mundi." The Lord Maguire seemed not to regard his discourse, but read out of his paper to the people as followeth :—

" Since I am here to die, I desire to depart with a quiet mind and with the marks of a good Christian, that is, asking forgiveness of God and next of the world. And I do forgive (from the bottom of my heart) all my enemies and offenders, even those that have a hand in my death. I die a Roman Catholick, and although I have been a great sinner, yet I am now by God's grace, heartily sorry for all my sins, and I do most confidently trust to be saved, not by my own works but only by the Passion, merits and mercy of my dear Saviour Jesus Christ, into whose Hand I commend my soul."

And then added " I beseech you gentlemen, let me have a little time to say my prayers."

SHERIFF GIBBS : Sir, if you answer ingenuously to those questions we shall ask you, you shall have time afterwards. Whether do you account the shedding of the Protestant blood to be a sin or not ? And whether do you desire pardon of God for that sin ?

MAGUIRE : I do desire pardon of God for all my sins ; I cannot resolve you in anything for my part.

SHERIFF GIBBS: You can tell what your conscience dictates to you. Do you think it was a sin or not?

MAGUIRE: For my part I cannot determine it.

SHERIFF GIBBS: Then now it seems nothing to you to kill so many?

MAGUIRE: How do you mean killing of them? To tell you my mind directly, for the killing I do not know that, but I think the Irish had a just cause for their wars. . . .

All this while his eye was mostly upon his papers, mumbling over something out of them to himself; whereupon one of the sheriffs demanding those papers of him, he flung them down. They were taken up and given to the Sheriff, and a copy of them hereafter follows. . . . After other suchlike talk, the Sheriff bidding him prepare himself for death, he said " I do beseech all the Catholicks that are here to pray for me, I beseech God to have mercy on my soul." And so was executed.

Conor Maguire, Baron of Enniskillen, arrested in 1641 for alleged complicity in the Insurrection, was tried and executed in London four years later.

The laſt Speeches
AND
CONFESSION
OF THE
Lord Maguire :

The *Iriſh* REBELL, that was Hanged at Tyburne, and Drawne, and Quartered on Thurſday laſt, the 20th. of *February, 1644.*

With all the Queſtions that were put to him, and his ſeverall Anſwers.

And the Coppies of thoſe Letters, and other Papers which he then had in his hands and made uſe of, that were afterwards delivered to Sheriffe *Gibbs.*

COL. HENRY MC T. O'NEILL (1646)

O NEILL in the spring waited on the Nuncio at Kilkenny, where the Supreme Council gave him a new power to levy a new army of northern men, which he compleated in May following to five thousand men strong, of which five hundred horse, such as they were ; with whom he marched to Benborbe, marching with six thousand foot in nine battalions, and eight hundred horse well accoutred, and encamped at the old place near Armagh, and within seven miles of O Neill's camp.

Next day, being the fifth, the scouts came in with news that the enemy was marching westward from Armagh towards Glasslagh, and at the same time that Colonel George Munroe marched with a party of five hundred foot from Coleraine to Dungannon, within seven miles of Benborbe, on the other side ; whereupon O Neill, with all his horse, went to the top of the hill (where the battle was fought the same afternoon) to take a view of the enemy in their march, as they passed the road the other side of the river towards Glasslagh (the place appointed for the Laganners and those of Coleraine to join the main body). . . .

The rout began two hours before night, in which the enemy left very rich booty of all sorts, which hindered the execution much, by the soldiers falling to plunder. My lord Montgomery was taken prisoner, and so was Major Cogheran ; Captain Hamilton, with several other officers slain, with four thousand private men on the spot ; and in the pursuit that night and the next day, about one hundred and fifty soldiers taken prisoners, and dismissed with a pass. To the best of my memory upwards of twenty colours taken, their artillery (being four field-pieces) with most of all their arms, tents, and baggage left behind (except Sir James Montgomery's regiment on their right, who escaped). Lost on the Irish side, Colonel Manus McNeale, Garve O Donnell, slain ; Lieutenant-General Farrall and Lieutenant-colonel Phelim McTuoll O Neill wounded ; Colonel Miles Reilly's cornet killed, with thirty-five private men, and two hundred and forty-five wounded. Next day O Neill ordered my lord Blayney's and captain Hamilton's corpse to be interred in Benburbe church with the proper ceremonies. If God had not put this timely stop to Munroe's career, his instructions and intentions were to harass the whole country before him 'till he came to Dunmore near Kilkenny, as was found by a memorial delivered by my lord Montgomery's own hand, when a prisoner.

A Journal of the most memorable transactions of General Owen O'Neill and his party, from the year 1641, to the year 1650. Faithfully related by Col. Henry McTully O'Neill, who served under him.

* * * * * *

CAPT. MULHOLLAND (1646)

M ACART made not his way to Charlemount but towards his Enemies, and marched a Myle from Benburb towards them, where he took his ground on a scroggred high hill, and sent out five hundred men more, half Pike half musket, to assist those returning from the Lord of Ardes. On which Ardes halted till Munroe came up with the Army, and drew on another Hill against MacArt, and a Bottom between them. Then men were commanded out from both sides down next the River in scroggie Woods, where Munroe's Men were often put to the worse and beaten back, and then [the parties] were relieved on both sides.

In the meantime that these parties or wings were so playing, Munroe's field pieces were not idle, but giving Fire, and most commonly overshot MacArt's men, and only twice struck down by two fyles. At this rate they were from two o'clock till an hour before Sunset, and MacArt's men crying to advance. But he desired them to have a little patience till the Horse would return ; who returning in great haste in a gallop, all in a sweat both Horse and Men, and drawn up in their ground ; then there was an intermission on both sides, being preparing to fight more close, on which MacArt spoke in the Front of his own Men these words, as I was told, or to that effect :—

" Gentlemen and Fellow Soldiers ! Know that those that stand before you ready to fight are those that banished you, your Wives and Children from your Lands and Houses, and make you seek your Bread and Livelihood in strange places. Now you have Arms in your hands as good as they have, and you are Gentlemen as good as they are. You are the Flower of Ulster, descended from as Ancient and Honourable a Stock of People as any in Europe. This Land you and your Predecessors having possessed about three thousand years. All Christendom knows your quarrel is good— to Fight for your native Birthright and for the Religion which your Forefathers professed and maintained since Christianity came first to this Land.

" Owen O'Neill, that very brave and noble Irish chieftain " (Pope Urban VIII).

" So as now is the time to consider your distressed and slavish condition ; you have Arms in your Hands, you are as numerous as they are ; and now try your Valour and your Strength on those who have banished you, and now resolve to destroy you Bud and Branch. So let your Manhood be seen by your push of Pike ; and I will engage, if you do so, by God's assistance and the Intercession of His Blessed Mother and all the Holy Saints in Heaven, that the Day will be your own. Your word is *Sancta Maria* ; and so in the Name of the Father, Son and Holy Ghost advance, and give not Fire till you are within Pikelength."

Which accordingly was observed. At which time the sun and Wind was against them, and blew the

Smoke in their faces, so that for a little moment the Musketeers could not see. At which charge the Scottish and British officers stood it Manfully, and left not their Ground till they were beaten down by push of Pike. But their men did not back them so vigorously as they should. One reason was, that since they left Mullow and Lisnegarvy they had not time to rest or refresh themselves till they came to front MacArt, and then standing from Two o'clock till Seven o'clock to their Arms, was enough to make them faint and heartless.

Another reason is that the Irish Pikes were longer by a Foot or two than the Scottish Pikes, and farr better to pierce, being four square and small and the others' Pikes broad-headed, which are the Worst in the World. Withall to my own knowledge, the Soldiers, I mean some that were not strong [enough] in the British Army for his Pike in a windy day, could cut off a foot, and some two, of their Pikes—which is a damned thing to be suffered. But the truth is, that Army did not expect to be faced by Ulstermen, much less to be fought with ; but too much confidence makes security, and security makes carelessness : and so it happened that day.

—*History of the War of Ireland from 1641 to 1653.* By a British officer of the regiment of Sir John Clotworthy. Ed. by Rev. E. Hogan, S.J. (Dublin, 1873).

*   *   *   *   *   *

THE *Confederate Wars* (1642–53)—*scenes and episodes from which have been described in the foregoing pages—were the greatest organised effort that the Irish people has ever made to preserve itself from complete destruction.   The Muster-Marshal of the Marquis of Ormond, Viceroy, computed in 1643 that 70,000 troops had been sent across the Channel to Ireland, the great majority of whom had been killed or taken prisoner. The Confederation then held most of Ireland, with many towns, ports, and fortresses, flew its flag on the high seas, and maintained diplomatic missions abroad.*

From the time of the Cessation (1643)—a truce between King Charles I and the Catholic Irish—the Confederate ranks were rent by dissensions. Prospects of victory, once bright, vanished with the arrival of Oliver Cromwell and the death of Eoghan Ruadh O Neill.   Cromwell, financed by a monied interest which claimed the land of Ireland as security, uprooted the whole social and religious order and ruined both the Irish nobility and the old families which had governed the towns for centuries.   What these twelve years did to the people in general is tersely described by J. P. Prendergast :

" Ireland, in the language of Scripture, now lay void as a wilderness. Five-sixths of her people had perished. Women and children were found daily in ditches, starved. The bodies of many wandering orphans whose fathers had embarked for Spain, and whose mothers had died of famine, were preyed upon by wolves. In the years 1652 and 1653 a man might travel twenty or thirty miles and not see a living creature. Man, beast and bird were all dead or had quit those desolate places. The troopers would tell stories of the places where they saw smoke, it was so rare to see either smoke by day or fire or candle by night."

CHAPTER V.

The Cromwellian Settlement

IS Israel a Servant? is he a home-born slave? why is he spoiled? The young lions roared upon him, and yelled, and they made his land waste : his cities are burnt without inhabitant.—*Jeremiah*, Ch. ii, 14, 15. (Quoted in Clarendon's *Historical View of the State of Ireland*).

When will this wild war be finished ; Ireland planted ; inhabitants disburthened ; soldiers settled ? The unsettling of a nation is easy ; the settling is not.—VINCENT GOOKIN, Surveyor-General of Ireland (1654)

The Cromwellian Settlement is the foundation of that deep and lasting division between the proprietary and the tenants which is the chief cause of the political and social evils of Ireland.—W. E. H. LECKY.

*　　*　　*　　*　　*　　*

W. C. ABBOTT (1939)

HOPE and fear are, indeed, among the most potent of political motives, but the invasion of Ireland had two other incentives. The first was the prospect of plunder, that is to say of the acquisition of Irish lands long since allotted to many of those who now took part in this enterprise, and expected by many others as their reward. The second was the necessity of keeping the army occupied ; and it may be noted that, beginning with this Irish expedition, there are few periods in the next eight years when some part of that army was not engaged in active service outside of England. Whatever may be thought of the Commonwealth and the Protectorate, they embraced or were compelled to adopt the oldest device of dictatorship—foreign war—which, consciously or unconsciously, diverted attention from domestic policy, and their chief support, the armed forces, from becoming the chief danger to their existence. . . .

It is apparent . . . that the Irish expedition was more than a military enterprise designed to break the power of the monarchy in Ireland. It was scarcely less a colonizing venture. Cromwell himself had claims to Irish lands which dated back to the first efforts to suppress the Irish rebellion, and there were many in his army and many more outside who had contributed to that enterprise and had substantial interest in the conquest of the Irish. Nor was it supposed that those who conquered it should not inherit it. These brethren of the Covenant and the sword looked forward to the accomplishment of a dream which they had long entertained, the vision of a rich and fertile country, a Promised Land, which should be the

OLIVARIVS CROMWELL EXERCITVVM ANGLIE   REIPVBLICE DVX GENERALIS LOCVM-
TENENS ET GVBERNATOR HIBERNIE OXO   NIENSIS ACADEMIE CANCELLARIVS

This striking print, engraved by Mazot, shows Cromwell at the height of his fame, with the City of London in background, and celebrates his triumphs as leader of the Army of the English Republic and Governor of Ireland. Entering London on his triumphant return from Ireland, Cromwell heard someone say: " What a crowd has come to see your Lordship's triumph ! " Cromwell: " Yes, but if it were to see me hanged, how many more would there come ? "

prize of victory and whose estates should be enjoyed by its conquerors. . . . In that spirit Cromwell and his men approached their task.—*The Writings and Speeches of Oliver Cromwell.* Vol. II.

★ ★ ★ ★ ★ ★

CLEMENT WALKER (1649)

SUNDAY after Easter-day [1649], six preachers militant at Whitehall tried the patience of their hearers ; one calling up another successively ; at last the Spirit of the Lord called up Oliver Cromwell, who standing a good while with lifted up eyes, as it were in a trance, and his neck inclining a little to one side, as if he had expected Mahomet's dove to descend and murmur in his ear ; and sending forth abundantly the groans of the Spirit, spent an hour in prayer, and an hour and a half in a Sermon. In his prayer he desired God to take off from him the government of this mighty People of England, as being too heavy for his shoulders to bear : An audacious, ambitious and hypocritical imitation of Moses. It is now reported of him that he pretendeth to Inspirations ; and that when any great or weighty matter is propounded, he usually retireth for a quarter or half an hour and then returneth and delivereth out the Oracles of the Spirit.—*History of Independency.*

Clement Walker, Member of Parliament, was a strong opponent of Cromwell's party, the Independents. He was imprisoned in the Tower of London for writing his " History of Independency " (1649), and died there while awaiting trial for high treason in 1651.

★ ★ ★ ★ ★ ★

ANTHONY A WOOD (1663)

IN 1650 . . . being often with his mother and brethren, he would tell them of the most terrible assaulting and storming of Tredagh [Drogheda], wherein he himself had been engaged. He told them that 3,000 at least, besides some women and children, were, after the assailants had taken part, and afterwards all the town, put to the sword on the 11 and 12 Sept., 1649 ; at which time Sir Arthur Aston, the governor had his brains beat out, and his body hack'd and chop'd to pieces.

He told them, that when they were to make their way up to the lofts and galleries in the church and up to the tower where the enemy had fled, each of the assailants would take up a child and use it as a buckler of defence, when they ascended the steps, to keep themselves from being shot or brain'd. After they had killed all in the church, they went into the vaults underneath where all the flower and choicest of the women and ladies had hid themselves.

One of these, a most handsome virgin and arrayed in costly and gorgeous apparel, kneeled down to Thomas Wood with tears and prayers to save her life : and being strucken with a profound pity, took her under his arm, went with her out of the church, with intention to put her over the works and to let her shift for herself ; but then a soldier perceiving his intentions, ran his sword . . . Whereupon Mr. Wood seeing her gasping, took away her money, jewels, &c., and flung her down over the works.

Anthony Wood (1632–95), or a Wood as he described himself, was a well-known Oxford historian. His brother, Thomas, served with Cromwell's army in Ireland.

* * * * * *

TO the Honourable John Bradshaw, Esquire, President of the Council of State : These

Dublin, 16th September, 1649.

Sir,

It hath pleased God to bless our endeavours at Tredah. After battery, we stormed it. The enemy were about 3,000 strong in the town. They made a stout resistance, and near 1,000 of our men being entered, the enemy forced them out again. But God giving a new courage to our men, they attempted again, and entered, beating the enemy from their defences.

The enemy had made three entrenchments, both to the right and left " of " where we entered ; all which they were forced to quit. Being thus entered, we refused them quarter ; having the day before, summoned the town. I believe we put to the sword the whole number of the defendants. I do not think thirty of the whole number escaped with their lives. Those that did, are in safe custody for Barbadoes. Since that time, the enemy quitted to us Trim and Dundalk. In Trim they were in such haste that they left their guns behind them.

This hath been a marvellous great mercy. The enemy, being not willing to put an issue upon a field-battle, had put into this garrison almost all their prime soldiers, being about 3,000 horse and foot, under the command of their best officers ; Sir Arthur Asthon being made governor. There were some seven or eight regiments, Ormond's being one, under the command of Sir Edmund Verney. I do not believe, neither do I hear, that any officer escaped with his life, save only one lieutenant, who, I hear, going to the enemy said, that he was the only man that escaped of all the garrison. The enemy were filled upon this with much terror. And truly I believe this bitterness will save much effusion of blood, through the goodness of God.

I wish that all honest hearts may give the glory of this to God alone, to whom indeed the praise of this mercy belongs. " As " for instruments, they were very inconsiderable the work throughout.

We are marching the army to Dublin, which we hope will be here to-morrow night, where we desire to recruit with victual, and shall then, God willing, advance towards the southern design—you know what—only we think Wexford will be our first undertaking in order to the other.

Captain Brandly did with forty or fifty of his men very gallantly storm the tentalia ; for which he deserves the thanks of the State.

I rest,

Your most humble servant,
OLIVER CROMWELL.

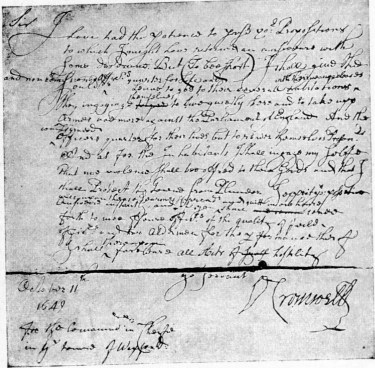

CROMWELL TO THE GOVERNOR OF WEXFORD

SIR,

I have had the patience to peruse your propositions, to which I might have returned an answeare with some disdaine. But (To bee short) I shall give the souldiers and noncommissioned officers quarter for life and leave to go to their severall habitations, with their wearing cloathes They ingaginge themselves to live quietly there and to take upp arms no more against the Parliament of England And the commissioned officers quarter for their lives, but to render themselves prisoners And as for the inhabitants, I shall ingage myselfe that noe violence shall bee offered to their goods, and that I shall protect the towne from plunder.

I expect your possetive answeare instantly and if you will upon these tearmes surrender and quitt in one houre shall send forth to mee four officers of the quality of feild officers and two Aldermen for the performance thereof I shall thereupon forbear all acts of hostility.

Your servant, O. CROMWELL.

For the Commander in Cheife in the towne of Wexford.

The original of the letter of which a facsimile is shown above from Cromwell to Col. David Sinnott, Commander of the Wexford garrison, is preserved in the Library of the Royal Irish Academy. When the terms had been agreed upon and signed, the Cromwellians broke into the town, slaughtered and plundered the inhabitants.

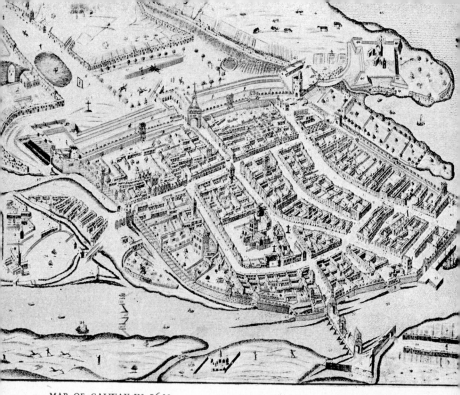

MAP OF GALWAY IN 1652

The Map in Trinity College,
Dublin, from which the above copy
is reproduced, measures six feet
six inches by four feet six. It
depicts Galway, then the second
city in Ireland. From it " a tolerably accurate idea may now be
formed of the former opulent state
and magnificence of Galway,
adorned with superb and highly
decorated buildings, and surrounded
by every requisite for security and
defence which either art could
suggest or wealth command."—
(James Hardiman: History of
Galway, 1820.)

CAPTAIN MULHOLLAND

AFTER this Hugh Duff [Hugh Dubh O'Neill] did set all Men and Maids to work, Townsmen and Soldiers, only those on duty attending the Breach and the Walls—to Draw dunghills, Morter, Stones, and Timber, and made a long Lane a Man's height, and about Eighty yards Length on both sides up from the Breach, with a foot Bank at the back of it; and caused [to be] place [d] Engines on both sides of the Same, and two Guns at the end of it invisible opposite to the Breach, and so ordered all things against a Storm.

Which [Storm] was about eight o'clock in the morning in the month of January, and [the English] entered without any opposition; and but few were to be seen in the town till they so Entered, that the Lane was cram'd full with Horsemen Armed with Helmets, back Breast Swords, Musquetoons and Pistols. On which those in the Front seeing themselves in a Pound, and could not make their way further, cryed out, "Halt! Halt!" On which those entering behind at the breach thought by those words, that all those of the Garrison were running away, and cryed out "Advance!" "Advance!" as fast as

*   *   *   *   *   *

FLIGHT OF JAMES II FROM DUNCANNON, CO. WEXFORD

(1690).

those before cryed, "Halt!" "Halt!" and so advanced till they thrust forward those before them, till that Pound or Lane was full, and could hold no more.

Then suddenly rushes a resolute party of Pikes and Musquetteers to the Breach, and scoured off and knocked back those entering. At which instance Hugh Duff's men within fell on those in the Pound with Shotts, Pikes, Scythes, Stones, and casting of great long pieces of Timber with the Engines amongst them; and then two Guns firing at them from the end of the Pound, slaughtering them by the Middle or Knees with chained Bullets, that in less than an hour's time about a thousand men were killed in that Pound, being a Top one another.

At this time Crumwell was on Horse back at the Gate, with his Guard, expecting the Gates to be opened by those entered, untill he saw those in the Breach beaten back, and heard the Cannons going off within. Then

By The Lord Lieutenant Generall of Ireland.

WHEREAS I am informed that the horſe vnder my Commande (ſince their being quartered within the *Black-water*) have and doe in their ſeverall quarters take away and waſt Wheate and Barly for their horſes, And doe behave themſelves outrageouſly towards the Inhabitants not contenting themſelves with ſuch Proviſions as they are able to afforde them, but doe kill their ſheepe and other cattle within and as often as they pleaſe. I doe hereby ſtraightly charge and Commande all Souldiers to forbeare ſuch like practices vpon paine of Death. And whereas ſuch offences as theſe cannot be comitted without the conſent, conniuance or at leaſt the neglect of the Officers, I doe hereby require them as they will anſwer it at their vtmoſt perills That they be diligent in governeing the Souldiers vnder their commands in their carriage to the Inhabitants in this Province of *Mounſter* in ſubjection to the Parliament, According to the Articles, Rules, and Diſcipline of War exerciſe in the Army, in the Army in *England* towards the Inhabitants there. And I doe hereby farther declare that if any Inhabitant within the lymitts aforeſaid ſhall make his greivance knowne vnto the Officer of any of the reſpective Souldiers that ſhall doe any wrong as aforeſaid and the ſaid Officer vpon proofe made ſhall refuſe to doe the ſaid party right, that then the ſaid party makeing complaint to me ſhall have ſatisfaction for his damage from the ſaid Officer. And I doe farther will and require all Officers and Souldiry within the lymitts aforeſaid, that they doe not breake downe any ſtackes of Barly or Wheate in their reſpective quarters, to give the ſame to their horſes; But that they content themſelves with Peaſe, Oates, Hay, and ſuch other forrage as the Country afords paying or giving Ticketts at ſuch reaſonable Rates for the ſame, as they were vſually ſold for, before their comeing into the ſaid quarters. Given vnder my hande this 8. day of December 1649.

O. CROMWELL.

Printed at Corcke in the yeare of our Lord God 1649.

Proclamation printed by Cromwell in Cork, 1649. From one of the very few copies extant, now in the National Library of Ireland.

he fell off as much Vexed as ever he was since he first put on a Helmet against the King, for such a repulse he did not usually meet with.

The Siege, at Distance and close, being about five or six weeks, and by several sallies out and on the Walls several of those within were lost, but many wounded and Sick, on which the Major General consulted with his officers [and seeing] that their ammunition was gone, concluded to leave the Town without Crumwell's leave, and so at Nightfall he imported the same to the Mayor, one Whyte, and advised him after he was gone half a Dozen miles off as he might guess, to send privately out to Crumwell for Licence to speak to him about conditions for the town ; but not to make mention of himself on any account till he had done. After which advice to the Mayor marches away with his men about two Hours after Night fall, and passed over the River undiscovered by a Guard of Horse that lay at the other side of the Bridge, and [he] made no great halt till he reached to a Town called Ballynasack, Twelve Miles from Clonmell, where he refreshed his Men, and then marched to Limerick.

Then the Mayor, according as he was advised, about Twelve o'clock at night sent out to Crumwell very privately for a conduct to wait upon his Excellency ; which forthwith was sent to him, and an Officer to conduct him from the Wall to Crumwell's Tent, who after some course compliments was not long capitulating, when he got good conditions for the Town, such in a manner as they desired.

After which Crumewll asked him if Hugh O'Neill knew of his coming out, to which he Answered he did not, for that he was gone two Hours after Night fell with all his Men, at which Crumwell stared and frowned at him and said, " You knave, have you served me so, and did not tell me so before." To which the Mayor replied, if his Excellency had demanded the question, he would tell him. Then he asked him what that Duff O'Neill was ; to which the Mayor answered, that he was an over sea Soldier, born in Spain ; on which Crumwell said " G—— d—— you, and your over sea ! " and desired the Mayor to give the Paper back again. To which the other answered, that he hoped his Excellency would not break his conditions or take them from him, which was not the repute his Excellency had, but to perform whatsoever he had promised. On which Crumwell was somewhat calm, but said in a fury, " By G—— above he would follow that Hugh Duff O'Neill wheresoever he went."

Then the Mayor delivered the keys of the gates to Cromwell, who immediately commanded guards on them, and next morning himself entered, where he saw his men killed in the Pound, notwithstanding which and his fury that Hugh Duff went off as he did, he kept his conditions with the Town.

— The History of the Warr of Ireland from 1641 to 1653. By a British Officer of the Regiment of Sir John Clotworthy. Ed. by Rev. E. Hogan, S.J. (Dublin, 1873).

This narrative is preserved at Clongowes-Wood College. Father Hogan thinks that the author was probably an Irishman, by name Mulholland. Though opposed to the Confederates, he writes of them without malice, and his outlook is honourable and humane. Of the shooting of Alaster MacDonnell after the battle of Knocknanoss, he says : " I am confident, that after an Enemy having surrendered his Sword and Armes, and is a Prisoner, 'tis murder to kill him."

By the Commissioners appointed for Stateing the Arreares of the Souldiery Ct and of Publique faith Debts in Ireland /

UPon Composition and Agreement made with M⁹ Esther Hunt Administratrix to her late Husband Capt Thomas Hunt Deceased in behalfe of her selfe And for her selfe of Henry Thomas Beniamin Anne, Hester and Sarah Hunt Children of the said Defunct for all the said Defunts — — Arreares for Service in *Ireland* from the Last Day of December 1646 to the 4th Day of June 1649 As Capt of a troope of Horse in Coll Chidley Cootes Regiment —

£ 76 8
714 17 06

There remains due from the Common-wealth to the said Esther Hunt and y⁹ said Children of the defunct their Executors, Administrators, or Aſſign's, the Sum of Seaven hundred and fowerteene Pounds Seaventeene shillings and Six pence — which is to be satiſfied to the said Esther Hunt and y⁹ said Children of y⁹ Defunct their Executors, Administrators, or Aſſign's, out of the Rebels Lands, Houſes, Tenements and Hereditaments in *Ireland*; or other Lands, Houſes, Tenements and Hereditaments there, in the diſpoſe of the *Commonwealth* of ENGLAND. Signed and Sealed at DUBLIN the Sixe and twentieth day of May 1658

Examined and entred

Tho Herbert
Gen Register

Edw Roberts
Robert Gorges
Robt Jeffreys

J. P. Prendergast says that he sought twenty years for a specimen of a Cromwellian Debenture before finding this " perfect facsimile."

J. P. PRENDERGAST (1863)

O F all possessions in a country, Land is the most desirable. It is the most fixed. It yields its returns in the form of rent with the least amount of labour or forethought to the owner. But, in addition to all these advantages, the possession of it confers such power, that the balance of power in a state rests with the class that has the balance of Land . . .

The term " Settlement," of such great import in the history of Ireland in the Seventeenth century, means nothing else than the settlement of the balance of land according to the will of the strongest ; for force, not reason, is the source of law. And by the term Cromwellian Settlement is to be understood the dealings of the Commonwealth of England with the lands and habitations of the people of Ireland after their conquest of the country in the year 1652. As their object was rather to extinguish a nation than to suppress a religion, they seized the lands of the Irish, and transferred them (and with them all the power of the state) to an overwhelming flood of new English settlers, filled with the intensest national and religious hatred of the Irish.

Two other settlements followed, which may be called the Restoration Settlement and the Revolution Settlement. The one was a counter revolution, by which some of the Royalist English of Ireland and a few of the native Irish were restored to their estates under the Acts of Settlement and Explanation. The other (or Revolution Settlement) followed the victory of William III at the Battle of the Boyne. By it the lands lately restored to the Royalist English and few native Irish were again seized by the Parliament of England, and distributed among the conquering nation. At the court for the sale of estates forfeited on account of the war of 1690, the lands could be purchased only by Englishmen. No Irishman, high or low, could purchase an acre of them, or occupy more than the site for a cabin ; for to the condition of labourers it was now intended that the relics of the nation should be reduced.

The Penal Laws, which lasted nearly in full force till the breaking out of the first American war, were nothing but the complement of the Forfeited Estates Act. . . . It will thus be seen that these three Settlements are only part of one whole, and that the Cromwellian Settlement is the foundation of the present settlement of Ireland.—

J. P Prendergast (1808-93) made a profound study of the history of the Irish land question. His " Cromwellian Settlement" appeared in 1863, the second edition in 1870, the year of the first of the series of Land Acts, which eventually reversed the Cromwellian Settlement and restored the land of Ireland to the Irish. The Debentures were given to Cromwell's soldiers for arrears of pay. A third edition is currently on sale published by Mellifont Press, Ltd., Dublin.

    ★   ★   ★   ★   ★   ★

CHAPTER VI.

The Boyne and Limerick

ᴀ Rí nᴀ Cruinne ᴅo Rín ise
'S ᵹᴀċ ní uirċe áċá ᴅéᴀnċᴀ
ᖴuᴀsᴄᴀil ᖴóᴅlᴀ ᴀ ᵹuᴀis ᴀn ᵹleo sᴀ
ıs ᖴuᴀiᵹ ᴀ ᖴóirne ı nᵹráᴅ ᴀ ċéıle.
—ᴅ. Uᴀ ᵬrúᴀᴅᴀır (1689).

(O King and Maker of the World and of all it contains, free Ireland
from the perils of this strife, and knit her factions together in love.)

* * * * * *

NICHOLAS PLUNKET, 1700.

I SAY then, that if managers of this affair were staunch in wisdom,
true to their trust, diligent in the execution, clean in their
conscience, and constant in unity, they might recover England
by such means as were found in Ireland at the king's arrival. For first,
there were at least sixty thousand men of an army, of which a considerable
proportion were veterans. The rest in two months' time, by constant
exercise, might be made skilful enough in the use of arms. Their cavalry
and dragoonry were not to be contemned. Some regiments of horse
and some of dragoons might vie with the best of Europe.

Of battering cannon, and field pieces they had enough to their purpose
in several towns of the realm, as at Kinsale fort, Duncannon fort, at
Dublin, Galway, Limerick, and in others. Of small arms they had some
store ; they had iron and artificers to form a sufficiency in a short time,
as also to cast mortars and bombs, pikes, half-pikes, scythes, spades,
pickaxes, and other utensils of war they might have in abundance.
Horses and oxen for draught abounded. A collection of merchant ships,
gabbards and boats might have been timely made out of several ports
of the kingdom to transport the army into Scotland, which might march
from thence into England.

To clothe and feed those forces there was an overflowing plenty in
the country; for no land in Europe, for its extent, could show such
flocks of sheep and so great stocks of black cattle. Corn was in redundancy.
You may be convinced of all this by the vast exportation of slaughtered
beef, of wool, of woollen manufacture, and of grain, that was made
every year. The city of Cork alone used to slaughter at the least ten
thousand bullocks in a season. The county of Tipperary was sufficient
to keep the army clothed constantly. The two counties of Roscommon
and Mayo, in the province of Connaught, could yearly maintain greater

79

numbers of troops with beef. Half of the county of Meath was able to give bread unto them. The province of Ulster produced linen sufficiently; if not, there might have been a supply had out of the other provinces. What shall I say of the butter, cheese, roots, fish and pork, of which there was abundance? Of all the plentiful product, there could be annually a fair proportion spared for transportation into France, and in exchange necessaries of war might be brought home; for Ireland, at the king's arrival received no increase of people—it had but the usual store of mouths to consume the growth of the country . . .

About this time we are to tell that the Prince of Orange, being established King of England, he entered immediately of himself into the grand confederacy which had been made the last winter between the Emperor, the King of Spain, the States of the United Netherlands, and the princes of the Empire against the King of France.
The little spark of fire, kindled in the Palatinate of the Rhine for the gaining and defending a few acres of land, raised such a flame through the extent of divers nations, that before it could be quenched, ten years' labour was spent, an ocean of blood spilt, mountains of treasure consumed, which might have bought twenty times more land than was in dispute; fleets destroyed; cities, towns and countries ruined; churches profaned; the service of God conculated; many a brave family extinguished; and thousands impoverished. Yet, in the end, the cause of this long, bloody strife was not ended, but left to a peaceable decision. The consideration of these calamities which must ensure upon a war, should make princes extremely timorous in the enterprise, and never to begin till all fair ways of accommodation are first used, and unless the thing in controversy be of transcendant value and of undoubted right. . .

Restoration of their estates, for forty years in the possession of Protestant usurpers.

Acts passed by the Irish Parliament, and sanctioned by the Lord Deputy to be absolutely valid, without having to send over previously prepared bills, for the king's approbation.

Causes to be determined by the Irish judicature, without appeal to English tribunals.

Full liberty to be given to Irish merchants to import and export, without being compelled to send their ships to English ports (thus avoiding iniquitous dock dues, etc.).

Studies of Law to be founded in Dublin.

The Viceroyalty to be given to Catholics.

A mint to be set up in Dublin.

The chief State appointments to be conferred on Catholics.

A standing army of 8,000 Catholics, a Catholic militia, and a fleet of 24 war ships of the Fourth rate, to be maintained.

Half the ecclesiastical livings to be given to Catholics during the life time of the present Protestant incumbents, and after their death all to Catholics.

Works to be set on foot to make the great rivers navigable, to deepen and defend the ports, and to drain the bogs.— *A Light to the Blind.*

The manuscript known as " A Light to the Blind," formerly in possession of the Plunkets, Earls of Fingall, is now in the National Library of Ireland. According to family tradition, the author was Nicholas Plunket, a lawyer and kinsman of the Earl. Sir John Gilbert, who published a considerable portion of this contemporary narrative of the Jacobite war in Ireland, says : " Few documents have come down to us from the Irish, whose resistance to England from 1688 to 1691 attracted the attention of Europe."

★　★　★　★　★　★

THE SIEGE OF SLIGO, 1689

The best skill of contemporary Dutch artists was employed to illustrate the campaigns of King William in Ireland. Among the Dutch engraved prints reproduced in this volume, the great panorama of the Battle of the Boyne, the central portion of which is shown at the end, was especially admired. Below is " La Ville de Slego prise par le Roy Jaques II." Sligo was besieged and taken by Sarsfield early in the war.

CAITRÉIM TAIDG.

Go bfuil rí dá rírib againne
Dobeir fáilte is fál da sagartaib
Is d'éis ar foronig Taog do tarcuisne
Go bfuil fórsa pórt is bailte aige.

Ní do breoigoin Seon is atarrac
Taog ón sliab do tiact san ngradam san
Fear " Cia súd " i gcuram sagairne
Is fear " Who's there " na seitleac airgte.

D'eis a ndeárna Ráif do radaireact
Féac a cloideam sa píce ag Flaitbeartac
Fós na céadta réad nac taitneann rís
Bandailiar ag triall cum Aifreann. . . .

Cuid dá ranncaib Flann is Fearadac
Is Muireadac Ó Duibdiorma an scaifaire
Bit a séis le céile ag reacaireact
I gcanmaim nac taigiuir le Sacsanaib.

I dtig na gárda is gnát ger b'annam san
Sórdán nac sólás le geamaraib
Fianuigeact ar fialríograid Danba
Píp trí mbeann is damsa an gadaraig.

—DÁIBID Ó BRUADAIR.

Nowhere is the Irish standpoint in the last great war fought on Irish soil so completely and movingly expressed as in the Gaelic poems of David O'Bruadair (1625?–98). The above verses are from a long poem, "The Triumph of Tadhg," in which the author describes with much satisfaction the dejected state and impending downfall of the Cromwellian planters : We have a real King to rule us, who knows how to protect our clergy. Tadhg, once derided, now has the towns and fortresses. "Cia súd" is up and "Who's there" is down. After all Ralph's prating and swaggering, Flaherty holds the sword and pike. Hundreds are marching to Mass. The gay-hearted Gaels talk in a tongue that Saxon ears do not love. The songs of the Fiana and drone of bagpipes are heard in the guardroom.

REV. GEORGE WALKER (1689)

BEING prevail'd on to give an account of the Siege of London-Derry, it is convenient, by way of preliminary, to take notice how that Town came to be out of the hands of the Irish, when all places of the Kingdom of any strength or consideration were possessed by them. It pleased God so to infatuate the councils of my Lord Tyrconnell, that when the three thousand men were sent to England to assist his master against the invasion of the Prince of Orange, he took particular care to send away the whole regiment quartered in and about this city.

He soon saw his error, and endeavoured to repair it by commanding my Lord Antrim to quarter there with his regiment, consisting of a numerous swarm of Irish and Highlanders. Upon the 6th of December they were upon their march in and about Newtown (a market town belonging to Col. George Philips, 12 miles distant from Derry). Col. Philips, having notice of this, and joining with it the apprehensions they were under, of a general insurrection of the Irish intended on the 9th of December, and considering that Derry as well as other places was to be presently possessed by the Irish . . . immediately dispatches a letter to Alderman Norman, giving an account of these matters and his opinion of them, and importuning him to consult with the sober people of the town and to set out the danger of admitting such guests among them . . .

Alderman Norman and the rest of the graver citizens were under great disorder and consternation, and knew not what to resolve upon. One of the companies was already in view of the town and two of the officers within it, but the younger sort who are seldom so dilatory in their resolutions, got together, run in all haste to the main-guard, snacht up the keys, and immediately shut up all the four gates and the magazine.
—*A true account of the siege of London-Derry* (1689).

REFUGEES

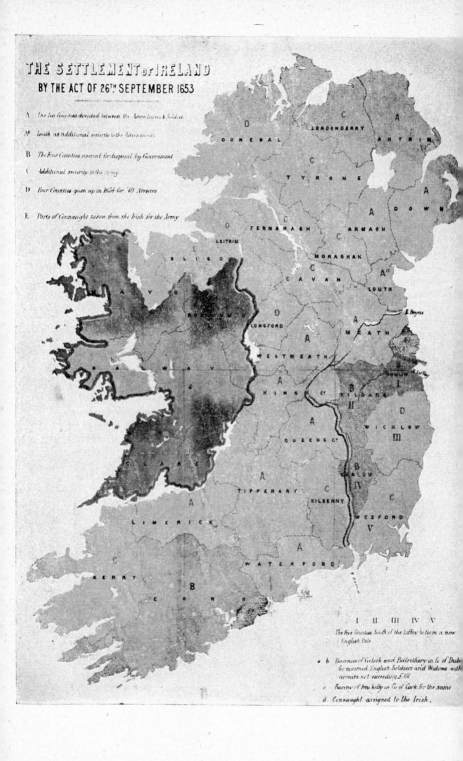

THE SETTLEMENT OF IRELAND
BY THE ACT OF 26TH SEPTEMBER 1653

A The ten Counties divided between the Adventurers & Soldiers.

Aᵃ Louth as additional security to the Adventurers

B The Four Counties reserved for disposal by Government

C Additional security to the Army

D Four Counties given up in 1654 for '49 Arrears

E Parts of Connaught taken from the Irish for the Army

The Five Counties South of the Liffey to form a new English Pale

a b Baronies of Golock and Balrothery in Co. of Dublin
       for maimed English Soldiers and Widows with
       arrears not exceeding £150

c Barony of Imokelly in Co. of Cork for the same

d Connaught assigned to the Irish.

Rev. Mr. Seth Whittle (1689)

WE have been surrounded in this poor city for divers months; beleaguer'd by a multitude of merciless and implacable enemies; exposed to danger without ceasing or intermission. We have been deserted by those who came to our relief; tempted by parlies and specious terms of capitulation; undermined by treacherous contrivances among ourselves; exercised with all the varieties of terror and amazement.

The small shot hath poured upon us like a shower of hail; the great guns, like thunder hath shaken our walls; and the bombs like lightning have ruin'd our houses. We have seen death in all its horrible shapes, and we are every moment entertain'd with spectacles of misery and mortality. Sickness and disease are entered within our gates, and pale famine is visible in every countenance. The fond mother hath not a morsel of bread to appease the languishing cry of her starved infant; the grateful son hath not wherewithal to sustain his aged parent.

One friend looks at another, and sees his misery, but cannot prevent a lingring death. He that formerly had his table cover'd with variety of dishes, knows not where to satisfie nature with one wholesome bit. We cannot refresh ourselves with such scraps and morsels as we formerly allow'd to our dogs; nay, we are constrain'd to eat of such things, as at another time human nature would nauseate and abhor. Nevertheless God has made us this day a defenced city and an iron pillar and brazen walls against the whole land.—*A Sermon.*

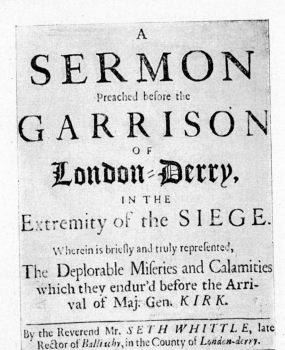

A
SERMON
Preached before the
GARRISON
OF
London-Derry,
IN THE
Extremity of the SIEGE.

Wherein is briefly and truly represented,
The Deplorable Miseries and Calamities
which they endur'd before the Arrival of Maj. Gen. KIRK.

By the Reverend Mr. SETH WHITTLE, late
Rector of Ballishy, in the County of London-derry.

REV. GEORGE WALKER (1689)

JULY 27.—The garrison is reduced to 4456 men, and under the greatest extremity for want of provision, which does appear by the following account, taken by a gentleman in the garrison, of the price of food:

	l.	s.	d
Horse flesh sold for, per pound,		1.	8
A quarter of a dog (fattened by eating the bodies of the slain Irish)	0.	5.	6
A dog's head,	0.	2.	6
A cat,	0.	4.	6
A rat,	0.	1.	0
A mouse,	0.	0.	6
A small stook taken in the river, not to be bought for money, or purchased under the rate of a quantity of meal.			
A pound of greaves,	0.	1.	0
A pound of tallow,	0.	4.	0
A pound of salted hides,	0.	1.	0
A quart of horse blood	0.	1.	0
A horse pudding.	0.	0.	6
An handful of sea-wreck,	0.	0.	2
————— of chick-weed,	0.	0.	1
A quart of meal, when found	0.	1.	0

We were under so great necessity that we had nothing left unless we could prey upon one another: A certain fat gentleman conceived himself in the greatest danger, and fancying several of the garrison looked on him with a greedy eye, thought fit to hide himself for three days. Our drink was nothing but water, which we paid very dear for, and could not get without great danger; we mixed in it ginger and anniseeds, of which we had great plenty: Our necessity of eating the composition of tallow and starch, did not only nourish and support us, but was an infallible cure of the looseness; and recovered a great many that were strangely reduced by that distemper, and preserved others from it.

MAP OF THE BOYNE

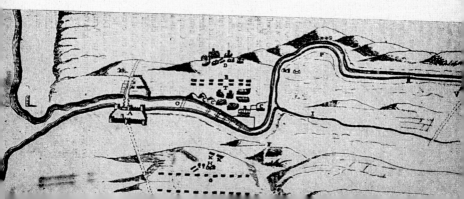

Cromwell's March ....
William's March .—.—.—.—.

This map shows the line of march of the two commanders, Cromwell and William of Orange, who decided the fate of Ireland in the seventeenth century. It will be noted that the operations of both were confined to the eastern side of the island. The military conquest in 1650-53, and again in 1690-91, was hard-fought and prolonged. The wars of Ireland ended with the Treaty of Limerick and departure of the Irish soldiers to France. The action of the Irish officers in consenting to the Treaty of Limerick was generally condemned by military opinion as premature and ill-advised. "They were much to blame," wrote James II's famous son, the Duke of Berwick, "for the generals of the enemy would have consented to everything for the sake of putting an end to this war."

THE BOYNE WATER

July the first, in Oldbridge town,
  There was a grievous battle,
Where many a man lay on the ground
  By the cannons that did rattle.
King James he pitched his tents between
  The lines for to retire ;
But King William threw his bomb-balls in,
  And set them all on fire . . .

When we the Boyne began to cross,
  The enemy they descended ;
But few of our brave men were lost,
  So stoutly we defended.
The horse were the first that marched o'er,
  The foot soon followed a'ter,
But brave Duke Schomberg was no more
  By venturing over the water.

These verses from " the Great Orange Song of Ireland " are from the version printed by T. C. Croker in his " Historical Songs of Ireland " (1844). Mr. Donal O'Sullivan in his edition of the Bunting collection of Irish music, says : " This celebrated tune is to Orangemen what the Seanbhean Bhoct is to nationalists. The words are worthy of the tune, which is a fine one."

When valiant Schomberg he was slain,
  King William thus accosted
His warlike men, for to march on,
  And he would be the foremost.
"Brave boys," he said, "be not dismayed
  For losing of one commander:
For God will be our king this day,
  And I'll be general under." . . .

Come, let us all, with heart and voice,
  Applaud our lives' defender
Who, at the Boyne, his valour showed,
  And made his foes surrender.
To God above the praise we'll give,
  Both now and ever a'ter;
And bless the "glorious memory"
  Of King William that crossed the Boyne Water.

KING WILLIAM CROSSING THE BOYNE

SIR WILLIAM WILDE (1850)

THE scene becomes truly picturesque. Upon the left, the rocky banks of Townly Hall demesne are clothed with the most splendid foliage; upon the right, the deep meadows and green inches are fringed by the woods of Oldbridge; and in the centre, upon a massive rock, which juts over the water, rises the obelisk raised to commemorate the passage of the Boyne when Stuart and Nassau contended for the Crown of these realms. Grander battle-fields,—more extensive plains, as that of Waterloo,—or with the mountains looking upon the sea, as at Marathon,—may easily be found; but for inland sylvan beauty, the diversity of hill and dale with wooded banks, and a shining river, this scene of action may well challenge comparison . . . situated about three miles from Donore . . .

William and his army marched in two columns from Ardee, upon the 30th of June. Having arrived within view of Drogheda, the position of the Irish encampment, stretching along the slopes of Donore, was at once recognised. A person standing upon any of the elevations in that neighbourhood, could with ease recognise every tent in the Irish camp; and, looking up the charming valley of the Boyne from this spot over the scene which the celebrated tourist, Arthur Young, said, was "one of the completest landscapes he had ever seen," William may well have given utterance to the exclamation, "Well it is a country worth fighting for!"

The English army then turned slightly westward along the northern slope of the ridge we have described, and by which it was in a great measure concealed from the Irish, and took up its position nearly parallel with the Boyne; its right descending into the hollow of the King's Glen, and its left resting in another narrow ravine, at the eastern extremity of the hill, and very similar to the former. It had thus the advantage of being able to reach the Boyne in a few minutes through either of those two deep, narrow ravines, and William not only had this advantage of position, but, while his own army was completely concealed from view, every tent in that of his opponent was plainly mapped before him, and many of them within point-blank range of his cannon.

The English being encamped and their batteries erected, the firing commenced upon both sides, and was continued during the greater portion of the day. The old ballad says, and perhaps truly:

> "King James he pitched his tents between
>   The lines, for to retire,
> But King William threw his bomb-balls in,
>   And set them all on fire,"

alluding, no doubt, to James's intention of retreating, and to the murderous effect of the heavy English artillery, which it is stated soon dismounted two of the enemy's guns.—SIR WILLIAM WILDE: *The Beauties of the Boyne and its Tributary the Blackwater*. 2nd edition. 1850.

JOHN SHIRLEY (1692)

ON the 30th of June the King marched early in the Morning from his Camp at Ardee towards Drogheda, and found the Irish Army Encamped along the Boyne above the Town; but the Foot not coming up before it was late, and with them the Artillery; nothing could be done that Night, but visiting the Posture of the Enemy, and the Fords of the River, which appeared very difficult to pass: However, the King Encamped within shot of the Enemies Cannon, which had like to have proved very fatal to these Kingdoms by sending Death so near a Precious Life that is so dear to them; for as his Majesty was taking a view of their Posture, a six pound shot bruised his shoulder, and razed the skin; making a large though not a deep Wound; yet he nothing daunted thereat, only caused it it to be dressed, and mounting again, kept on Horseback for several hours after.

Toward the dusk of the Evening, he commanded Count Schomberg, with the right Wing of the Horse, two Regiments of Dragoons, and Trelawney's Brigade, to take five Field-pieces, and go early in the Morning to try the Fords some Miles above the Enemies Camp, and if he found an Opportunity to pass over and Attaque them in the Flank, or oblige them to Decamp. And almost beyond Expectation, he passed with good Success, beating off 8 Squadrons that stood ready to oppose him; and having gained firm ground on the other side the River, drew up his Men in Battalia, sending to acquaint the King what he had done, and to receive his further Orders: But the King no sooner received the News, and perceived the Enemy were drawing up to Charge the right Wing, but he caused the Attaque to be made in three places; the first before a small Village, at a very good Ford; at the Second the Foot waded the middle; and at the Third the Horse were forced to swim.

The Dutch Foot Guards that first passed over, sustained the shock of the Enemies shot, whilst they were in the Water, not firing til they came up close, and then pouring in their Bullets. Those that were in the Village and behind the Ditches gave way; but five of the Enemies Battalions came up to charge them, before the Third Battalion of that Regiment had passed the River, yet ours maintained their ground, and made them retreat in disorder, leaving one of their Colours, and many dead Men upon the place; but our Men pressing eagerly on, and advancing beyond the Village, were twice vigorously attacqued by the Enemies Horse, but received no great damage; whereupon the Danish Forces advanced to the Left, and the Brigadiers Melionere and Hanmore came on the Right, one being attacqued by the Dragoons, and the other by the Horse, but neither did any great matter, by reason they had no Pikes: and now the thundering of the Guns, clashing of Swords, and the Cries and Shouts made a confused noise; so that the Irish trembled at the Din of War.—JOHN SHIRLEY: *The true and impartial history and wars of the Kingdom of Ireland . . . more particularly relating to all the memorable skirmishes, battles, sieges and other extraordinary occurrences* (1692).

REV. GEORGE STORY (1691)

IT will be convenient that I here give as good a description of the city and its situation as I can of a place that I had not the liberty to go into, though I have been sometimes very near it. It's therefore for circumference one of the largest in the Kingdom, except Dublin, and the houses are generally built very strong within the walls, being made most of them castle-ways, with battlements.

It stands upon the River Shannon, and though it be nigh sixty miles from the sea, yet ships of burden can come up to the bridge ; for the river below the town looks like an arm of the sea. One part stands on Munster side, and is called Irish Town, being compassed about with a very strong stone wall, and without this a counterscarp with pallisados and also several forts and bastions ; and on the inside the wall they had

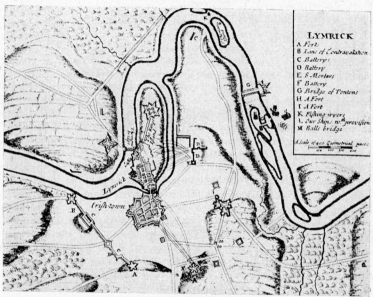

PLAN OF LIMERICK BESIEGED. FROM STORY'S "IMPARTIAL HISTORY" (1691)

cast up a vast ditch, with an huge bank of earth and stones, having only a place left to go in and out.

The River about a quarter of a mile above the town, splits itself in two, and between the branches lies a most pleasant spot of ground, called the King's Island. being about two miles circumference, on the lower end of which stands the greater part of Limerick, where there is a castle and a cathedral church. This also is invested with a stone wall, and is called the English town, between which and the Irish town there is a very large stone bridge ; and beyond the English town, upon the further brancn of the river, there is another bridge that leads into the County of Clare, near which stands a considerable fort of stone, and the Irish cast up several more of earth, and made great fortifications in the King's Island, at which they were busy all the while we continued there. Here the Irish kept continually a strong guard, having also during our stay two or three regiments entrenched, opposite to the Danes on Munster side, towards the west of the Irish town . . .

Wednesday the 27th (August) . . . About half an hour after three the signal being given by firing three pieces of cannon, the Grenadiers being in the furthest angle of our trenches leapt over and ran towards the counterscarp firing their pieces and throwing their grenades. This gave the alarm to the Irish, who had their guns all ready, and discharged great and small shot up at us as fast as 'twas possible. Our men were not behind them in either ; so that in less than two minutes the noise was so terrible that one would have thought the very skies ready to rent in sunder. This was seconded with dust, smoke, and all the terrors that the art of man could invent, to ruin and undo one another ; and to make it the more uneasy, the day itself was excessive hot to the bystanders, and much more sure in all respects to those upon action. . . .

The Irish then ventured upon the breach again, and from the walls and every place so pestered us upon the counterscarp, that after nigh three hours resisting bullets, stones (broken bottles from the very women, who boldly stood in the breach, and were nearer our men than their own), and whatever ways could be thought on to destroy us, our ammunition being spent, it was judged safest to return to our trenches. When the work was at the hottest, the Brandenburgh Regiment (who behaved themselves very well) were got upon the black battery, where the Enemy's powder happened to take fire, and blew up a great many of them, the men, faggots, stones, and what not, flying into the air with a most terrible noise. . . .

The Danes were not idle all this while, but fired upon the enemy with all imaginable fury, and had several killed ; but the mischief was we had one breach, and all towards the left it was impossible to get into the Town when the gates were shut, [even] if there had been no Enemy to oppose us, without a great many scaling-ladders, which we had not. From half an hour after three, till after seven, there was one continued fire of both great and small shot, without any intermission ; insomuch that the smoke that went from the town reached in one continued cloud to the top of a mountain at least six miles off . . .

The King stood nigh Cromwell's fort all the time, and the business being over, he went to his camp very much concerned, as indeed was the whole Army ; for you might have seen a mixture of anger and sorrow in everybody's countenance. . . . We lost at least five hundred upon the spot, and had a thousand more wounded, as I understood by the surgeons of our hospitals, who are the properest judges. The Irish lost a great many by our cannon and other ways ; but it cannot be supposed that their loss should be equal to ours, since it's a much easier thing to

93

defend walls, than 'tis by plain strength to force people from them; and one man within has the advantage of four without. . . .

Next day the King sent a drummer, in order to a truce, that the dead might be buried, but the Irish had no mind to it; and now the soldiers were in hopes that the King would make a second attack, and seemed resolved to have the Town or die every man. But this was too great a hazard to run at one place, and they did not know how scarce our ammunition was, it being very much wasted the day before. This day however we continued battering the wall, and it began to rain; and next day it was very cloudy all about, and rained very fast, so that everybody began to dread the consequences of it. The King therefore calls a Council of War, wherein it was resolved to quit the Town and raise the Siege, which as the case stood then with us, was no doubt the most prudent thing that could be done. . . . Therefore, on Sunday the last of August, all the Army drew off (having a good Body of Horse in the Rear). As soon as the Irish perceived we had quitted our Trenches, they soon took possession of them with great joy, and were in a small time after over all the ground whereon we had encamped.—G. STORY: *Impartial History* (1691).

Rev. George Story was a chaplain to King William's army in Ireland (1689–91). His "Impartial History" (1691) and its "Continuation" (1694) are the principal Williamite authorities for the campaign.

SARSFIELD DESTROYING WILLIAM'S SIEGE TRAIN

COL. CHARLES O'KELLY (1692)

THE army of Ginkell appeared in Sight of Aughrim, on the 12th July. The Irish Army, composed of about 10,000 Foot, 2,000 Men at Arms, and as many light Horse, were soon drawn up by St. Ruth in two Lynes, the Cavalry on both Wings flanking the Foot ; and having placed Chevalier de Tessé on the right Wing of the Horse, and Sarsfield on the left, and given their severall Posts to the Rest of the chief Commanders, he obliged himself to noe certaine place, but rode constantly from one side to another, to give the necessary orders where he saw Occasion. Ginkell being come up at so near a Distance that his Rams and other battering Engins might doe Execution, he ordered them to be discharged, and having a vast Number of them, he made them play incessantly upon the Irish Army, hopeing by that Meanes to force them from the Hill which was of great Advantage. But the Irish encouraged by the Presence and Conduct of St. Ruth, kept their Ground, and beat the English as often as they advanced towards them.

The Fight continued from Noon till Sunsett, the Irish Foot haveing still the better of the Enemy ; and St. Ruth, observeing the Advantage of his Side, and that the Enemy's Foot were much disordered, he was resolved by advancing with the Cavalrie, to make the Victory compleat, when an unlucky Shott from one of the terrible new Engines hitting him in the Head, made an end of his Life, and took away the Courage of his Army. For Ginkell, observeing that the Irish were in some Disorder, gave a notable Conjecture that the General was either killed or wounded, whereuppon he commanded his Army to advance.

The Irish Cavalrie being discouraged by the Death of St. Ruth, and none of the Generall Officers comeing to lead them in that Place, they gave back and quitted the Field. The Foot, who were engaged with the Enemy, and knowing nothing of the Generall's Death or the Retreat of their Cavalrie, continued fighting till they were surrounded by the whole English Army, soe that most of them were cutt off, and noe Quarter given but to a very few ; the Rest, by the Favour of the Night then approaching, (for St. Ruth was killed about Sunsett) made their Escape.

In this Battle, Lord Galway, a most hopefull Youth, Son to the first Peer of Connaught, Colonel Maguire and Colonel Charles Moore, the chief Men of two illustrious Families in Ulster and Leinster, Brigadier Henry O'Neill, Grandchild of Sir Phelim O'Neill, and Colonel Maurice Connell, all stout officers, with many more brave Heros, gloriously fell with Arms in Hand, fighting to the last Breath, for the ancient Faith and Liberty of Ireland. Gordon O'Neill was mortally wounded, and left for dead in the Field, but being happily known by some Scottish Officers of his Relation (for his Mother was Daughter to one of the chiefe Peers of Scotland) he was carefully attended by them, untill the Gods were pleased to restore him to Life and Health, and being, by the Treaty of Limerick, released from his Imprisonment, he followed King James into France.

This was the Issue of that famous Engagement of Aughrim, soe glorious to Ginkell, and soe fatall to St. Ruth and the Irish . . .

After this notable Victory at Aughrim Ginkell only wanted the Reduceing of Limerick and Galway to compleat the Conquest of the whole Kingdom. Galway is the Head City of Connaught, not much above a Daye's journey from Aughrim. It is built uppon a Neck of Land between the Sea and the River Corrib, which comes out of a great Lake riseing from high Mountains in the West of Connaught, 24 Miles from Galway, and separating that Part of the Country from the Rest of the Province ; for there is noe Passage thither but by Boats over the Lake, or by the Conveniency of a stone Bridge at Galway, soe that the Town, haveing the Sea on the South, the River Corrib and the Lake on the West and North lyes exposed to an Attack only on the East Side, where Ginkell encamped on the 19th July and that Night he gained an Outwork upon the Hill, very near the Walls, by the Treachery of an Officer who deserted from thence to the Enemy.—*The Destruction of Cyprus. A secret History of the War of the Revolution in Ireland.*

Col. O'Kelly's narrative, written immediately after the Williamite war, was circulated among his friends with the names and places disguised, as the author was still living in Ireland. It was edited and published, with the names and places identified by J. C. O'Callaghan, for the Irish Archæological Society (1850). Father E. Hogan, S.J., who, with Count Plunket, edited another copy of " The Destruction of Cyprus " in 1894, says that it " has the distinction of being the only statement of the old Irish or nationalists during the war."

★ ★ ★ ★ ★ ★

A LIGHT TO THE BLIND

IN a fortnight after Limerick was surrounded, the expected French fleet, under count de Chateau-Renaud, arrived about the twentieth of October, at Scattery, in the river of Limerick, being eighteen men of war, four fire-ships, and twenty ships of burden, bringing victuals, ammunition, money, and all other necessaries of war. In this fleet was Col. Simon Luttrell, who had taken great care for its speedy arrival, though afterwards the arrival was too late.

When this fleet arrived, there was at Limerick, in that moiety thereof which is called the English Town, a good body of the Irish soldiers destined for France, who now, with the assistance of the fleet, might retake the other half of the city, and maintain it all winter, if they had a mind to break the peace, and thereby they could renew the war, for none of their army was shipped off as yet, and the English host was gone into winter quarters. But men of honour will rather suffer than break their word, which is a doctrine little regarded by the Protestants of England and Ireland.

The French fleet being informed of the surrender of Limerick, returned within a few days to France, with deep resentment at their unexpected disappointment. There went aboard them a part of the Irish soldiers. The most Christian King, hearing of this affair, was in great rage, and was like to punish severely those commanders (as above said) who had the chief hand in giving up the town, until receiving some sort of apology for the fact, his majesty was pleased to smother his passion.

Here we cannot omit to tell our opinion, that the King of France made a false step in politics by letting the Irish war fall, because that war was the

ARTICLES

Agreed upon the Third Day of *Octob.*

One Thousand Six Hundred and Ninety One.

Between the Right Honourable, Sir *Charles Porter*, Knight, and *Thomas Coningsby*, Esq; Lords Justices of *Ireland*; and His Excellency the Baron *De Ginckle*, Lieutenant General, and Commander in Chief of the *English* Army ; *On the One Part ·*
And the Right Honourable, *Patrick* Earl of *Lucan*, *Piercy* Viscount *Gallmoy*, Colonel *Nicholas Purcel*, Colonel *Nicholas Cusack*, Sir *Toby Butler*, Colonel *Garret Dillon*, and Colonel *John Brown* ; *On the other Part :*
In the behalf of the *Irish* Inhabitants in the City and County of *Lymerick*, the Counties of *Clare*, *Kerry*, *Cork*, *Sligo*, and *Mayo*.

In Consideration of the Surrender of the City of Lymerick, *and other Agreements made between the said Lieutenant General* Ginckle, *the Governor of the City of* Lymerick, *and the Generals of the Irish Army, bearing Date with these Presents, for the Surrender of the said City, and Submission of the said Army : It is Agreed, That*

I.

THE *Roman Catholicks* of this Kingdom, shall enjoy such Privileges in the Exercise of their Religion, as are consistent with the Laws of *Ireland*; or as they did enjoy in the Reign of King *Charles* the II : And their Majesties, as soon as their Affairs will permit them to Summon a Parliament in this Kingdom, will endeavour to procure the said *Roman Catholicks* such farther Security in that particular, as may preserve them from any Disturbance, upon the Account of their said Religion.

FIRST PAGE OF THE TREATY OF LIMERICK,
REPRODUCED FROM THE ARTICLES AS PUBLISHED OFFICIALLY IN DUBLIN
BY THE WILLIAMITE GOVERNMENT, 1691

best medium in the world for destroying soon the confederacy abroad, by reason that the confederate princes could not prolong the foreign war without the army and money of England, which were employed in the war of Ireland, the sequel to which would be the re-enthronement of the King, at which juncture the forces of France and England, by sea and land conjoined, would give laws to the earth.

*   *   *   *   *   *

COL. CHARLES O'KELLY

THE Treaty began on the 26th September and continued to the 3rd October, and then it was concluded, to the Satisfaction of some, and to the sensible Affliction of others. But that which raised the Admiration of all People, and begat an Astonishment which seemed universall over all Ireland, was the sudden, unexpected, prodigious Change of Sarsfield, who appeared now the most active of all the Commanders to forward the Treaty, and took most pains to perswade the Colonels and Captains to a Complyance ; representing that there was but a small Quantity of Provisions left, and noe Expectation of any Supply out of France till next Spring ; that if they rejected the conditions now offered, they were to hope for none when their Provisions were all spent ; and that, therefore, the Necessity to capitulate, at present was absolute and unavoidable. The authority of Sarsfield, and the Opinion which all the World conceived of his untainted Loyalty and Zeal for his Country, expressed uppon severall Occasions, made them approve what he expressed or proposed, tho' with a great Deal of Reluctancy, and a Regrett equall thereunto.

And now, alas ! the saddest Day is come, that ever appeared above the Horizon of Ireland. The sun was darkened, and covered over with a black cloud, as if unwilling to behold such a wofull spectacle : there needed noe Rain to bedew the Earth, for the Tears of the disconsolate Irish did abundantly moisten their native Soile to which they were that Day, to bid the last Farewell. Those who resolved to leave it never hoped to see it again ; and those who made the unfortunate Choise to continue therein, could at the same Time have Nothing in Prospect but Contempt and Poverty, Chains and Imprisonment, and, in a Word all the Miserys that a conquered Nation could rationally expect from Power and Malice . . .

What the Reasons might be for these prodigious Transactions, and what performance the conquered Irish (whether living in voluntary Exile abroad, or in a forced Bondage at home) have hitherto received, after soe many large Promises of both sides, must be the Work of another Time, and likely of an other Pen : the publick Calamity of my Countrymen, unfortunate Countrymen in generall, and the lamentable Condition of some particular friends, added to the Incommodities of old age, rendring me unable to pursue that Remnant of a wofull History, that requires Ink mixed with the Writer's Teares ; and the Fountain of my weak Eyes hath been drained up already by the too frequent Remembrance of the slaughter at Aughrim and the sad Separation at Limerick.—*The Destruction of Cyprus.*

PATRICK SARSFIELD, EARL OF LUCAN.

The portrait shown above is in the Convent of the Franciscan Fathers, Merchant's Quay, Dublin. Sarsfield's handsome face, fine appearance (he was six feet five inches in height), charm and dash made him an ideal popular hero. The Gaelic ballad from which some verses, with Mangan's translation, are quoted on page 100, illustrates how much he was loved and admired, but contemporaries like the Duke of Berwick did not rate his abilities very highly and regarded the Treaty of Limerick as a tragic and unnecessary surrender.

SLÁN CUM PÁORAIC SÁIRSÉAL

A Páoraic Sáirséal, slán ʒo oci cú,
Ó cuaóais oo'n Frainac, 's oo campaí scaoilce,
Aʒ oéanaṁ oo ʒearáin leis na ríʒciḃ
As o'fáʒ cú Éire aʒus ʒaeóil ḃocc' claoióce.

A Páoraic Sáirséal, ʒuióe ʒac nouine leac,
Mo ʒuióe-se féin, as ʒuióe Mic Muire leac,
Ó cóʒ cú an cát Caol aʒ ʒaḃáil crí ḃiorra óuic,
'S ʒur aʒ Cuileann Ó ʒCuanac buaóaó leac Luimneac.

Ʒeoḃaó-sa siar an sliaḃ so im' aonar,
As ʒeoḃaó aniar arís má's féioir;
Is ann oo connaic mé an campa Ʒaeóealac,
An oream ḃocc silce nár cuir le n-a céile.

*   *   *   *   *   *

Farewell O Patrick Sarsfield, may luck be on your path!
   Your camp is broken up, your work is marred for years;
But you go to kindle into flame the King of France's wrath,
   Though you leave sick Eire in tears—

The Son of Mary guard you, and bless you to the end!
   'Tis altered is the time when your legions were astir,
When at Cullen you were hailed as conqueror and friend,
   And you crossed Narrow-water near Birr—

I'll journey to the north, over mount, moor and wave;
   'Twas there I first beheld drawn up, in file and line,
The brilliant Irish hosts; they were bravest of the brave,
   But, alas, they scorned to combine.

JAMES CLARENCE MANGAN.

CHAPTER VII

Country and People in the XVIIIth Century

WERE I to devise an emblematical figure of Ireland, in her present state, it should not be a Minerva-like figure, with her spear and harp; nor should it be a Diana with her wolf dogs coupled, and the moose deer in the thicket of the background. . . . But my picture of Ireland should be *mulier formosa superne*, a woman exquisitely beautiful, with her head and neck richly attired, her bosom full, but meanly dressed, her lower parts lean and emaciated, half covered with tattered weeds, her legs and feet bare, with burned shins, and all the squalor of indigent sloth.—REV. THOMAS CAMPBELL: *A Philosophical Survey of the South of Ireland* (1777).

* * * * * *

cúigiȯ na h-éireann

Tá Connaċt molta ȯá mbéinn 'mo ṫost,
Connaċt aoibinn gan aon-loċt—
Tá ór le fágail ann ag luċt aiṫris rann—
'Sí Connaċt cruiṫneaċt Éireann.

Ní liaċtaiġe fuinín ar fáit
Ná maiġȯean álainn as árȯ-flaiṫ
I ȯtír Ulaȯ na lann mear,
Na sciaṫ, na n-eaċ, 'sna ȯtréinfear.

Is mín clár Laiġean go léir,
Iomaȯ stéaȯ agus ȯeaġ-laoċ—
Ȯeasbean suáilceaċ, caoin, ceoil,
Iomaȯ uaisle agus onóir.

Laoċ go rat gaċ flaiṫ 'san Mumain
Ag cosaint críce gaċ anbfainn—
Tír lán ȯe mil as ȯe beoir
As fír-ȯíȯean gaċ ȯíċleoir.

This Eighteenth-century poem in praise of the provinces of Ireland—an escape in the poet's mind to a remoter past—salutes Connacht as the "Wheat of Eire," Ulster for its beautiful women and great chieftains, Leinster for its level plains, its music and song, Munster land of honey and beer and shelter of the poor. In contrast there follows Swift's "plain, pathetic and truthful" 'Short View of the State of Ireland' under its newest rulers.

101

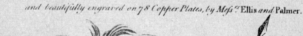

AN

HIBERNIAN ATLAS;

OR

GENERAL DESCRIPTION

OF THE

KINGDOM OF IRELAND:

Divided into PROVINCES; with its sub-divisions of COUNTIES,

BARONIES, &c.

Shewing their Boundaries, Extent, Soil, Produce, Contents, Measure,

Members of Parliament, and Number of Inhabitants;

ALSO THE

Cities, Boroughs, Villages, Mountains, Bogs, Lakes, Rivers and

NATURAL CURIOSITIES

Together with the Great and Bye POST ROADS.

The whole taken from actual SURVEYS and OBSERVATIONS,

By BERNARD SCALE, Land Surveyor.

and beautifully engraved on 78 Copper Plates, by Mess.rs Ellis and Palmer.

Published as the Act directs 1 Feb.1776.

LONDON:

Printed for Robert Sayer, and John Bennet, Map and Printsellers, N.o 53 in Fleet Street; and may

be had of the Author, at his House in DUBLIN, and at Mangroves, near Brentwood, ESSEX.

TITLE-PAGE OF BERNARD SCALE'S HIBERNIAN ATLAS (1776).

RODERICK O'FLAHERTY (1629–1718)

IT is replenished with rivers, brooks, lakes, and standing waters, even on the tops of the highest mountains. On the sea side there are many excellent large and safe harbours for ships to ride on anchor; the climate is wholesome, soe as divers attain to the age of ninety years, a hundred and upwards. The land produces wild beasts, as wolves, deere, foxes, badgers, hedgehogs, hares, rabbets, squirrells, martens, weasels, and the amphibious otter, of which kind the white-faced otter is very rare. It is never killed, they say, but with loss of man or dog, and its skin is mighty precious. It admits no rats to live anywhere within it, except the Isles of Aran and the district of the west liberties of Galway.

The water streames, besides lampreys, roaches, and the like of no value, breed salmons (where there is recourse to the sea), eels, and divers sorts of trouts. There was never a pike or bream as yet engendered in all this countrey, nor in the adjacent parts of Mayo or Galway counteys. The sea here is plentifully stored with fish, as cods, lings, hawkfish, coalefish, turbots, plaices, hadogs, whitings, gurnards, macrels, herrings, &c.

The greatest number of cattle in this country is of cows, the soil being for the most part good only for pasture and grazing, and very fertile of all kinds of herbs. The chiefest product therefore, and greatest commodity is beefe, butter, tallow, hides, and of late cheese out of the Isles of Aran; yet it yields as much corn, of wheat, barley, oats, and rye as is enough to sustaine the inhabitants, and furnish the market besides.

The inhabitants are so observant of law, that now for above thirty years of peace, there was not one body executed out of the whole territories for any transgression; and scarce any brought to the bar for misdemeanour. They dwell for the most part next the borders of the countrey where commonly is the best land; and in summer time they drive their cattle to the mountaines, where such as looke to the cattle live in small cabbins for that season. . . .

The tract of land on the south side of the barony, by the Bay of Galway, divided among the four parishes, and separated from Lough Orbsen and the river's tract by a large space of mountain land, is good pasture for cattle; but so craggy and full of stones, and so destitute of deep mold, that in very few spots of it a plough can goe; yet the tenants, by digging, manure it so well, that they have corn for themselves, their landlords and the market. Never was garden with more paines tilled for black seeds. They carry on horses, out of the shore, all the seaweeds cast in daily, as long as they can get it, from Michaelmas till sowing time past; and sometimes on spring tide low waters, they goe as far down as they can, man, woman and child, and cut the sea weed with knives, to have it cast up again by the sea. With this they muck the land, and dig up daily, earth to cover it, out of watery furrows which serve for conveying away the water from the ridges.—*A Chorographical Description of West or h-Iar Connaught.*

This account of Western Connaught in the later seventeenth century is by a great Gaelic scholar who lost his estates in the confiscations and died very poor in 1718.

THE first cause of a Kingdom's thriving is the fruitfulness of the soil, to produce the necessaries and conveniences of life, not only sufficient for the inhabitants, but for exportation into other countries.

The second, is the industry of the people in working up all their native commodities to the last degree of manufacture.

The third, is the conveniency of safe ports and havens, to carry out their own goods, as much manufactured, and bring in those of others, as little manufactured as the nature of mutual commerce will allow.

The fourth, is that the natives should as much as possible, export and import their goods in vessels of their own timber, made in their own country.

The fifth, is the liberty of a free trade in all foreign countries, which will permit them, except those who are in war with their own Prince or State.

The sixth, is, by being governed only by laws made with their own consent, for otherwise they are not a free People. And therefore all appeals for justice, or applications, for favour or preferment to another country, are so many grievous impoverishments.

The seventh, is, by improvement of land, encouragement of agriculture, and thereby increasing the number of their people, without which any country, however blessed by Nature, must continue poor.

The eighth, is the residence of the Princes, or chief administrators of the civil power.

The ninth, is the concourse of foreigners for education, curiosity or pleasure, or as to a general mart of trade.

The tenth, is by disposing all offices of honour, profit or trust, only to the natives, or at least with very few exceptions, where strangers have long inhabited the country, and are supposed to understand, and regard the interest of it as their own.

The eleventh is, when the rents of lands, and profits of employments are spent in the country which produced them, and not in another, the former of which will certainly happen, where the love of our native country prevails.

The twelfth, is by the public revenues being all spent and employed at home, except on the occasions of a foreign war.

The thirteenth, is where the people are not obliged, unless they find it for their own interest, or conveniently, to receive any monies, except of their own coinage by a public mint, after the manner of all civilized nations.

The fourteenth, is a disposition of the people of a country to wear their own manufactures, and import as few incitements to luxury, either in clothes, furniture, food or drink, as they possibly can live conveniently without. . . .

As to the first cause of a Nation's riches, being the fertility of the soil, as well as temperature of climate, we have no reason to complain; for although the quantity of unprofitable land in this Kingdom, reckoning bog, and rock, and barren mountain, be double in proportion to what it is in England, yet the native productions which both Kingdoms deal in, are very near on equality in point of goodness, and might with the same encouragement be as well manufactured. I except mines and minerals, in some of which however we are only defective in point of skill and industry.

BUST OF DEAN SWIFT IN ST. PATRICK'S CATHEDRAL, DUBLIN.

105

In the second, which is the industry of the people, our misfortune is not altogether owing to our own fault, but to a million of discouragements.

The conveniency of ports and havens which Nature bestowed us so liberally is of no more use to us, than a beautiful prospect to a man shut up in a dungeon.

As to shipping of its own, this Kingdom is so utterly unprovided, that of all the excellent timber cut down within these fifty or sixty years, it can hardly be said that the Nation hath received the benefit of one valuable house to dwell in, or one ship to trade with.

Ireland is the only Kingdom I ever heard or read of, either in ancient or modern story, which was denied the liberty of exporting their native commodities and manufactures wherever they pleased, except to countries at war with their own Prince or State, yet this by the superiority of mere power is refused us in the most momentous parts of commerce, besides an Act of Navigation to which we never consented, pinned down upon us, and rigorously executed, and a thousand other unexampled circumstances as grievous as they are invidious to mention. To go unto the rest.

It is too well known that we are forced to obey some laws we never consented to, which is a condition I must not call by its true uncontroverted name for fear of my Lord Chief Justice Whitshed's ghost with his *Libertas et natale solum*, written as a motto on his coach, as it stood at the door of the court, while he was perjuring himself to betray both. Thus, we are in the condition of patients who have physic sent them by doctors at a distance, strangers to their constitution, and the nature of their disease : And thus, we are forced to pay five hundred *per cent.* to divide our properties, in all which we have likewise the honour to be distinguished from the whole race of mankind.

As to improvement of land, those few who attempt that or planting, through covetousness or want of skill, generally leave things worse than they were, neither succeeding in trees nor hedges, and by running into the fancy of grazing after the manner of the Scythians, are every day depopulating the country.

We are so far from having a King to reside among us, that even the Viceroy is generally absent four-fifths of his time in the Government.

No strangers from other countries make this a part of their travels, where they can expect to see nothing but scenes of misery and desolation.

Those who have the misfortune to be born here, have the least title to any considerable employment to which they are seldom preferred, but upon a political consideration.

One third part of the rents of Ireland is spent in England, which with the profit of employments, pensions, appeals, journeys of pleasure or health, education at the Inns of Court, and both Universities, remittances at pleasure, the pay of all superior officers in the army and other incidents, will amount to a full half of the income of the whole Kingdom, all clear profit to England. . . . .

As to the last, or fourteenth article, we take special care to act diametrically contrary to it in the whole course of our lives. Both sexes, but

A MODEST
PROPOSAL

For preventing the

CHILDREN

OF

POOR PEOPLE

From being a Burthen to

Their Parents or Country,

AND

For making them Beneficial to the PUBLICK.

By Dr. SWIFT.

Dublin, Printed by *S. Harding* :
London, Re-printed ; and fold by *J. Roberts*
in *Warwick-lane*, and the Pamphlet-Shops.
M. DCC, XXIX.

especially the women, despise and abhor to wear any of their own manufactures, even those which are better made than in other countries, particularly a sort of silk plaid, through which the workmen are forced to run a sort of gold thread that it may pass for Indian. Even ale and potatoes in great quantity are imported from England as well as corn, and our foreign trade is little more than importation of French wine. for which I am told we pay ready money.

Now if all this be true, upon which I could easily enlarge, I would be glad to know by what secret method it is that we grow a rich and flourishing people, without liberty, trade, manufactures, inhabitants, money, or the privilege of coining ; without industry, labour or improvement of lands, and with more than half of the rent and profits of the whole Kingdom, annually exported, for which we receive not a single farthing : And to make up all this, nothing worth mentioning, except the linen of the North, a trade casual, corrupted, and at mercy, and some butter from Cork. If we do flourish, it must be against every law of Nature and Reason, like the thorn at Glastonbury, that blossoms in the midst of winter.

But my heart is too heavy to continue this journey longer, for it is manifest that whatever stranger took such a journey, would be apt to think himself travelling in Lapland or Ysland, rather than in a country so favoured by Nature as ours, both in fruitfulness of soil, and temperature of climate. The miserable dress, and diet, and dwelling of the people. The general desolation in most parts of the Kingdom. The old seats of the nobility and gentry all in ruins, and no new ones in their stead. The families of farmers who pay great rents, living in filth and nastiness upon butter-milk and potatoes, without a shoe or stocking to their feet, or a house so convenient as an English hog-sty to receive them. These indeed may be comfortable sights to an English spectator, who comes for a short time only to learn the language, and returns back to his own country, whither he finds all our wealth transmitted.

Nostra miseria magnus es.

There is not one argument used to prove the riches of Ireland, which is not a logical demonstration of its poverty. The rise of our rents is squeezed out of the very blood and vitals, and clothes, and dwellings of the tenants who live worse than English beggars.—*A Short View of the state of Ireland* (1728).

This famous tract, filled with the " cruel indignation " that glowed in the great heart of the author to his dying day, was published shortly after ' Gulliver's Travels. It circulated freely in Ireland, but the publisher of the English edition was prosecuted and sent to prison.

BISHOP BERKELEY (1750)

123. Whether one may be allowed to conceive and suppose a society or nation of human creatures clad in woollen cloths and stuffs, eating good bread, beef and mutton, poultry and fish in great plenty, drinking ale, mead, and cyder, inhabiting decent houses built of brick and marble, taking their pleasure in fair parks and gardens, depending on no foreign imports either for food or raiment? And whether such people ought much to be pitied?

132. Whether there be upon earth any Christian or civilised people so beggarly, wretched, and destitute, as the common *Irish*?

133. Whether, nevertheless, there is any other people whose wants may be more easily supplied from home?

134. Whether if there was a wall of brass a thousand cubits high round this kingdom our natives, might not, nevertheless, live cleanly and comfortably, till the land, and reap the fruits of it?

142. Whether it be not certain that from the single town of *Cork* were exported, in one year, no less than one hundred and seven thousand one hundred and sixty-one barrels of beef; seven thousand three hundred and seventy-nine barrels of pork; thirteen thousand and sixty-one casks, and eighty-five thousand seven hundred and twenty-seven firkins of butter? And what hands were employed in this manufacture?

143. Whether a foreigner could imagine that one-half of the people were starving in a country which sent out such plenty of provisions?

173. Whether the quantities of beef, butter, wool, and leather, exported from this island, can be reckoned the superfluities of a country where there are so many natives naked and famished?

175. Whether she would not be a very vile matron, and justly thought either mad or foolish, that would give away the necessaries of life, from her naked and famished children, in exchange for pearls to stick in her hair and sweet meats to please her own palate?

199. Whether it was not an *Irish* professor who first opened the public schools at *Oxford*? Whether this island hath not been antiently famous for learning? And whether at this day it hath any better chance of being considerable?

271. Whether there be any country in Christendom more capable of improvement than Ireland?

272. Whether we are not as far before other nations with respect to natural advantages, as we are behind them with respect to arts?

274. Whether my countrymen are not readier at finding excuses than remedies?

109

433. Whether London is not to be considered as the metropolis of *Ireland*? And whether our wealth (such as it is) doth not circulate through *London*, and throughout all *England*, as freely as that of any part of his Majesty's dominions?

526. Whether of late years our Irish labourers do not carry on the same business in England, to the great discontent of many there? But whether we have not much more reason than the people of England to be displeased at this commerce?

527. Whether, notwithstanding the cash supposed to be brought into it, any nation is, in truth, a gainer by such traffic?

528. Whether the industry of our people employed in foreign land while our own are left uncultivated, be not a great loss to the country?

532. Whether it be not a good rule to judge of the trade of any city, and its usefulness, to observe whether there is a circulation in the extremities, and whether the people round about are busy and warm?—*The Querist*.

George Berkeley (1685–1753), Bishop of Cloyne, has a notable place in modern English philosophy. Residing in a south Irish diocese at a time of Irish national and economic collapse, he turned his mind to social reform. His incisive " Querist " was published in sections—in 1735, 1736 and 1737. The author's final revision appeared in 1750. " After a lapse of nearly two centuries, many of the queries are still pertinent, and deserve attention from those in whom an acute sense of Ireland's political wrongs is not incompatible with an insight into the real possibilities of her welfare." (Works of George Berkeley, edited by G. Sampson, with an introduction by the Rt. Hon. A. J. Balfour, 1898).

THE INNY BRIDGE, CO. KERRY (1756).

"Éamonn an Cnuic"

Cia hé sin amuiġ
'n-a ḃfuil faoḃar ar a ġut
Aġ réaḃaḋ mo ḋorais ḋúnta?
Mise Éamonn an Cnuic
'Tá báiḋte fuar fliuċ
Ó síor-ṡiuḃal sléiḃte is ġleannta.
A laoġ ġil 's a ċuid,
Céard ḋéanfainn-se ḋuit,
Muna ġcuirfinn ort beinn ḋom' ġúna,
'S go ḃfuil púdar go tiuġ
Ḋ'á síor-ṡéiḋeaḋ leat,
'S go mbeimís araon múċta.

Is fada mise amuiġ
Faoi ṡneaċta 'ġus faoi ṡioc
'S gan ḋánaċt agam ar éinneaċ:
Mo ṡeisreaċ gan scur,
Mo ḃranar gan cur,
As gan iad agam ar aon ċor!
Níl caraid agam,
Is ḋanaid liom soin,
Do ġlacfaḋ mé moċ ná ḋéiḋ'naċ,
'S go ġcaiṫfeaḋ mé ḋul
Tar fairrge soir
O's ann naċ ḃfuil mo ġaolta.

NED OF THE HILL

—Who is that out there still
With voice sharp and shrill
Beating my door and calling?
—I am Ned of the Hill
Wet, weary and chill
The mountains and glens long walking.

O my dear love and true
What could I do for you
But under my mantle draw you?
For the bullets like hail
Fall thick on your trail,
And together we both may be slaughtered.

111

—Long lonely I go,
Under frost, under snow
Hunted through hill and through hollow.
　No comrade I know :
　No furrow I sow
My team stands unyoked in the fallow :

No friend will give ear
Or harbour me here—
'Tis that makes the weight of my sorrow !
　So my journey must be
　To the east o'er the sea
Where no kindred will find me or follow.

Translated by THOMAS MacDONAGH.

Edmund O'Ryan—" Edmund of the Hill "—a famous Tipperary outlaw—flourished in the early eighteenth century. He was " an outlaw'd gentleman, whose confiscated lands and forfeited life fired him to the resolution of heading a band of robbers and committing many acts of desperation, which were frequently counteracted by a generosity almost romantic or performed with a spirit truly heroic." He was himself the author of this, one of the most popular of all Irish songs. " Eamonn an Chnuic " was originally a love song, but in national tradition the outlaw came to symbolise Ireland itself.

Thomas MacDonagh, whose fine translation is quoted above, refers to it as " that untranslatable Eamonn an Chnuic, which yet we would all translate." MacDonagh was himself a Tipperaryman. He was a signatory to the Proclamation of Easter Week, 1916, and was executed as a leader of the Rising.

✶　✶　✶　✶　✶　✶

ARTHUR YOUNG (1780)

THE age has improved so much in humanity, that even the poor Irish have experienced its influence, and are every day treated better and better ; but still the remnant of the old manners, the abominable distinction of religion, united with the oppressive conduct of the little country gentlemen, or rather vermin of the kingdom, who never were out of it, altogether bear still very heavy on the poor people, and subject them to situations more mortifying than we ever behold in England. The landlord of an Irish estate, inhabited by Roman Catholicks, is a sort of despot who yields obedience, in whatever concerns the poor, to no law but that of his own will.

To discover what the liberty of a people is, we must live among them, and not look for it in the statutes of the realm : the language of written law may be that of liberty, but the situation of the poor may speak no language but that of slavery ; there is too much of this contradiction in Ireland ; a long series of oppressions, aided by many very ill-judged laws, have brought landlords into a habit of exerting a very lofty superiority, and their vassals into that of an almost unlimited submission : speaking a language that is despised, professing a religion that is abhorred, and being disarmed, the poor find themselves in many cases slaves even in the bosom of *written* liberty. Landlords that have resided much abroad, are usually humane in their ideas; but the habit of tyranny naturally contracts the mind, so that even in this polished age, there are instances of a severe carriage towards the poor, which is quite unknown in England.

A landlord in Ireland can scarcely invent an order which a servant, labourer or cottar dares to refuse to execute. Nothing satisfies him but an unlimited submission. Disrespect or any thing tending towards sauciness he may punish with his cane or his horsewhip with the most perfect security; a poor man would have his bones broke if he offered to lift his hand in his own defence. Knocking down is spoken of in the country in a manner that makes an Englishman stare. It must strike the most careless traveller to see whole strings of cars whipt into a ditch by a gentleman's footman, to make way for his carriage; if they

"AN IRISH PEASANT"
(From the *London Magazine*, 1788).

are overturned or broken in pieces, no matter, it is taken in patience; were they to complain they would perhaps be horsewhipped.

The execution of the laws lies very much in the hands of justices of the peace, many of whom are drawn from the most illiberal class in the kingdom. If a poor man lodges a complaint against a gentleman, or any animal that chuses to call itself a gentleman, and the justice issues out a summons for his appearance, it is a fixed affront, and he will infallibly be *called out.* Where MANNERS are in conspiracy against LAW, to whom are the oppressed people to have recourse? It is a fact that a poor man having a contest with a gentleman must—but I am talking nonsense, they know their situation too well to think of it; they can have no defence but by means of protection from one gentleman against another, who probably protects his vassal as he would the sheep he intends to eat. . . .

THE cottages of the Irish, which are all called cabbins, are the most miserable looking hovels that can well be conceived: they generally consist of only one room: mud kneaded with straw is the common material of the walls; these are rarely above seven feet high, and not always above five or six; they are about two feet thick, and have only a door, which lets in light instead of a window, and should let the smoak out instead of a chimney, but they had rather keep it in: these two conveniences they hold so cheap, that I have seen them both stopped up in stone cottages, built by improving landlords; the smoak warms them, but certainly is as injurious to their eyes as it is to the complexions of the women, which in general in the cabbins of Ireland has a near resemblance to that of a smoaked ham. The number of the blind poor I think greater there than in England, which is probably owing to this cause.

The roofs of the cabbins are rafters, raised from the tops of the mud walls, and the covering varies; some are thatched with straw, potatoe stalks, or with heath, others only covered with sods of turf cut from a grass field; and I have seen several that were partly composed of all three; the bad repair these roofs are kept in, a hole in the thatch being often mended with turf, and weeds sprouting from every part, gives them the appearance of a weedy dunghill, especially when the cabbin is not built with regular walls, but supported on one, or perhaps on both sides by the banks of a broad dry ditch, the roof then seems a hillock, upon which perhaps the pig grazes.

Some of these cabbins are much less and more miserable habitations than I have ever seen in England. I was told they were the worst in Connaught; but I found it an error; I saw many in Leinster to the full as bad; and in Wicklow, some worse than any in Connaught. When they are well roofed, and built, not of stones, ill put together, but of mud, they are much warmer, independently of smoak, than the clay, or lath and mortar cottages of England, the walls of which are so thin, that a rat hole lets in the wind, to the annoyance of the whole family. The furniture of the cabbins is as bad as the architecture; in very many consisting only of a pot for boiling their potatoes, a bit of a table, and one or two broken stools; beds are not found universally, the family lying on straw . . . .

This is a general description, but the exceptions are very numerous. I have been in a multitude of cabbins that had much useful furniture, and some even superfluous; chairs, tables, boxes, chests of drawers, earthen ware, and in short most of the articles found in a middling English cottage; but, upon enquiry, I very generally found that these acquisitions were all made within the last ten years; a sure sign of a rising national prosperity. I think the bad cabbins and furniture the greatest instances of Irish poverty; and this must flow from the mode of payment for labour, which makes cattle so valuable to the peasant, that every farthing they can spare is saved for their purchase; from hence also results another observation, which is, that the apparent poverty of it is greater than the real; for the house of a man that is master of four or five cows, will have scarcely any thing but deficiencies; nay, I was in the cabbins of dairymen and farmers, not small ones, whose cabbins were not at all better, nor better furnished than those of the poorest labourer: before, therefore, we can attribute it to absolute poverty, we must take into the account the customs and inclinations of the people. In England a man's cottage will be filled with superfluities before he possesses a cow. I think the comparison much in favour of the Irishman.

A LURID CARTOON OF " AN IRISH CABIN." FROM ARTHUR YOUNG'S *Travels*.

The cabbins of the poor Irish, being such apparently miserable habitations, is another very evident encouragement to population. In England, where the poor are in many respects in such a superior state, a couple will not marry unless they can get a house, to build which, take the kingdom through, will cost from twenty-five to sixty pounds ; half the life, and all the vigour and youth of a man and woman are passed, before they can save such a sum ; and when they have got it, so burthensome are poor to a parish, that it is twenty to one if they get permission to erect their cottage. But in Ireland the cabbin is not an object of a moment's consideration ; to possess a cow and a pig is an earlier aim ; the cabbin begins with a hovel, that is erected with two days' labour ; and the young couple pass not their youth in celibacy for want of a nest to produce their young in. If it comes to a matter of calculation, it will then be but as four pounds to thirty.

Marriage is certainly more general in Ireland than in England : I scarce ever found an unmarried farmer or cottar ; but it is seen more in other classes, which with us do not marry at all ; such as servants ; the generality of footmen and maids, in gentlemen's families, are married, a circumstance we very rarely see in England.

Another point of importance is their children not being burthensome. In all the enquiries I made into the state of the poor, I found their happiness and ease generally relative to the number of their children, and nothing considered as such a misfortune as having none : whenever this is the fact,

115

or the general idea, it must necessarily have a considerable effect in promoting early marriages, and consequently population.

The food of the people being potatoes is a point not of less importance : for when the common food of the poor is so dear as to be an object of attentive economy, the children will want that plenty which is essential to rearing them ; the article of milk, so general in the Irish cabbins, is a matter of the first consequence in rearing infants. The Irish poor in the Catholick parts of that country are subsisted entirely upon land ; whereas the poor in England have so little to do with it, that they subsist almost entirely from shops, by a purchase of their necessaries ; in the former case it must be a matter of prodigious consequence, that the product should be yielded by as small a space of land as possible ; this is the case with potatoes more than with any other crop whatever.

Generally speaking the Irish poor have a fair belly-full of potatoes, and they have milk the greatest part of the year. What I would particularly insist on here is the value of his labour being food not money ; food not for himself only, but for his wife and children. An Irishman loves whisky as well as an Englishman does strong beer ; but he cannot go on Saturday night to the whisky-house, and drink out the week's support of himself, his wife, and his children, not uncommon in the ale-house of the Englishman. It may indeed be said that we should not argue against a mode of payment because it may be abused, which is very true ; but we certainly may reason against that which carries in its very principles the seed of abuse.—*A Tour in Ireland ; with general observations on the present state of that Kingdom made in the years* 1776, 1777, *and* 1778, *and brought down to the end of the year* 1779 *(London,* 1780).

Arthur Young was famous throughout Western Europe as an authority on agriculture. His Irish tour is, perhaps, the most useful and impartial of the many accounts of this country written by English visitors in the eighteenth century—though it suffers from the loss of the most interesting portion which was stolen with the author's luggage by a dishonest servant.

*   *   *   *   *   *

DR. R. TWISS (1775)

I LANDED in Ireland with an opinion that the inhabitants were addicted to drinking, given to hospitality, and apt to blunder, or make bulls ; in which I found myself mistaken. Hospitality and drinking went formerly hand in hand, but since the excesses of the table have been so judically abolished, hospitality is not so violently practised as heretofore, when it might have been imputed as a fault.

Some years ago (perhaps half a century), when the English language was but little understood by the common Irish, it was not to be wondered at, that they frequently used improper words, and blundered, because, as the Irish was their native tongue, and the English an acquired one, they thought in one language, and expressed themselves in another, the disadvantage of which is obvious ; but as at present almost all th peasants understand the English language, they converse with as much propriety as any persons of their class in England, or anywhere else.

MAP PRINTED AS A FRONTISPIECE TO "A TOUR IN IRELAND" BY DR. R. TWISS (1776).

Dr. R. Twiss (1747–1821) is said to have travelled 27,000 miles in Europe. He offended many people in Ireland by his comments. Dublin manufacturers took revenge by having his portrait painted on china with an opprobrious rhyme.

117

Gaming and duelling are also attributed to the Irish, but probably with little foundation. As to the science of gaming, possibly it may prevail in Dublin, as it does in every great city in Europe ; and with regard to the art of duelling, a prudent traveller may as easily avoid any such disagreeable encounters there, as elsewhere.—*A Tour in Ireland.*

* * * * * *

JOSEPH WALKER (1787)

OF the dresses of the turbulent reign of James II I cannot speak with certainty ; for little is certainly known. If any particular fashion prevailed at that time, it was probably of English origin. Some of the female peasantry, however, still continued attached to their old habits. Of these I will here describe one, as worn to the hour of her death by Mary Morgan, a poor woman, who was married before the battle of the Boyne, and lived to the year 1786. On her head she wore a roll of linen, not unlike that on which milk-maids carry their pails, but with this difference, that it was higher behind than before ; over this she combed her hair, and covered the whole with a little round-eared cap, or coif, with a border sewed on plain ; over all this was thrown a kerchief, which, in her youth, was made fast to the top of her head, and let to fall carelessly behind ; in her old age it was pinned under her chin.

Her jacket was of brown cloth, or pressed frize, and made to fit close to the shape by means of whale-bone wrought into it before and behind ; this was laced in front, but not so as to meet, and through the lacing were drawn the ends of her neckerchief. The sleeves, half-way to the elbows, were made of the same kind of cloth with the jacket ; thence continued to the wrist of red chamlet striped with green ferreting ; and there, being turned up, formed a little cuff embraced with three circles of green riband. Her petticoat was invariably of either scarlet frize or cloth, bordered with three rows of green riband. Her apron green serge, striped longitudinally with scarlet ferreting, and bound with the same. Her hose were blue worsted. And her shoes of black leather, fastened with thongs, or strings.

This fashion of habit, however, had not been always peculiar to the peasantry ; it appears to have prevailed formerly in the principal Irish families. About the close of the last century, there lived at Credan, near Waterford, a Mrs. Power, a lady of considerable fortune, who, as being lineally descended from some of the Kings of Munster, was vulgarly called, The Queen of Credan. This lady, proud of her country and descent, always spoke the Irish language, and affected the dress and manners of the ancient Irish. Her dress, in point of fashion, answered exactly to that of Mary Morgan as just described ; but was made of richer materials. The border of her coif was of the finest Brussels-lace ; her kerchief of clear muslin ; her jacket of the finest brown cloth, trimmed with narrow gold lace, and the sleeves of crimson velvet striped with the same ; and her petticoat of the finest scarlet cloth, bordered with two rows of broad gold lace.—*An historical essay on the dress of the ancient and modern Irish* (Dublin, 1787).

JUSTIN MACCARTHY, VISCOUNT MOUNTCASHEL, FIRST COMMANDER OF THE IRISH
BRIGADE IN THE SERVICE OF FRANCE

*Justin MacCarthy, cousin of the Earl of Clancarty, " who had lost his land," to
whom Egan O'Rahilly referred in " Valentine Brown" (page 120), shared in the fall
and exile of the great Irish house " under whom," says O'Rahilly, " my ancestors were
before the death of Christ." He led the Irish regiments on the Rhine and in Savoy.
The " Gazette de France" announces his death in 1694 : "My Lord Mountcashel, Lt.-
Gen. of the Armies of the King, died the first of the month of wounds received on
several occasions on which he had always been extremely distinguished."*

From a portrait by Sir Peter Lely.

Bailintín Brún

Do leaṫnuiġ an ciaċ diaċrac fá m' ṡeana-ċroiḋe dúr
Ar dtaisteal na nduaḃal iasaċta i ḃfearann Cuinn ċuġainn
Scamall ar ġriain iartair d'ár ceartas ríoġaċt Muṁan
Fá ndeara ḋam triall riaṁ ort, a Ḃailintín Ḃrún.

Caiseal gan ċliar, fial-teaċ ná marcraiḋe ar dtúis,
As beanna-ḃruiġ Ḃriain ciar-ṫuilte 'maḋraiḋiḃ úisc,
Ealla gan triair triaiṫe de ṁacaiḃ ríoġ Muṁan
Fá ndeara ḋam triall riaṁ ort, a Ḃailintín Ḃrún.

D'aistriġ fiaḋ an fial-ċruiṫ do ċleaċtaḋ sí ar dtúis,
Ó neaḋuiġ an fiaċ iasaċta i nDaingean-ċoill Rúis,
Seaċnaid iasc grian-tsruiṫ as caise caoin ciúin
Fá ndeara ḋam triall riaṁ ort, a Ḃailintín Ḃrún.

Dairinis tiar, Iarla 'ní'l aici 'en ċloinn úir,
i Hamburg mo ċiaċ ! Iarla na seaḃac síoḋac súḃac ;
Seana-rosc liat ag dian-ġol fé ceaċtar díoḃ súd
Fá ndeara ḋam triall riaṁ ort, a Ḃailintín Ḃrún. . . .
                                        —Aoḋaġán Ó Raṫaille.

These verses were addressed to Valentine Brown, 3rd Viscount Kenmare, by the famous Munster poet, Egan O'Rahilly. O'Rahilly wrote a fine Epithalamium for Valentine Brown's marriage to Honora Butler of Kilcash in 1720, but he had been bitterly offended by Valentine's subsequent coldness and neglect. O'Rahilly felt the humiliation of having to turn in his old age to a family, the members of which to his mind were still intruders, though Catholic and Jacobite.

The prospect of Killarney here reproduced from Dr. C. Smith's " Antient and Present State of Kerry" (1756) was dedicated by Smith to Lord Kenmare.

VALENTINE BROWN

That my old mournful heart was pierced in this black doom,
That foreign devils have made our land a tomb,
That the sun that was Munster's glory has gone down
Has made me travel to seek you, Valentine Brown.

That royal Cashel is bare of house and guest,
That Brian's turreted home is the otter's nest,
That the kings of the land have neither land nor crown
Has made me travel to seek you, Valentine Brown.

That the wild deer wanders afar, that it perishes now,
That alien ravens croak on the topmost bough,
That fish are no more in stream or streamlet lit by the sun
Has made me travel to seek you, Valentine Brown.

Dernish away in the west and her master banned;
Hamburg the refuge of him who has lost his land;
Two old grey eyes that weep; great verse that lacks renown,
Have made me travel to seek you, Valentine Brown.

Translated by FRANK O'CONNOR.

A
LIST
OF
LORDS,
GENTLEMEN, and OTHERS,

Who having ESTATES, EMPLOYMENTS, *and* PENSIONS *in* Ireland, *spend the same abroad; together with an Estimate of the Yearly Value of the same, as taken in the Months of* May, June *and* July 1729.

The Lords and Gentlemen of Estate, are divided into Three Classes.

FIRST CLASS comprehends those, who live constantly abroad, and are seldom, or never seen in *Ireland*.

SECOND CLASS comprehends those, who live generally abroad, and visit *Ireland* now and then, for a Month or two.

THIRD CLASS takes in those, who live generally in *Ireland*, but were occasionally absent, at the Time the said List was taken, either for Health, Pleasure, or Business; but their Number is commonly the same, for if some come home, others go abroad, and supply their Places.

A   FIRST

The Absentee landlord "with his one foot Irish and one foot English" was a long-standing burden on the country. Above is reproduced a page from Thomas Prior's "List of the Absentees of Ireland".

SIR JONAH BARRINGTON (1760-1834)

IN those days, then, the common people ideally separated the gentry of the country into three classes, and treated each class according to the relative degree of respect to which they considered it was entitled. They generally divided them thus :—

    1. *Half-mounted* gentlemen.
    2. Gentlemen every *inch of them*.
    3. Gentlemen to the *back bone*.

The first-named class formed the only species of independent yeomanry then existing in Ireland. They were the descendants of the small grantees of Queen Elizabeth, Cromwell, and King William ; possessed about 200 acres of land each, in fee farm, from the Crown ; and were occasionally admitted into the society of gentlemen—particularly hunters—living at other times amongst each other, with an intermixture of their own servants, with whom they were always on terms of intimacy. They generally had good clever horses, which could leap over any thing, but had never felt the trimming-scissors or currycomb. The riders commonly wore buck-skin breeches, and boots well greased, (blacking was never used in the country), and carried large thong whips heavily loaded with lead at the butt-end, so that they were always prepared either to horsewhip a man or knock his brains out, as circumstances might dictate.

These half-mounted gentlemen exercised the hereditary authority of keeping the ground clear at horse-races, hurlings, and all public meetings as the soldiers keep the lines at a review. Their business was to ride round the inside of the ground, which they generally did with becoming spirit, trampling over some, knocking down others, and slashing every body who encroached on the proper limits. Bones being but very *seldom* broken, and skulls still seldomer fractured, every body approved of their exertions, because all the by-standers gained therefrom a full view of the sport which was going forward. A shout of merriment was always set up when a half-mounted gentleman knocked down an interloper ; and some of the *poets* present, if they had an opportunity, roared out their verses by way of a song to encourage the gentlemen.

The second class, or gentlemen every *inch of them*, were of excellent old families—whose finances were not in so good order as they might have been, but who were popular amongst all ranks. They were far above the first degree, somewhat inferior to the third ; but had great influence, were much beloved, and carried more sway at popular elections and general county meetings than the other two classes put together.

The third class, or gentlemen to the *back bone*, were of the oldest families and settlers, universally respected, and idolized by the peasantry, although they also were generally a little out at elbows. Their word was law ; their nod would have immediately collected an army of cottagers, or colliers, or whatever the population was composed of. Men, women, and children, were always ready and willing to execute any thing " the squire " required.—*Personal Sketches*.

REV. G. STORY : (1693)

NOR will it be amiss, once for all, to give you a brief account how the Irish managed this affair, to make the Rapparees so considerable as they really were, doing much more mischief at this time o' th' year, than any thing that had the face of an Army could pretend to. When the Irish understood therefore how our men were posted all along the line . . . they let loose a great part of their Army to manage the best for themselves, that time and opportunity would allow them ; to all these they gave passes, signifying to what Regiment they belonged, that in case they were taken, they might not be dealt with as Rapparees but Souldiers.

These men knew the country, nay, all the secret corners, woods and bogs ; keeping a constant correspondence with one another, and also with the Army, who furnished them with all necessaries, especially ammunition. When they had any project on foot, their method was not to appear in a body, for then they would have been discovered. . . . Their way was to make a private appointment to meet at such a pass or wood, precisely at such a time a' th' night or day as it stood with their conveniency ; and tho' you could not see a man over night, yet exactly at their hour, you might find three or four hundred, more or less, as they had occasion, all well armed, and ready for what design they had formerly projected ; but if they happened to be discovered, or over-powered, they presently dispersed, having beforehand appointed another place of rendezvous, ten or twelve miles (it may be) from the place they then were at ; by which means our men could never fix any close engagement upon them during the winter ; so that if they could have held out another year, the Rapparees would have continued still very prejudicial to our Army, as well by killing our men privately, as stealing our horses, and intercepting our provisions. But after all, least the next age may not be of the same humour with this, and the name of a Rapparee may possibly be thought a finer thing than it really is, I do assure you that in my style they never can be reputed other than Tories, Robbers, Thieves, and Bogg-Trotters.—*A Continuation of . . . the Wars of Ireland* (1693).

* * *

The Rapparees were a constant trouble to English settlers, and many measures such as this were taken against them.

AN
ACT
FOR
Explaining and Amending
Two feveral
ACTS
AGAINST
Tories, Robbers,
AND
RAPPAREES.

DUBLIN:
Printed by *Andrew Crook*, Printer to the Queen's Moft

JOHN BUSH (1769)

YOU have frequently met with accounts, in the public papers, of the insurrections of the Whiteboys, as they are called in this country. From the people of fortune who have been sufferers by them, and who, too generally in this kingdom, look on the miserable and oppressed poor of their country in the most contemptible light, the accounts of these insurgents have, for the most part, been too much exaggerated to be depended on. . . . The original of their denomination of Whiteboys was from the practice of wearing their shirts withoutside of their clothes, the better to distinguish each other in the night-time. It happened that we were at Kilkenny, in our road to Waterford, at the very time of the late considerable insurrection of these unhappy wretches, in the south of Kilkenny county, not far from Waterford.

I was naturally led to enquire into the cause of these insurrections and the pretensions of the insurgents themselves for creating these disturbances. From the people of easy and affluent circumstances it is natural to suppose the accounts would be very different from such as were given by those of the same class with the delinquents. By comparing these, however, with the obvious appearance of things in the country, I soon had sufficient reason to believe their disquiet arose, in general, from the severe treatment they met with from their landlords, and the lords of the manors and principally from their clergy. Our road to Waterford lay through the very midst of these unhappy insurgents, and we were, consequently, advised to take a different route. Why, whence should be the fear? We have neither deprived them of their common rights nor their potatoes. They have no quarrel with us, who have never injured them.

We rode through the country, in which they were assembled in great number, but the very day before the last considerable engagement they had with the troops quartered at the towns in the neighbourhood; but met with no molestation from any of them. The very next day after we came to Waterford, the news was brought of this engagement, about four or five miles from the town. The opinions and representations of the inhabitants of the town were various on the merits of the affair; but it was easy to distinguish the sentiments of the humane from the aggravated representations of inveterate prejudice. . . .

There are many little commons, or vacant spots of ground, adjacent to the road, upon which the inhabitants of the cabbins by the highwayside have been used, from time immemorial, to rare, as they express it, a pig or a goose, which they have bought very young, the sale of which has helped to furnish them with a few necessaries. Many of these have been taken into the fields or enclosures on the road side by the landlords, who have farmed or purchased them, or the lords of the manor. From an impartial view of their situation, I could not, from my soul, blame these unhappy delinquents. They are attacked and reduced on all sides, so hardly, as to have barely their potatoes left them to subsist on.—*Hibernia Curiosa.*

125

EARL OF BELMORE (1894)

AFTER the Revolution of 1688, and when the country had settled down, the gentry owning the larger estates appear to have begun to build more pretentious houses. To take the writer's own estate as an example—the original house, built by Captain Roger Atkinson, the original patentee or grantee, is described by Pynnar as being "a strong stone house, situated in a strong Bawne of Lime and stone, 60 feet square, in which his (Atkinson's) wife with his family dwelleth." This house suffered in the Rebellion of 1641, but was sold with the estate by Atkinson's successors to Mr. John Corry, of Belfast, in 1656. Mr. Corry, from whom the writer is the descendant in the seventh generation through one female descent, inhabited the house apparently for the remainder of his life, and afterwards his son, Captain (and subsequently Colonel) James Corry, until the Revolution. It was burnt by order of the Governor of Enniskillen in 1688 or 1689 (in the absence apparently of the owner), to prevent it from falling into the hands of the Duke of Berwick's forces.

SPINNING AND REELING FLAX IN CO. DOWN

This house is described in a Patent of William and Mary, given in Harris, as having been "one of the best in that Country." In 1709 Colonel Corry, then M.P. for the county, had plans prepared for a new house, which would seem to have been attached to the old house (a building of some twenty feet in width, described in the plan as "the new house"), the latter being no doubt used for the kitchen and other offices. The new house was, according to the still existing plans, a rectangular building,

126

60 feet long by about 50 wide. It had a basement, with cellar, and probably some servants' rooms, like a town house. Above this was the entrance hall, with a greater and lesser parlour to right and left, facing west. Facing east was the withdrawing room, principal staircase, and a bedroom. On the next floor were the principal bedrooms, and over this again, attics with dormer windows.

This house lasted until the end of the century, when the first Earl of Belmore, having on the death of his mother, Sarah Corry, become possessed of the Corry in addition to his own Lowry Estates, built the existing house of Castlecoole on a palatial scale, and upon a higher site, at a distance of about 400 yards from the old house.

THE LINEN HALL, BURGH QUAY, DUBLIN, 1783.

The smaller gentry and the clergy resided, as a rule, in long low, thatched houses, with a ground floor, and some rooms in the slope of the roof, of which some specimens still remain. In the earlier part of the last century it appears to have been the fashion to divide the demesnes into rectangular fields, called " parks "—hence probably the origin of the term " townparks " As time went on, these were often thrown together into larger enclosures, and planted with single trees and plantations. The old " parks " were apt to be fenced with what is called a " double-ditch," with a great bank in the centre and a hedge and ditch on each side. The bank was planted with forest trees, and in the absence of plantations, such as we now find, was no doubt very useful for shelter, although terribly wasteful of good land. Some fine specimens of beech trees grown in this way still exist at Castlecoole.—*Some Social Notes on the Ulster Plantation.*

127

THE CUSTOM HOUSE, DUBLIN.

This masterpiece of Georgian architecture, designed by Gandon in 1781, was " the most costly, and excepting the Exchange, the most highly-decorated building in the city ; whether taken in the general effect or immediately considered, its appearance is magnificent, and on the whole it is acknowledged the most sumptuous edifice appropriated to such a use in Europe ". (Malton's Views of Dublin, 1797.)

*   *   *   *   *   *

REV. T. CAMPBELL (1777)

BOATE, who wrote about a hundred years since, arranges the Irish cities in the following order : Dublin, Galway, Waterford, Limerick, Cork and Londonderry. As to the other towns, he says, the best of them, which are Drogheda, Kilkenny, Belfast, &c., are hardly comparable to those market-towns which are to be found in all parts of England. But how greatly must this order be now deranged, when it is universally believed, that the third town, in trade and consequence, is Belfast. In extent also, it comes next to Cork, for it has 5,295 houses, Limerick but 3,859, and Waterford 2,628. It is remarkable that Newry, a town not so much as named by Boate, has now more trade, houses, and people than Galway.

DUBLIN. The magnitude of this city is much greater than I imagined ; I conclude it to be nearer a fourth, than a fifth of that of London. Viewing it from any of its towers, it seems to be more ; but from walking the streets, I should take it to be less . . . and reckoning six to a family, or twelve to a house, there will be above 160,000 souls in Dublin.

The bulk of this city is like the worst parts of St. Giles's, but the new streets are just as good as ours. They have finished one side of a square called Merion's Square, in a very elegant style. Near it is a square called Stephen's Green, round which is a gravel walk of near a mile ; here, genteel company walk in the evenings, and on Sundays, after two o'clock, as with us in St. James's Park. This square has some grand houses, and is in general well built. The great inequality of the houses instead of diminishing, does, in my opinion, add to its beauty. The situation is cheerful, and the buildings around it multiply very fast. Almost all the tolerable houses and streets have been built within forty years. Since the year 1685, the increase has been amazing. . . .

The quays of Dublin are its principal beauty ; they lie on each side the river, which is banked and walled in, the whole length of the city ; and at the breadth of a wide street from the river on each side, the houses are built fronting each other, which has a grand effect. When these streets are paved like the streets of London, we shall have nothing to compare wiht them.

Yesterday I went down the North Strand, catching the sea breezes as I rode along. Before you is the sea covered with ships ; on the left of the bay, is a country beautifully varied, and sufficiently dressed by art, to enrich the landskip ; to the right, the conical mountains of Wicklow terminate your view. The river Liffey and part of the city compose the foreground of this exquisite piece. . . .

If you prefer the men of this country for their hospitality and the women for their beauty, you are likely to live well with them. The ladies are, I believe, full as handsome as ours, yet it was sometime before I could bring myself to think so. . . . They are said not to walk as well as with us. If the fact be so I would rather attribute it to the badness of the streets, than to any wrong conformation of limbs. . . . In another generation, when the sides of these streets are flagged, the ladies of Dublin may be as much praised for their way of walking, as those of London.

It is deemed almost a reproach for a gentlewoman to be seen walking these streets. An old lady of quality told me last night, when speaking on this subject, that for her part, truly she had not once walked over Essex Bridge, since she was a girl. Now Essex Bridge is the grand pass here, as Charing Cross is in London. If it were not for dancing, of which they are passionately fond, the poor girls must all become cripples. It is impossible they should excel in what they do not practise ; but, if they walk ill, they certainly dance well. For last night, you must know, I was at a ball, and never enjoyed one more in my life. There is a sweet affability and sparkling vivacity in these girls, which is very captivating.

129

CORK is a city large and extensive, beyond my expectation. I had been taught to think worse of it, in all respects, than it deserves. . . . And as it is the great shambles of the Kingdom, I was predisposed to credit these reports; but is really as clean, in general, as the metropolis. The slaughter houses are all in the suburbs, and there, indeed, the gale is not untainted but in the city properly so called, all is tolerably clean and consequently sweet. . . . There are two large stone bridges, one to the north, and the other to the south, over the grand branches of the Lee, besides several small ones and some draw-bridges thrown over the lesser branches or canals. There are seven churches, an exchange, a custom-house, a barrack, several hospitals, and other public structures, yet none of them worth a second look. I have not seen a single monument of antiquity in the whole town, nor heard a bell in any of the churches, too good for the dinner-bell of a country squire. But here is something infinitely better. Here is the busy bustle of prosperous trade, and all its concomitant blessings; here is a most magnificent temple, erected to plenty in the midst of a marsh." . . . Smith's history of Cork, quoting Stanihurst, reports that 120 years ago, Cork was but the third city in Munster, now it is the second in the kingdom, and therefore called the Bristol of Ireland.

KILKENNY values itself upon its superior gentility and urbanity. It is much frequented by the neighbouring gentry as a country residence, has a stand of nine sedan chairs, and is not without the appearance of an agreeable place. I went last night to their weekly assembly, and was soon given to understand, by one of my partners that Kilkenny has always been esteemed the most polite and well-bred part of the kingdom. Knowing so little of this country, I am not furnished with any arguments from either reason or authority, to dispute this pretension. My partner was so beautiful a woman and so striking an example of the doctrine she taught that she led me away an easy captive to the opinion. For which I can see the justest grounds. This was the site for the old Ormond family, here the last duke kept a court, as several of his predecessors had done, in a style much more magnificent than any of the modern viceroys. The people imbibed the court manners, and manners remain long after their causes are removed.

At present the inheritor of the castle and some of the appendant manors, a Roman Catholic gentleman, affects the state of his ancestors; his wife receives company as, I am told, the old Ormond ladies used to do; she never returns visits; and people seem disposed to yield her this pre-eminence. The cook belonging to this inn, the Sheaf of Wheat, wears ruffles; and, though an old man, is full of vivacity as politeness. . . .

I am not singular in remarking that the peasants of this country are a most comely breed of men. They are generally middle sized, and have almost universally dark brown hair, and eyes of the same colour. The complexions are clear, their countenances grave, and their faces of that oval character, which the Italian painters so much admire.

130

BELFAST is a very handsome, thriving, well-peopled Town; a great many new houses and good shops in it. The folks seemed all very busy and employed in trade, the inhabitants being for the most part merchants, or employ'd under 'em, in this sea-port, which stands, conveniently enough, at the very inner part of Carrickfergus. Thro' the town there runs a small rivulet, not much better than that they call the Glibb in Dublin, which, however, is of great use for bringing their goods to the Key when the tide serves. . . . Here we saw a very good manufacture of earthenware which nearest Delft of any made in Ireland, and really is not much short of it. 'Tis very clean and pretty, and universally used in the north, and I think not so much owing to any peculiar happiness in their clay but rather to the manner of beating and mixing it up."

LIMERICK is a place fortified by nature; for, without the annoyance of circumjacent hills, it is built upon an island, encircled by a strong barrier, the arms of the Shannon. It is now happily dismantled, and scarce a trace of its old walls and seventeen gates are to be seen. The substitution of spacious quays and commodious houses, in place of lofty battlements and massive bastions, has given it a thorough and healthy ventilation. Limerick, like London, was formerly and frequently visited by the plague; but the effect has here also been removed by the removal of the cause. . . .

I can easily believe that the women here deserve their celebrated character for beauty; for I have seen great numbers of pretty faces in the streets and public walks. In general, the common people, too, are of a very comely personage. The streets are always crowded with them; having no staple manufacture to employ them, they walk about, like the sluggard, with their hands in their bosom. They once had a manufacture of serges, but that is nearly extinct. They are, however, famous for making gloves. . . . A few years ago the town stood on sixty-four acres of ground; now it covers one hundred, equal to 160 of our measure.

AND now having finished my little tour through two provinces of Ireland and ruminating upon what I have seen, I must say, and I cannot say it in words so authoritative as those of Sir John Davies:

'I have observed the good temperature of the air, the fruitfulness of the soil, the pleasant and commodious seats for habitation, the safe and large ports and havens, lying open for traffic into all the western parts of the world, the long inlets of many naviggable rivers and so many great lakes and fresh ponds within the land, as the like are not to be seen in any part of Europe; and, lastly, the bodies and minds of the people endued with extraordinary abilities of nature.'

After considering all this, yet seeing at the same time that the greater, and certainly the best part of what I have seen, instead of being in a progressive state of improvement, is verging to depopulation; that the

131

inhabitants are either moping under the sullen gloom of inactive indigence, or blindly asserting the rights of nature in nocturnal insurrections, attended with circumstances of ruinous devastation and savage cruelty, must we not conclude that there are political errors somewhere?

Cruelty is not in the nature of these people more than of other men, for they have many customs among them, which discover uncommon gentleness, kindness and affection. Nor are they singular in their hatred of labour. . . . There is no necessity for recurring to natural disposition, when the political constitution obtrudes upon us so many obvious and sufficient causes of the sad effects we complain of.

The first is, the suffering avarice to convert the arable lands into pasture. The evils arising from this custom in England were so grievous . . . so great was the discontent of the people, from poverty occasioned by decay of tillage and increase of pasturage, that they rose in actual rebellion in the reign of Edward VI and sharpened by indigence and oppression, demolished in many countries the greatest part of the inclosures.

Here you see an exact prototype of the present disturbances in Munster, carried on by the rabble, originally called *Levellers*, from their levelling the inclosures of commons, but now *White Boys*, from their wearing their shirts over their coats, for the sake of distinction in the night. There it was a rebellion, here it is only a star-light insurrection, disavowed by everybody; and the impotence of those engaged to do anything effectual, drives them into wanton and malignant acts of cruelty on individuals. Hopeless of redress, they are provoked to acts of desperation. . . . And as little wonder that insurrection should rear its head in this ill-fated country; the first landlords of which are absentees, the second either forestallers or graziers, and where the only tiller of the ground stands in a third, and sometimes in a fourth degree from the original proprietor. Something should be thought of, something done, to restore the rights of human nature, in a country almost usurped by bullocks and sheep. —*A Philosophical Survey of the South of Ireland* (London, 1777; Dublin, 1778).

Rev. T. Campbell (1733–89), well-known as a preacher, wit, and writer, was " the Irish Dr. Campbell" mentioned in ' Boswell's Life of Johnson.'

* * * * * *

CHAPTER VIII.

The Penal Times

THE Penal Code is the shell in which Protestant power has been hatched. It has become a bird. It must burst the shell or perish in it.—HENRY GRATTAN.

* * * * * *

Catholics in Ireland were liable to various disfranchisements and other penalties by law during the seventeenth and eighteenth centuries. Periods of active persecution alternated with longer intervals, when there was toleration by connivance, the laws were not strictly enforced, and there was much kindness and friendship among neighbours of different creeds. The extraordinary Penal Code of the eighteenth century was summarised by Lord Chancellor Bowes (1758-67) when he ruled that " the law does not suppose any such person to exist as an Irish Roman Catholic."

* * * * * *

JOHN MITCHEL (1815-75)

I KNOW the spots, within my own part of Ireland, where venerable Archbishops hid themselves, as it were, in a hole in the rocks. In a remote part of Louth County, near the base of the Fews mountains, is a retired nook called Ballymascanlon. There dwelt for years, in a farm house which would attract no attention, the Primate of Ireland and successor of St. Patrick, Bernard MacMahon, a prelate accomplished in all the learning of his time, and assiduous in the government of his archdiocese ; but he moved with danger, if not with fear, and often encountered hardships in travelling by day and by night. His next successor but one was Michael O'Reilly, and he dwelt in a cabin at Termonfechin, near Clogher Head, a very wild place, and greatly out of the way, as it lay between the Great Northern Road and the sea, and could only be found by those who searched for it. Here he died.

And if such were the toils, hardships, and dangers of the highest ecclesiastics, we may conjecture what kind of life awaited the simple priests who devoted themselves to the mission ; yet it was with full knowledge of all this, with full resolution to brave all this, that many hundreds of educated Irishmen, fresh from the colleges of Belgium or of Spain, came to the French sea coast of Brest or St. Malo, bent on finding some way of crossing to where their work lay.

Imagine a priest ordained at Seville or Salamanca, a gentleman of high old name, a man of eloquence and genius, who has sustained disputations in the college halls on questions of literature or theology ; imagine him on the quays of Brest, treating with the skipper of some

133

vessel to let him work his passage; he wears tarry breeches and a tarpaulin hat (for disguise was generally needful); he flings himself on board, takes his full part in all hard work, scarce feels the cold spray and the fierce tempests; and he knows, too, that the end of it all, for him, may be a row of sugar canes to hoe, under the blazing sun of Barbadoes, overlooked by a broad-hatted agent of a Bristol planter; yet he goes eagerly to meet his fate, for he carries in his hand a sacred deposit, bears in his heart a sacred message, and must deliver it or die. Imagine him then springing ashore, and repairing to seek the bishop of the diocese in some cave, or behind some hedge, but proceeding with caution by reason of the priest-catchers and their wolf-dogs.— *Reply to the falsification of history by James Anthony Froude.*

DE ROCHEFORD (1670)

PASSING over a bridge, which joins this part of the town to the larger, you come to a great quay, bordered by vessels, which come hither from all parts of Europe. . . . From this bridge you come to a fine and broad street, which forms a square in its centre, which

Catholic devotional works in Irish had to be printed abroad in the seventeenth and eighteenth centuries, owing to the penal laws. On this page and on the opposite page are facsimiles of Catechisms published in Louvain and Paris. (From the National Library of Ireland collection.)

serves for a parade : here is the town-house, towards which tend most of the best streets of the town. I was there on a Sunday, and was told that if I was desirous of hearing mass, one would be said at two miles distance from the town. It would be astonishing to relate the number of Catholics that I saw arrive from across the woods and mountains, to assemble at this Mass, which was said in a little hamlet, and in a chamber poorly fitted up. Here I saw, before Mass, above fifty persons confess, and afterwards communicate with a devotion truly catholic and sufficient to draw these religionists to the true faith.

The chapel in which the priest celebrated Mass was not better adorned than the chamber ; but God does not seek grand palaces, he chuses poverty and pureness of heart in those that serve him. This priest informed me that the Irish were naturally inclined to the Catholic faith, but that there were many in different parts of the kingdom who found great difficulty to perform freely the functions of their religion. He had studied long in France, and spoke the French language well. He told me the Irish Catholics did not eat either flesh or eggs on Wednesdays, Fridays, or Saturdays ; that they followed the commandments of the Church, and of our holy father the Pope, whom they acknowledged for chief of the Catholic, Apostolic, and Roman Church.—*Le voyage d'Europe* (1672).

* * * * * *

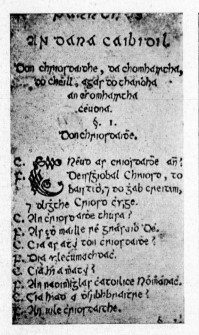

SUPERIOR OF CARMELITES (1629)

FOR a few years Ireland has at length enjoyed some sort of toleration in professing the Catholic faith. During the past summer, some of the nobility, selected from all Ireland, were sent as a deputation to the king [Charles I], that by offering a large pecuniary subsidy they might obtain for their country an exemption from many calamities which have hitherto oppressed her. . . . On account of this, all the ecclesiatics now publicly perform their sacred functions, and prepare suitable places for offering the holy sacrifice; with open doors they now preach to the people, say Mass, and discharge all their other duties, without being molested by anyone. . . .

In the present toleration, the Catholics enjoy some repose, and they attend at the chapels and frequent the sacraments; in which matter I myself, indeed, can testify as an eye-witness, how each week they flock in such crowds to the sacraments of penance and the holy eucharist, that scarcely is it possible for the priests to meet their demands. Our church, which is a fair size, cannot contain a sixth part of the congregation on Sundays and holydays, and four confessors are not sufficient for our confessionals. . . . In the same city of Dublin, there are very many other distinguished spiritual labourers, forsooth, the Franciscans, Dominicans, Capuchins, and Jesuits, all of whom untiringly labour in that vineyard. There are also pastors residing in their parishes, as best they can, supported by a stipend and casual offerings from their parishioners.—SUPERIOR OF THE CARMELITES IN DUBLIN—TO THE VATICAN (1629).

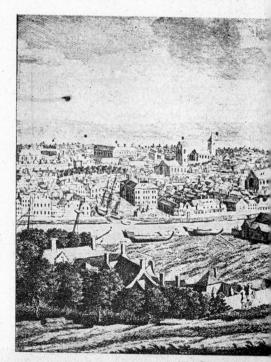

Cork, fifth city in Ireland in the 17th century, had become second by the middle of the 18th. This fine prospect, of which only the central portion is shown here, may be contrasted with the little walled town from " Pacata Hibernia " (1632), on page 12 of this book. Dr. Charles Smith, who published it in his History of Cork (1750), dedicated it to the Mayor, Sheriffs, and Council.

MATTHEW O'CONOR (1813)

LORD BERKELEY was a man of probity and moderate principles, who substituted a mild and merciful administration for the unrelenting tyranny of oppressors; the penal statutes of Elizabeth were relaxed, the public exercise of the Catholic religion allowed, its professors were admitted to all situations of trust and emolument, civil and military, to all franchises and corporations, to the rights and privileges of subjects, protected in their persons and properties, invested with political power, with shrievalties and magistracies, to secure them against oppression and injustice. Under this system Ireland began to flourish and prosper, to recover from the miseries of the late war, and the desolation of Cromwell; arts and manufactures revived. The English statutes against the exportation of wool gave rise to a native woollen manufacture, and that against the importation of live cattle into England gave a provision trade. Commerce again displayed her sails on the Irish shores. . . .

The liberal and enlightened Berkeley was removed, to make room for Lord Essex, a bigot, . . . and a storm of persecution let loose against the Catholics. They were disfranchised in all corporations, and deprived of corporate honours and emoluments. . . . Oliver Plunket, Primate of Armagh, was carried away to be tried at Westminster, contrary to the fundamental laws of the realm, was convicted upon suborned evidence of an impossible crime, hanged, and quartered at Tyburn.—*The history of the Irish Catholics.*

BLESSED OLIVER PLUNKET, ARCHBISHOP OF ARMAGH AND PRIMATE OF ALL IRELAND (1681)

O N the first of July, 1681, Mr. Sheriff demanded his prisoner, who was carryed by him on a Sledge to be Hang'd, Drawn, and Quarter'd, in his Passage to the Place of Execution. He made many Ejaculatory Prayers, full of the Love of God, and Charity to his Neighbours : When he arrived at TYBURN, and was ty'd up before the Cart was drawn from under him, he made with wonderful Cheerfulness this following Discourse.

" I have some few days past abided my Tryal at the *Kings Bench,* and now very soon I must hold up my Hand at the *King* of *King's Bench,* and appear before a Judge who cannot be deceived by false Witnesses or corrupted Allegations, for he knoweth the Secrets of Hearts. Neither can he deceive any, or give an unjust Sentence, or be mislead by Respect of Persons, he being all Goodness and a most just Judge, will infallibly decree an Eternal Reward for all good Works, and condign Punishment for the smallest Transgressions against his Commandments. Which being a most certain and undoubted Truth ; it wou'd be a wicked Act and contrary to my perpetual Welfare, that I shou'd now by declaring at any Thing contrary to Truth, commit a detestable Sin, for which within a short Time I must receive Sentence of Everlasting Damnation.

. . .

'Tis to be observ'd that I have been accus'd in *Ireland* of Treason and *Premunire ;* and that there I was arraign'd, and brought to my Tryal. But the Prosecutors (Men of flagitious and infamous Lives) perceiving that I had Records and Witnesses, they voluntarily absented themselves ; and came to this City, to procure that I should be brought hither to my Tryal ; (where the Crimes objected were not committed) where the Jury did not know me, or the Qualities of my Accusers, and were not informed of several other Circumstances conducing to a fair Tryal. Hereafter six Months close Imprisonment, (or there abouts) I was brought to the Bar the 3d of *May,* and arraign'd for a Crime, for which I was before Arraign'd in *Ireland,* a strange Resolution ; a rare Fact ; of which you will hardly find a Precedent these 500 Years past. But whereas my Witnesses and Records were in *Ireland,* the Lord chief Justice gave me 5 Weeks Time to get them brought hither ; but by reason of the Uncertainty of the Winds, the Seas, and of the Difficulty of getting Copies of Records, and bringing many Witnesses from several Counties in *Ireland,* and for many other Impediments, (of which Affidavit was made (I cou'd not at the end of 5 Weeks get the Records and Witnesses brought hither. I therefore begg'd for 12 Days more, that I might be in a Readiness for my Tryal ; which the Lord chief Justice denyed : And so I was brought to my Tryal, and expos'd, (as it were with my Hands ty'd) to those merciless Perjurors, who did aim at my Life. . . .

Oliverus Plunkett, Archi Episcopus Armachan...

...tor Bonus, Animam suam pro Ovibus suis posuit London Die ...

Marshen pinxit. I Vander Vaart... ...Bedtor Ex.

MEZZOTINT FROM A CONTEMPORARY PORTRAIT.

I dare venture farther to affirm, that if these Points of . . . had been sworn before any Protestant jury in *Ireland*, and had been acknowledged by me at the Bar, they would not believe me, no more that if it had been deposed, and confess'd by me, that I had flown in the Air from *Dublin* to *Holly-head.*

You see therefore what a Condition I am in, and you have heard what Protestations I have made of Innocency, and I hope you will believe the Words of a dying Man. And that you may be the more induced to give me Credit, I assure you that a great Peer sent me Notice, ' That he would save my Life, if I wou'd accuse others, but I answer'd, that I never knew any Conspirators in *Ireland*, but such (as I said before) as were publickly known Outlaws ; and that to save my Life, I wou'd not falsly accuse any, or prejudice my own Soul.' *S. Mat*, 16. 26. What availeth a Man, if he gain the whole world and loses his own Soul ? To take away any Man's Life or Goods wrongfully ill becometh any Christian, especially a Man of my Calling, being a Clergyman of the Catholick Church, and also an unworthy Prelate, which I do openly confess.

And now that I have shew'd sufficiently (as I think) how innocent I am of any Plot or Conspiracy ; I wou'd I were able with the like Truth to clear my self of high Crimes committed against the divine Majesty's Commandments, (often transgressed by me) for which I am sorry with all my Heart ; and if I shou'd or cou'd live a thousand Years, I have a firm Resolution, and a strong Purpose, by your Grace (o my God) never to offend you, and I beseech your divine Majesty, by the Merits of Christ, and by the Intercession of his blessed Mother, and all the Holy Angels and Saints to forgive me my Sins, and to grant my Soul eternal Rest. *Be merciful unto me O Lord, &c. Spare my Soul, &c. Into thy Hands I commend my Spirit, &c.*

THE

HONESTY

AND

TRUE ZEAL

OF THE

Kings Witneſſes

Juſtified and Vindicated againſt thoſe Un-christian-like Equivocal Proteſtations of

Dr. Oliver Plunkett,

Aſſerting in his laſt Speech his own inno-cency; being as great Damnation to his Soul, as any of his former Trayterous and Helliſh Practices againſt his King and Countrey, as breathing them upon the point of Death, with-out any time of repenting the Enormity of them with true Con-trition.

By Florence Weyer, Gent.

LONDON, Printed for T. Baldwin, 1681.

This is a facsimile of a pamphlet against the Archbishop published in London during his trial.

The Beatification of Oliver Plunket took place in St. Peter's, Rome, on May 23rd, 1920, and was attended by many visitors from Ireland.

To the final Satisfaction of all Persons that have the Charity to believe the Words of a dying Man ; I again declare before God, as I hope for Salvation, that what is contained in this Paper, is the plain and naked Truth, without any Equivocation, mental Reservation, or secret Evasion whatsoever ; taking the Words in the usual Sense and meaning Protestants do, when they discourse with all Candor and Sincerity. To all which I have here subscrib'd my Hand, *OLIVER PLUNKET*."
—HUGH REILY : *Ireland's Case briefly stated* (1695).

Blessed Oliver Plunket (1629–81) was educated at the Irish College, Rome. He returned to Ireland as Primate at the age of forty, and displayed great zeal in his arch-episcopate, confirming 48,655 people in his first four years. He was honoured and respected by Protestant as well as Catholic Irishmen. He lost his life in the " Popish Plot," the invention of the depraved ruffian, Titus Oates. Lord Macaulay thus describes the popular frenzy in London when Blessed Oliver was arrested and tried : " The capital and the whole nation went mad with hatred and fear. The penal laws, which had begun to lose something of their edge, were sharpened anew. . . . All the gaols were filled with Papists. . . . No citizen thought himself safe unless he carried under his coat a small flail loaded with lead to brain the Popish assassins. . . . The death of an innocent man gave no more uneasiness than the death of a partridge. The juries partook of the feelings then common throughout the nation, and were encouraged by the bench to encourage their feelings without restraint."

*   *   *   *   *   *

HUGH REILY (1695)

THEY (the Roman Catholicks of Ireland) capitulated with the generals of King William's troops and the Lords Justices of Ireland ; and obtained Articles commonly called the Articles of Limerick. . . . For the religious performance of which Articles, according to the true intent and meaning of the same, the said Lords Justices and generals, under the sanction of public faith, solemnly plighted their words and honours, and promised to get the same ratified by King William, which they accordingly did, King William ratifying them in Council under the Broad seal of England.

Now by the first of these Articles, the Roman Catholicks of Ireland were to enjoy such privileges in the exercise of their religion, as they did in the reign of King Charles the Second ; in whose reign it is manifest, the Roman Catholicks had bishops, dignitaries, priests, and religious orders of their own communion to instruct and govern them in religious matters.

By the second Article, all the Roman Catholicks of Ireland (except those who left the Kingdom, and submitted not to King William's Government) were to enjoy all their real and personal estates, and all rights, title and interest, privileges, and immunities, which they, and every, or any of them held or enjoyed in the reign of King Charles the Second ; in whose reign it is also manifest that all the Roman Catholick peers and gentlemen of Ireland and all others who would or could purchase them,

141

carried arms ; and that some of them were in posts of honours as that of sheriffs, Justices of the Peace, and other posts of profit and trust. That their lawyers, attorneys, and solicitors practised their respective callings with the same freedom and liberty as the Protestants. As also that the Roman Catholick merchants, dealers, and tradesmen were aldermen and burgesses in cities and freemen in towns and corporations, over all the Kingdom.

By the Ninth Article, the oath to be administered to such Roman Catholicks, as submitted to King William, was the oath of allegiance and no other.

The Impartial

HISTORY

OF

IRELAND.

Containing a Summary Account of all the Battles, Sieges, Rebellions, and Massacres. As also the Valour and Loyalty of the Irish, and the many Calumnys thrown on that Country and People whip'd off. Together with the most Remarkable Transactions both in Church and State, since the Reformation. In Two Parts.

By HUGH REILY Esq;

To which is annex'd,
The Nobility and Gentry of Ireland's Remonstrance to King Charles the Second, on his Restoration.

Also the Speech and dying Words of OLIVER PLUNKET, Arch Bishop of Armagh, and Primate of Ireland.

The Civil and Military Articles of Limerick.

Likewise the CASE of the Roman Catholick of Ireland Humbly Represented to both Houses of Parliament, with Remarks on the Conditions of Limerick, and the Nature of taking the Oaths of Allegiance, and Abjuration.   The latter,

By the Rever'd Doctor Nary.

Great is Truth, and Mighty above all things. 3. Esdras, 4. 41.
Strive for the Truth unto Death, and the Lord shall fight for thee. Ecclef. 4. 28.

London : Reprinted in the Year, 1744.

In confidence of this sacred tye of public faith solemnly given to them under the hands and seals of the said Lords Justices and generals, the said Roman Catholicks surrendered the City of Limerick and all the towns and garrisons then in their possession, and have ever since to this day, lived peaceably and quietly under the government of the respective Kings and Queens of Great Britain, without ever attempting to molest or disturb or raise any rebellion or tumult in it, as is evident to all the world. But how well the said Articles and this sacred tye have been kept to them ; or rather how manifestly they have been broken in upon and violated is a theme which the Roman Catholicks cannot with tears of blood sufficiently lament, *Hinc illa Lachryma.*

It would be tedious to recite all the acts of Parliament since made in this Kingdom to that purpose. Let it suffice to say that by Laws since made, all and every Roman Catholick of the Kingdom (bating a few lords and three or four colonels of the troops that were actually in Limerick and Galway at the time they surrendered) are disabled under severe penalties to carry arms defensive or offensive for their own or the defence of their houses and goods other than pitch forks or such instruments as the peasants till the earth with. Nay many gentlemen who formerly made a considerable figure in the Kingdom are nowadays when they walk with canes or sticks only in their hands, insulted by men armed with swords and pistols who of late rose from the very dregs of the people. *Servi dominati sunt nobis! Lamenta Jeremiae.*

142

All Roman Catholick lawyers, attorneys, and solicitors are disabled to practice their respective callings, except they take the Oath of Abjuration, the Oath of Supremacy and the Test, that is become Protestants. So that of about an hundred Roman Catholick lawyers and attorneys that attended the courts in Dublin and in the country, not one of them is allowed to get a morsel of bread by those studies upon which they spent their youth and their time.

All the Roman Catholicks of the Kingdom in general without any exception or saving, are disabled to purchase any lands or tenements, to take mortgages for security of money, or even to take any lease or farm exceeding the term of 30 years, and that at no less than two thirds of the improved rent. So that all encouragement for natural industry is taken away from them, and are left under an impossibility of ever being anything but slaves. By the same laws their children, though never so profligate or undutiful to their parents, upon their becoming Protestants are encouraged to compel their parents to give them a maintenance such as the Lord Chancellor for the time being shall see fit. And all heirs apparent of such parents upon their becoming Protestants make their fathers tenants for life ; so that fathers cannot, may not, provide for their other dutiful children or other extraordinary exigencies of life. Now if this be not encouraging children to transgress God's law I own I know not what it is. And will not the great Legislator of Heaven require this at men's hands ? —*Ireland's Case briefly stated* (1695).

Hugh Reily, descended from the famous Gaelic family, O Raghaille of Cavan, was Master of Chancery and Clerk of the King's Council for Ireland under James II. He accompanied James into exile, and was made Lord Chancellor of Ireland. His 'Case for Ireland' (1695), the only printed history of the country by an Irish nationalist, widely circulated during the penal times, was several times reprinted as 'The Impartial History of Ireland.'

* . * * * * *

LORD MACARTNEY (1773)

BUT the most remarkable transaction in Ireland, during the reign of Queen Anne, was the passing what are called the Popery laws ; laws, which, have yet remained unrepealed and unmitigated since their first institution.

If they have in any wise undergone alterations and amendments, those alterations and amendments have been only to sharpen their acrimony and invigorate their blows. As these laws have been represented by many as the true basis of civil liberty and the protestant religion in Ireland, I shall here endeavor to trace their origin, and describe their progress and operation. . . .

A new army of new settlers, and mostly of a newer religion . . . obtained large grants of forfeited lands in Ireland and from these adventurers are descended some of the principal persons of the kingdom in opulence and power. Most of these settlers were men of an untoward republican spirit, and of the sourest leaven, who eagerly adopted the most harsh and oppressive measures against those upon whose ruin they rose. The Restoration had secured to them their property, and the Revolution armed them with power. This power, instead of using it with justice and moderation, they stretched to the utmost rigour, and seemed determined ultimately to crush, if they could not immediately destroy. They did not, however, all at once unmask their design : they proceeded by cautious steps, and in the reign of King William, most of their provisions against popery may be justified on the principles of sound policy : but in the reign of Queen Anne they threw off all reserve, they avowed their intentions and executed them to the full. For this purpose they passed those acts, which have now for these seventy years past been the established law of the land. and which form the most compleat code of persecution that ingenious bigotry ever compiled.

It is but justice to the administration of England, to mention that they did not willingly give their consent to these severe statutes ; but not chusing, or not venturing to avow their disapprobation, they cunningly clogged the bills with a clause which they imagined would infallibly occasion them to be rejected. This clause, which introduced the sacramental test as a necessary qualification of office and employment, could not be very palatable to an assembly, where some of the principal leaders were Covenanters and Presbyterians. But these leaders on this occasion, in their severity to the scruples of others, forgot their own, and conscience was suffered to sleep while persecution raged.

The bills were passed, and the edict against popery, like the laws of the Medes and Persians, was never to be changed ; but the test clause relative to the dissenters, it was hoped, might at a favourable opportunity, either be repealed or evaded.

The laws of Ireland against Papists are the harsh dictates of persecution, not the calm suggestions of reason and policy. They threaten the Papists with penalties in case of foreign education, and yet allow them no education at home. They shut the doors of their own university against them, and forbid them to enter any other. No man shall go to lecture who will not go to church. A Papist shall not be a divine, a physician, or a soldier ; he shall be nothing but a Papist. He cannot be a lawyer, for the law is not his friend : he cannot be a soldier, and draw his sword for his country, for he is forced to draw it against it : we will not admit him into our own service and yet denounce vengeance against him if he engages in another. If he becomes a trader or mechanic, he shall scarcely enjoy the rights of a citizen. If a farmer, he shall not cultivate or improve his possessions, being discouraged by the short limitations of his tenure ; and yet we complain of the dulness and laziness of a people, whose spirit is restrained from exertion, and whose industry has no reward to excite it. This is one great cause why the Irish do not take a more rapid progress in tillage and manufactures.—*An account of Ireland in* 1773. *By a late Chief Secretary in that Kingdom.*

George Macartney (1737–1806), said to have been descended from an Ulster branch of the MacCarthys, won a great reputation as British envoy to Russia and China and Governor of Madras. He was Chief Secretary for Ireland, 1769–72.

An ACT for Banishing

all *Papists* exercising any Ecclesiastical Jurisdiction, and all Regulars of the *Popish Clergy* out of
this Kingdom.

CHAP. XXVI.

WHEREAS, it is Notoriously known, That the late Rebellions in this King-dom have been Contrived, Promoted and Carried on by Popish Arch=Bi-shops, Bishops, Jesuits, and other Ecclesias-tical Persons of the Romish Clergy. And for-asmuch as the Peace and Publick Safety of this Kingdom is in Danger, by the great number of the said Arch=Bishops, Bishops, Jesuits, Friers, and other Regular Romish Clergy, now residing here, and settling in Fra-ternities and Societies, contrary to Law, and to the great Impoverishing of many of His Ma-jesty's Subjects of this Kingdom, who are forc'd to maintain and support them; which said Romish Clergy do, not only endeavour to withdraw His Majesty's Subjects from their Obedience, but do daily stir up, and move Se-dition, and Rebellion, to the great hazard of the Ruine and Desolation of this Kingdom. For

A 2   the

Short-titles of the laws against Catholics occupy many pages in the Indexes to the Irish Statutes from William of Orange to George II. Above is shown a facsimile of a typical penal law (1739).

FATHER LUKE WADDING, O.F.M. (see page 175)

REV. T. CAMPBELL (1778)

THERE are but two churches in this large town, or rather city (Kilkenny) consisting of between two and three thousand houses ; but there are several mass-houses, each of which has congregations, vastly more numerous than both the churches. . . . You would be amazed, considering how thinly the country is inhabited, at the number of Romanists I saw on Sunday assembled together. Round the altar were several pictures, which, being at the distance of a very long nave of an old monastery, I went round to the door of one of the transepts, in order to see more distinctly. The people made way for me, and some of them offered to conduct me to where the quality sat, but this I declined. . . . The priest was very decently habited in vestments of partly-coloured silk, with a large cross embroidered on the outside. . . . Yet even here it is possible that God may be worshipped in spirit and truth. . . .

It must too be observed, that though the monasteries are destroyed, the monks remain to this day, and have regular services in their distinct houses, as in the parish mass-house. In all of which they have a succession of service on Sundays and holy-days, from early in the morning, till late at night, for the accomodation of their numerous votaries. . . . The prevalence of the Popish interest in Cork may be argued from the following trivial circumstance : bidding a fellow whom I had picked up for my *ciceroni*, to conduct me from the cathedral to the bishop's house, he asked me *which bishop?* The same conclusion I drew at Kilkenny, from another trifle ; I there heard the titular bishop greeted in the style of his dignity.

On Sunday morning early I stepped into one of their mass-houses, and a spacious one it was. The priest had just finished the celebration of mass. On the altar stood six candles. A servitor came in, after the priest had withdrawn, and, kneeling before the altar, he entered the rails like those of our chancels ; and, after kneeling again, he snuffed out two of the candles ; then he kneeled again, and snuffed out two more ; he kneeled a fourth time and extinguished the fifth ; the sixth he left burning. There were several elegant carriages standing before the door when I entered, and a prodigious crowd of people in the street ; as motley an assemblage of human creatures as I had ever seen.—*Survey of Ireland* (1778).

*   *   *   *   *   *

DR. D. A. CHART (1933)

IT is not easy to say how far the Penal Laws were actually enforced in Ireland, though it is certain that they were never enforced with the same rigour as the similar laws in France. The unpublished evidences, especially that of the King and the Southwell correspondence, suggest that when there was imminent danger of a French invasion the Roman Catholics were repressed, and that when the danger was past the Penal Code, like so many Irish laws, became a dead letter. The system of persecution was certainly very irregular. In times when the State sought to apply the laws many a tenant sought and found the protection of the

Protestant squire, or the Protestant rector of the parish, to whom he transferred his estates and who acted privately as his trustee. . . . Of the English Roman Catholic the Jesuits themselves reported that he is " either by his own position or by the good esteem of his neighbours superior to the action of the laws," and the same is true of the Irish Roman Catholic. This is clearly proved by the fact that, more than forty years after the application of the Penal Laws in 1691, the Roman Catholics still greatly outnumbered the Protestants in every part of Ireland except the counties of Antrim, Down, Derry and Armagh, in which alone the latter had a real majority. This is plain proof that the laws, though never in abeyance, were never completely enforced. The very reasons which Sir John Davies assigned for the failure of England to conquer Ireland are, with slight change, those which accounted for the failure of the Penal Laws. Those who put these ferocious enactments on the Statute Book, and kept them there without any consistent attempt to enforce them, forgot the wise maxim of Machiavelli that half measures are fatal and that the Prince must either crush or conciliate.—*History of the Church of Ireland*, Vol. III.

*   *   *   *   *   *

THE BANNER OF IRELAND, CARRIED BY THE EARL OF CLANRICARD, AT THE FUNERAL OF QUEEN ELIZABETH

Fram an early 17th Century English print.

CHAPTER IX.

State and Parliament

IN kingdoms conquered nothing but time, and that also must be the flux of hundreds of years, has power to unite the conqueror's issue and the ancient inhabitants in perfect amity.—SIR GEORGE CAREW : *A Discourse of the Present State of Ireland* (1614).

* * * * * *

THE pageantry of the procession to the House of Lords and the homage paid to the Lord Lieutenant did not enchant me ; for it exceeded even what I had expected ; and the grenadiers on horse-back, the principal officers of the household with their wands, and the pages in their liveries, paddling on foot through the mud, with grooms of chambers and footmen, through the streets lined with soldiers, had an air of absolute monarchy and of military force to support it, that had I been an Irishman I could not have endured the sight of.—LORD NUNEHAM : *Harcourt Papers*, III, 118 (1772).

* * * * * *

cúirt an meaðon oiðce

Mar o'imtiş şac oít ar críocaib Páil—
Şan sealb şan saoirse aş síolrac seanoa,
Ceannus a nolişe ná cíos ná ceannpoirt,
Scriosao an tír is ní'l 'na noiaio
In mao na luibna act plíşeac is piaoail ;
An uaisle b'pearr cum páin mar leaşoar
Is uactar láime aş páslaiş sárobre
Aş peallao le ponn is poşail şan péacaint
O'peannao na lobar 's an lom oá léirscrios.
Is oocrac oúbac mar oiuşa şac oaoirse
Ooilbe oúr i noubceilt olişte
An pann şan peróm ná paşaro ó éinne
Act clampar ooimin is luişe cum léirscrios,
Pallsact pear olişe is pactnaioe áronirt,
Cam is calşais paillişe is pábar,
Scamal an olişe aşus píoroat panncirt.
Oallaş le bríb, le *fee* 's le pallsact.

—BRIAN MERRIMAN.

149

THE MIDNIGHT COURT

That Erin lingers in thraldom long,
Wasted by woe without respite,
To misery's hand abandoned quite,
Her land purloined, her laws decayed,
Her wealth destroyed, and her trust betrayed,
Her fields and pastures with weeds o'ergrown,
Her ground untilled and her crops unsown,
Her chieftains banished and an upstart band
Of hirelings holding the upper hand.
Who'd skin the widow and orphan child
And grind the weak and the meek and mild.
Same 'tis, sure, that the poor oppressed
By lawless might, in plight distressed,
Get nought for ought but extortion vile,
The judge's fraud and the lawyer's wile,
The tyrant's frown and the sycophant's sneer
Bribing with fee and with fawning leer

—Translated by Arland Ussher.

*　　*　　*　　*　　*　　*

ALICE STOPFORD GREEN (1847–1929)

WE may observe that the extension of shires, the violent fetching in of districts in Ulster, was only the last stage in a work nearly a hundred years old. This was true also of the manipulation of boroughs, so as to neutralise the old Anglo-Irish county members 'predominantly patriotic in feeling.' A steady increase of numbers had always naturally followed on the successive plantations of Munster and of Ulster, and on the political use of the boroughs by the Crown. The introduction in a tempered and guarded way of men of 'Irish blood and Irish opinion' had formed part of the Tudor policy since Henry VIII.

Davis worked on the same lines as the officials before him, adding new shires, and making boroughs to control the shires ; this last, indeed, on a larger scale than had yet been done. He boasted in words of giving ' the new British colony and the old Irish nations ' equal and indifferent rights to make laws for themselves : in deeds he adopted the common official measures to annihilate any constitutional expression of the opinion of either. In the safeguards to prevent the will of the nation, Irish or Anglo-Irish, from having any effect there was nothing new : he merely furbished up the old Tudor methods, so well known to Ireland. His profession fitted him to elaborate the 'constitutional' methods by which the 'representative' system, piously permitted in name, should be defeated in fact. Parliamentary government remained as complete as it had been any time the last hundred years.

The legislation, moreover, of 1613 was in importance far below that of successive Tudor Parliaments. In one point, indeed, it was similar, and the confiscation of Ulster to prepare the way of plantation was merely the last of a series of Acts of forfeiture begun in 1537, and continued in 1541, 1556, 1569, and 1585. Here there was nothing new. The 'great administrator' of 1613, in fact, put the corner-stone on an old edifice of corruption and tyranny. The novelty lay in a more cynical use of force. The Attorney-General's new and original reforms were the sessions in the Castle, and the overawing of the 'representatives' of the people by the army.

Davis's parliamentary system, the seal of his 'great administration', had certain forseen and designed effects. . . . It permanently fixed in Irish ecclesiastics a civil power which was not allowed in Great Britain, and the disposal of ecclesiastical patronage became so important an element in the scheme, not of religion but of English domination, that the Church was kept as a mere servant of the ministerial interests in the House of Lords, and did in fact completely manage that House for its masters—a bitter heritage to both Church and Nation. The Lower House was expressly put 'at the service of the Government' by skilled manipulation both of the country and of the borough members : means were thus prepared to defy and defeat those national aspirations which . . . were now beginning to find 'organised constitutional expression'. Representation of 'Irish thought and opinion' was so managed as to detach the members completely from the 'patriotic' movement. . . . However England might boast of its struggles for free discussion and control of affairs by Parliament, the Houses in Dublin were from the outset signed with the mark of corruption and death. . . .

We miss the clash of vital principles. The sphere becomes contracted and dull. The story is only too liable to fall into a kind of sublimated gossip of Dublin colonists—who is bribed, who is troublesome, and who is cowardly, who can be lured to betray his country ? Round and round goes the talk of the ante-chamber. All problems and principles are brought to one monotonous test, the predominance of the English interest, and that as seen, not even in the English colony, but in London or the Castle. . . . On this lower platform the actors seem stunted and diminished. They seem to need the breath of a larger air, the proportions of a broader horizon. Irish history, indeed can have no vigorous life unless it can strike root in a deeper soil.—The Irish Parliament in the 17th Century (*Scottish Historical Review*, VII).

An eminent Irish historian of modern times, who had made a deep study of constitutional history in Ireland and England, offered the above criticism of the Irish Parliament in the seventeenth century from the standpoint of the historic Irish nation.

SIR CHRISTOPHER PLUNKET (1613)

UPON the 18th day of May, being Tuesday, the lord deputy, with all the peers of the realm, and the noblemen, the clergy, both bishops and archbishops, attired in scarlet robes very sumptuously, with sound of trumpets ; the lord David Barry, viscount Buttevant, bearing the sword of estate ; the earl of Thomond, bearing the cap of maintenance : and after all these, the lord deputy followed, riding upon a most stately horse, very richly trapped, himself attired in a very rich and stately robe of purple velvet, which the king's majesty had sent him, having his train borne up by eight gentlemen of worth : and thus, in most stately and sumptuous manner, they rode from the castle of Dublin, to the cathedral church of St. Patrick, to hear divine service, and a sermon preached by the reverend father in God, Christopher Hampton, D.D. archbishop of Armagh, and primate of all Ireland.

But as many of the nobility of Ireland, as were of the recusant [Catholic] faction, went not into the church, neither heard divine service or sermon notwithstanding that they were lords of the parliament house, and rode

A contemporary French print, reproduced on page 159, shows the Irish House of Lords in session in the reign of Queen Anne, the Duke of Ormond presiding. The Irish Parliament met at Chichester House in the reigns of Charles II, William III, and Anne. Here the Cromwellian Settlement was virtually confirmed, the Williamite confiscation completed and the foundations of the Penal Code well laid. Parliament first met in the new House in College Green in 1731. This fine building, afterwards extended, was much admired.

towards the church with other lords of estate, yet they stayed without during the time of service and sermon. Now when service was done, the lord deputy returned back to the castle, those recusant lords joined themselves again with the rest of the estate, and rode to the castle in manner as before they came from thence. . . .

And when the whole high court of parliament was set, the lord chancellor made a grave and worthy speech, concerning many great and worthy causes of estate, there to be debated upon, for the good of the kingdom, and for the commonwealth thereof ; and among many other things, his lordship declared the king's majesty's pleasure, concerning Sir John Davis, his majesty's attorney-general in Ireland ; and how his highness was pleased that he should be the speaker of the lower parliament house, and for that purpose, his majesty had by his gracious letters, recommended the said Sir John Davis unto the lord deputy, and the whole state of the parliament house, willing them to accept of him for that purpose.

After this oration ended, and other matters debated upon, as fitly appertained to the first days action of the parliament, the lord deputy rose up, and made an end for that day, being the 18th of May, 1613.

The next day, being the 19th of May, and the 2d of the parliament,

the said Sir John Davis was brought into the parliament house, to be presented, and to take his place according to his majesty's good meaning . . . and thereupon arose a great tumult, because there were two elections, *viz.*, those of the recusants sect had chosen Sir John Everard knight, for the speaker, and therefore, would in no wise accept of Sir John Davis, and in this division grew an uncertainty who had most voices ; whereupon Sir John Davis, with all those of the protestancy, went out to be numbered, and before they came in again those of the recusancy had shut the door, and had set Sir John Everard in the chair of the speaker ; but when the protestants saw that, they quietly pulled Sir John Everard out of the chair, and held Sir John Davis therein ; and thus, with great contention the 2d and 3d days were spent : but the recusants prevailed not, for Sir John Davis was maintained in the place, according to his highness's good meaning. Then did the recusants of both houses of parliament withdraw themselves, and resorted not thither any more, notwithstanding that they were often sent for by the lord deputy.

This was the first Irish Parliament since 1586, and the first in any way representative of the entire island. It signalised the suppression of Gaelic political institutions, after a struggle of four and a half centuries, crowned by the Flight of the Earls and the Ulster Plantation. To ensure a safe majority for the new administration, 39 Boroughs were created, 19 in Ulster. The Catholic nobility, mainly Anglo-Irish, strongly protested against the packing of Parliament, the overawing of its deliberations in the Castle by the Viceroy's troops, and the " extreme penal laws." King James I made a long reply in characteristic style, which concluded : "What if I have created 40 noblemen and 400 boroughs, the more the merrier, the fewer the better cheer ? "

* * * * * *

SIR RICHARD BELLINGS (1642)

THE English being now [1642] engaged in a civil war at home, the Confederate Catholics of Ireland had leisure to mould such a government as might best suit with the condition of the times, and constitution of their affairs ; to which end there met in the city of Kilkenny a very numerous assembly of prelates, of noblemen and trustees, chosen from all the counties and corporations having right to send burgesses to Parliament. . . .

In some large room appointed for the place of meeting, seats were built to the height of three ascents. Those at the upper end were designed for the lords and prelates, not so particularly, as others of the trustees did not frequently sit there with them. The chair of the Prolocutor was placed at the side of the room, somewhat nearer that end. The precedence of speaking, as to the other members of the house, was determined by the Prolocutor ; but a nobleman or prelate that offered to speak was always preferred. . . . Although they regulated their assemblies after the model of the most orderly meetings, yet they avoided, as far as was possible for them, all circumstances that might make it be thought they had usurped a power of convening a parliament. . . .

The choice of those, who as representatives of the assembly, were to govern by the name of a Supreme Council, was the work wherein they expressed the most rigorous exactness . . . . and those thus chosen, having taken the oath of counsellors, were, after the recess of the assembly, accepted and obeyed as the supreme magistrates of the Confederate Catholics.

At this meeting general orders were established, thenceforth to be observed as the model of their government; by which, after declaring that the Roman Catholick church in Ireland should have and enjoy all the privileges and immunities according to the great charter that the common law of England and all the statutes of force, in Ireland, which were not against religion, or the liberties of the natives, should be observed; that all men should bear faith and true allegiance to the king and his lawful successors, and maintain and uphold his and their rights and lawful prerogatives, against all manner of persons whatever.

They then descended to institute a settled government in the hands of trustees, to whom they continued the name of Supreme Council, with ample power in all causes, capital, criminal, and civil (the right and title of land only excepted), and over all persons of what degree or quality soever; next after it was ordered that provincial and county councils should be established, and the limits of their respective power were set forth.

Sheriffs and all other ministerial officers appointed for conserving the publick peace of the Kingdom were to execute their charge as they were wont, and no temporal government or jurisdiction was to be assumed or exercised in any part of their quarters, without it were instituted or appointed by the General Assembly, or Supreme Council.

Care was likewise taken to refrain men's violent entering into possession of such lands as they were not lawfully seized of the first of October one thousand six hundred and forty-one, a decree very necessary in such distracted times. . . .

For encouragement likewise of traffick and manufacture, they gave all artizans, artificers, makers of ships and mariners that would settle themselves and their families in the kingdom, the liberties and privileges of free denizons.

They gave order likewise for making a public seal,* and ordained many other things which were thought, both for continuing that union among themselves, to which by the oath of association then confirmed and enjoined to be taken by all the confederates, they were obliged and for advancing the war in which they were unanimously embarked.

The Supreme Council chosen in this assembly presently upon the recess of it, according to the resolution taken therein, authorized by their commission Col. Thomas Preston in Leinster, Col. Owen O'Neale in Ulster, Major Barry in Munster, and Major Roorke in Connaught, to command in chief the forces of those provinces, limiting by such instructions as they thought necessary, the ample power conferred upon them by their commission, and because the courts of foreign princes before the now establishment of the government swarmed with multitudes of agents . . . abusing the credulity of strangers, the name of their country, and the reverence

* See page 58.

155

SVPREAME
COVNCEL
OF THE
CONFEDERATE
CATHOLICQVES
OF
IRELAND.

VVEE the fupreame Councell of the faid Confederate Catholickes, hauing of a long tyme, wi
pe fenfe of the fufferings of the people, and the wayes taken to heape miferies on this a
Kingdome, beene equally diftracted betweene the care wee were oblidged to haue taken of the fafetie a

*Head of one of the Proclamations issued by the Confederation of Kilkenny (1648).
Hundreds of pamphlets and newsletters against the Confederation were published
in London. Of the proclamations printed on behalf of the Confederation in Kilkenny
and Waterford, very few copies are now in existence. The Confederation official
records, seized by the Cromwellians in 1654, were nearly all destroyed by fire in 1711.*

*   *   *   *   *   *

borne the cause for their own private benefit ; the Council after they had
intrusted several persons to agitate their affairs abroad . . . suppressed
those self intruding solicitors.

These grounds of intelligence from abroad and the conduct of their
forces at home being laid, they endeavoured to provide betimes for such
wants as did most afflict them ; and because the price of corn by reason of
much land which the distraction of the times hindered from being tilled
began to rise, and that there was a general scarcity of arms and ammunition, they commanded the magistrates of the maritime towns in their
obedience to engage such as trafficked beyond the seas to import a third
part of their lading, in wheat, iron, arms and ammunition, and to encourage
them therein, they suspended for a time the payment of custom for such
commodities.

They gave order likewise for fortifying the harbour of Wexford, both
to prevent the enemies landing there, and to encourage as well home as
foreign traffick, which now began to be set on foot ; the good market they
came to, and the example of capt. Antonio Vandezipen, who was the first
that adventured to supply the country with arms and ammunition, inviting
thereunto.—RICHARD BELLINGS (Secretary to the Supreme Council of the
Confederate Catholicks of Ireland) : *Fragmentum historicum, or the War
of Ireland . . . 1642 to 1647.*

156

SIR WILLIAM PETTY (1672)

THE government of Ireland is by the King, 21 bishops (whereof four are Archbishops), and the Temporal Peers; whereof some part, so, by reason of the late rebellion [1641-53], do not sit in Parliament.

By about 3,000 freeholders, and the members of about 100 corporations, the University at Dublin reckoned for one, represented in the House of Commons, by about 270 knights, citizens, and burgesses.

The Parliament so constituted, have a negative upon any law that the Lord Lieutenant and Council shall offer to the King, and which the King and his Council in England shall under the great seal remit to the said Parliament.

The sheriffs of counties, and of cities and counties in Ireland are 40 finally appointed by the Lord Lieutenant, each of which hath about ten bailiffs.

The Chief Governor, called sometimes Lord Lieutenant, sometimes Lord Deputy, sometimes Lords Justices, with a Council, at this time consisting of about 50 members, do govern in all matters belonging to the peace, prerogative, &c. . . .

The ecclesiastical government is by Archbishops, Bishops, Archdeacons, Deans of Cathedral Churches, in all which there are now actually but one quire entire, and that in Dublin, serving both at Christ Church and St. Patrick's. And the parsons, vicars, and curates for the Protestant religion, are in all Ireland at this day near five hundred, and about half the tythes are impropriate, and belonging to laymen.

This is the state of the external and apparent government of Ireland, so far as it concerns the number and species of persons managing the same. But the internal and mystical government of Ireland is thus, *viz.*

1. There are always about twenty gentlemen of the Irish nation and Popish religion, who by reason of their families, good parts, courtly education and carriage, are supported by the Irish to negotiate their concernments at the Court of England, and of the Viceroy in Ireland.

These men raise their contributions by the priests (who actually and immediately govern the people). The priests are governed by at least 24 Romish Bishops, all of whom have a long time been conversant in France, Spain, Italy, Germany, England, where as chaplains and almoners, &c., they have made an interest with the governing men and Ministers of State in those several kingdoms, and have obtained some benefits and preferments from them.

So as the body of the Irish Papists (being about 800,000, whereof near 700,000 do live in wretched cabbins, without chimney or window) are governed by about 1,000 secular priests, and 2,500 friars and regulars of several orders; whereof most are Franciscans, next Dominicans and Augustins, but few Capuchins and Jesuits or Carthusians.—*The Political Anatomy of Ireland*

157

THE PARLIAMENT OF JAMES II (1689)

JAMES landed at Kinsale, 12th March, 1689, about a month after the election of William and Mary by the English convention. He entered Dublin in state on the 24th March, accompanied by D'Avaux as Ambassador from France, and a splendid court. . . . On the 7th May, Ireland possessed a complete and independent government. Leaving the castle, over which floated the national flag, James proceeded in full procession to the King's Inns, where the Parliament sat. . . .

The first of (its) acts, asserting the independence of the Parliament of Ireland, is in accordance with the principle enunciated many years previously by the Supreme Council of the Irish Confederates. It is noteworthy that neither Molyneux, in his " Case of Ireland being bound by acts of Parliament in England ", nor Grattan, in his motion on the declaration of right, 1782, made any reference to the circumstance that the independence of the parliament of Ireland had been specifically asserted by the Irish Confederates in 1642, and by the parliament in Dublin in 1689.—THOMAS DAVIS : *The Patriot Parliament of 1689.*

*   *   *   *   *   *

1 . AN Act declaring that the Parliament of England cannot bind Ireland against writs of error and appeals to be brought for removing judgments, decrees, and sentences given in Ireland into England :

Whereas his Majesty's realm of Ireland is, and hath been always a distinct kingdom from that of his majesty's realm of England, always governed by his majesty and his predecessors according to the ancient customs, laws, and statutes thereof : and as the people of this kingdom did never send members to any Parliament ever held in England, but had their laws continually made and established by their own parliaments, so no acts passed in any Parliament held in England were ever binding here, excepting such of them as by acts of parliament passed in this kingdom were made into laws here ; yet of late times (especially in the times of distractions) some have pretended that acts of Parliament passed in England, mentioning Ireland, were binding in Ireland ; and as these late opinions are against justice and natural equity, and so they tend to the great oppression of the people here, and to the overthrow of the fundamental constitutions of this realm ; and to the end that by these modern and late opinions no person may be further deluded, be it therefore enacted by the King's most excellent majesty, by the advice and consent of the lords spiritual and temporal, and the commons in this present parliament assembled, and by the authority of the same, and it is hereby declared, that no act of parliament passed or to be passed in the Parliament of England, though Ireland should be therein mentioned, can be or shall be any way binding in Ireland ; excepting such acts passed or to be passed in England as are or shall be made into law by the Parliament of Ireland—*Acts of the Parliament of James II* (1689).

ON THE IRISH PARLIAMENT (1733)

Ye paltry underlings of state,
Ye senators who love to prate
Ye rascals of inferior note,
Who, for a dinner, sell a vote
Ye pack of pensionary peers,
Whose fingers itch for poets' ears
Ye bishops, far removed from saints,
Why all this rage? Why these complaints?
The point is plain; remove the cause;
Defend your liberties and laws.
Be sometimes to your country true;
Have once the public good in view;
Bravely despise champagne in court,
And choose to dine at home with port;
Let prelates by their good behaviour
Convince us they believe a Saviour;
Nor sell what they so dearly bought—
This country—now their own—for nought.

—JONATHAN SWIFT.

THE IRISH HOUSE OF LORDS IN SESSION.

JONATHAN SWIFT (1724)

MY dear Countrymen,

Having already written three letters upon so disagreeable
subject as Mr. Wood and his half pence; I conceived my t
was at an end : But I find, that cordials must be frequently applied
weak constitutions, political as well as natural. A people long used
hardships, lose by degrees the very notions of liberty, they look up
themselves as creatures at mercy, and that all impositions laid on them
a stronger hand, are, in the phrase of the Report, legal and obligato
Hence proceeds that poverty and lowness of spirit to which a kingdom m
be subject as well as a particular person. And when Esau came faint
from the field at the point to die, it is no wonder that he sold his birthri
for a mess of pottage. . . .

For let us take the whole matter nakedly, as it lies before us, with
the refinements of some people, with which we have nothing to do. H
is a patent granted under the great seal of England, upon false suggestio

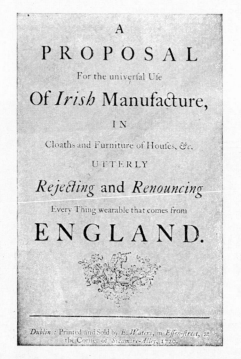

*Title pages of two famous pamphlets by Dean Swift (1720 and 1724). "Mone
the great divider of the world," said the Drapier, " hath by a strange revolution be
the great uniter of a most divided people."*

to one William Wood for coining copper halfpence for Ireland : The
Parliament here, upon apprehensions of the worst consequences from the
said patent, address the King to have it recalled ; this is refused, and a
committee of the Privy-council report to His Majesty, that Wood has
performed the conditions of his patent. He then is left to do the best he
can with his halfpence ; no man being obliged to receive them ; the people
here, being likewise left to themselves, unite as one man, resolving they
will have nothing to do with his ware. By this plain account of the fact
it is manifest, that the King and his ministry are wholly out of the case,
and the matter is left to be disputed between him and us. Will any man
therefore attempt to persuade me, that a Lord Lieutenant is to be
dispatched over in great haste by anticipating a prorogation, merely to
put an hundred thousand pounds into the pockets of a sharper by the
ruin of a most loyal kingdom. . . .

And this gives me an opportunity of explaining, to those who are
ignorant, another point, which hath often swelled in my breast. Those
who come over hither to us from England, and some weak people among
ourselves, whenever in discourse we make mention of liberty and property,
shake their heads, and tell us, that Ireland is a ' depending kingdom ',
as if they would seem, by this phrase, to intend that the people of Ireland
is in some state of slavery or dependence different from those of England ;
whereas a ' depending kingdom ', there is no more understood than that
by a statute made here in the 33d year of Henry 8th. ' The King and his
successors are to be kings imperial of this realm as united and knit to the
imperial crown of England '. I have looked over all the English and Irish
statutes without finding any law that makes Ireland depend upon England,
any more than England does upon Ireland. We have indeed obliged
ourselves to have the same king with them, and consequently they are
obliged to have the same king with us. For the law was made by our own
Parliament, and our ancestors then were not such fools (whatever they
were in the preceding reign) to bring themselves under I know not what
dependence, which is now talked of without any ground of law, reason or
common sense. . . .

'Tis true indeed, that within the memory of man, the Parliaments of
England have sometimes assumed the power of binding this kingdom by
laws enacted there, wherein they were at first openly opposed (as far as
truth, reason and justice are capable of opposing) by the famous Mr.
Molineux, an English gentleman born here, as well as by several of the
greatest patriots, and best Whigs in England ; but the love and torrent of
power prevailed. Indeed the arguments on both sides were invincible.
For in reason, all government without the consent of the governed is the
very definition of slavery : But in fact, eleven men well armed will certainly
subdue one single man in his shirt. But I have done. For those who have
used power to cramp liberty have gone so far as to resent even the liberty
of complaining, although a man upon the rack was never known to be
refused the liberty of roaring as loud as he thought fit. . . . The remedy
is wholly in your hands, and therefore I have digressed a little in order to
refresh and continue that spirit so seasonably raised amongst you, and to

161

let you see that by the laws of GOD, of NATURE, of NATIONS, and of your
OWN COUNTRY, YOU ARE and OUGHT to be as FREE a people as your brethren
in England.—*A Letter to the Whole People of Ireland. By M. B. Drapier.*

*National spirit in Ireland was at a low ebb in 1724, when Dean Swift, writing as
M. B. Drapier, began his pamphlets against Wood's copper coinage. Ireland had no
mint, and the contract for coining money was a gift from the crown. Melusina von der
Schulenberg, Duchess of Kendal, mistress of George I, sold the contract for Irish
copper coinage to William Wood, an English ironmaster, for £10,000 and profits.
Swift roused the Irish people to furious indignation about this transaction—not only by
the " Drapier's Letters " but by verses and street-ballads:*
> *"When late a feminine magician,*
> *Join'd with a brazen politician,*
> *Expos'd to blind a nation's eyes,*
> *A parchment of prodigious size."*

*" At the Drapier's call," said Lord Orrery, " a spirit arose among the people,
that in the eastern phrase, was like unto a trumpet in the day of the whirlwind. . . .
The Papist, the fanatic, the Tory, the Whig—all enlisted themselves under the banners
of M. B. Drapier." In the Fourth and most famous of the Letters, which appeared
October, 1724, Swift struck at the root of the controversy and challenged the right
of the British Parliament to make laws binding on Ireland.*

★   ★   ★   ★   ★   ★

LORD MACARTNEY (1773)

WHETHER Ireland be a conquered country, or not, has been the
subject of much idle disquisition. If the question means simply,
whether Ireland was subdued by force of arms, and I allow that
it was, what inference can be drawn from the concession? Every country
under the sun has been conquered in its turn, and almost every region
of the civilised world has undergone the revolutions of splendour and
declension. The spot of earth perhaps changes its name, and the form or
mode of its government is altered; but the rights of mankind are in
themselves the same under every sovereign and every administration.
Of what consequence then is it to the antient Irish or the later settler,
whether their country was conquered, or not? . . .

The government of Ireland is in the Lord Lieutenant and Council.
The Council can do no act without the Lord Lieutenant and his deputy,
and there are many things which the Lord Lieutenant cannot do without
the Council. The Lord Lieutenant is appointed by letters patent under
the great seal of England. . . .*

There are two Houses of Parliament, which, in antient times, were
seldom assembled but on extraordinary occasions. From 1615 to 1631,
and from 1677 to the Revolution, they were totally intermitted. At present,
there is usually a session held once in two years, and, by a late act, the same
parliament cannot be continued longer than eight years. It has been
shewn in the historical sketch that, by the law of Poynings, no Parliament
can be called, unless the causes and considerations for calling it be certified,

* There was just occupation enough as [Lord Lieutenant] to prevent a man
going to sleep, but not sufficient to keep him awake.—DUKE OF SHREWSBURY
(*Marchmont Papers,* i, 91).

162

and transmitted to England, by the Lord Lieutenant and Council. Should a Parliament be summoned without this formality, all its acts would be absolutely void. . . .

The House of Commons, being the assembly in which all motions for money and supplies usually arise, is of consequence the principal theatre of business. As the course of passing an Irish law, is, and must be, different from the course of passing an English one, I shall here state the manner of it in a few words.

Heads and sketches of a Bill or Bills, when agreed to by either House of Parliament, are sent up to the Lord Lieutenant, with a desire that his excellency will transmit them to Great Britain in due form. This form is given to them by the Lord Lieutenant and Council, by whom they are taken into consideration, and, if not rejected, are altered and amended in such manner as appears to be necessary. They are then engrossed, and become a Bill, which is certified by the Lord Lieutenant and Council as proper to be passed into a law, and, so certified, is transmitted to England under the great seal of Ireland. It is there referred, by the King and Council, to the Attorney General and Solicitor-General ; and, when revised and reported upon by them, it is then examined and considered by the King and Council, who either reject it or alter and amend it, and, so altered and amended, return it to Ireland, under the great seal of England.—*An account of Ireland in 1773. By a late Chief Secretary in that kingdom.*

*   *   *   *   *   *

SIR JONAH BARRINGTON (1760–1834)

EARLY on the 16th of April, 1782, the great street before the House of Parliament was thronged by a multitude of people, of every class and of every description, though many hours must elapse before the House would meet, or business be proceeded on. . . . Not the slightest appearance of tumult was observable ; on the contrary, such perfect order prevailed that not even an angry word or offensive expression escaped their lips. Nothing could more completely prove the good disposition of the Dublin populace than this correctness of demeanour, at a time when they had been taught that the very existence of their trade and manufactures and consequently the future subsistence of themselves and their families, was to be decided by the conduct of their representatives that very evening ; and it was gratifying to see that those who were supposed, or even proved to have been their decided enemies, were permitted to pass through this immense assemblage, without receiving the slightest token of incivility, and with the same ease as those who were known to be their determined friends.

The Parliament had been summoned to attend this momentous question by an unusual and special call of the House ; and by 4 o'clock a full meeting took place. The body of the House of Commons was crowded with its Members ; a great proportion of the Peerage attended as auditors, and the capacious gallery which surrounded the interior magnificent dome of the house contained above 400 ladies of the highest distinction,

PADDY'S RESOURCE

A cartoon published in 1780, with the words :—
"Ireland long tuned her harp in vain,
The Cannon seconds now the strain."

who partook of the same national fire which had enlightened their parents, their husbands, and their relatives, and by the sympathetic influence of their presence and zeal communicated an instinctive chivalrous impulse to eloquence and to patriotism.

Those who have only seen the tumultuous rush of Imperial Parliaments can form no idea of the interesting appearance of the Irish House of

Commons.—The cheerful magnificence of its splendid architecture—the number—the decorum and brilliancy of the anxious auditory—the vital question that night to be determined, and the solemn dignity which closed the proceedings of that awful moment—collectively produced impressions, even on disinterested strangers, which perhaps had never been so strongly or so justly excited by the appearance and proceedings of any house of legislature. Mr Pery the Speaker took the Chair at 4 o'clock. The singular wording of the summonses had its complete effect, and procured the attendance of almost every Member resident within the kingdom.

A calm but deep solicitude was apparent on almost every countenance, when Mr. Grattan entered, accompanied by Mr. Brownlow, and several others, the determined and important advocates for the Declaration of Irish Independence. Mr. Grattan's preceding exertions and anxiety had manifestly injured his health ; his tottering frame seemed barely sufficient to sustain his labouring mind, replete with the unprecedented importance and responsibility of the measure he was about to bring forward. He was unacquainted with the reception it would obtain from the connexions of the Government ; he was that day irretrievably to commit his country with Great Britain, and through him Ireland was either to assert her liberty, or start from the connexion. . . .

For a short time a profound silence ensued :—it was expected that Mr. Grattan would immediately rise—when the wisdom and discretion of the Government gave a turn to the proceedings, which in a moment eased the Parliament of its solicitude, Mr. Grattan of the weight that oppressed him, and the people of their anxiety. Mr. Hely Hutchinson (then Secretary of State in Ireland) rose. He said that his Excellency the Lord Lieutenant had ordered him to deliver a message from the King, importing that, ' His Majesty being concerned to find that discontents and jealousies were prevailing amongst his loyal subjects of Ireland, upon matters of great weight and importance, recommended to the House to take the same into their most serious consideration, in order to effect such a *final* adjustment as might give satisfaction to both kingdomss'. And Mr. Hutchinson accompanied this message with a statement of his own views on the subject, and his determination to support a declaration of *Irish Rights* and Constitutional *Independence*.—Thus, on the 16th of April, 1782, did the King of Ireland, through his Irish Secretary of State, at length himself propose to redress those grievances through his Irish Parliament ; an authority which, as King of England, his Minister had never before recognised or admitted.

In a moment the whole scene was completely changed ; those miserable prospects which had so long disgusted, and at length so completely agitated the Irish people, vanished from their view. . . . Another solemn pause now ensued. Mr. Grattan remained silent—when Mr. George Ponsonby rose, and, after eulogizing the King, the British Minister, and the Irish Government, simply proposed an humble address in reply. —It is an observation not unworthy of remark, that in describing the events of that important evening, the structure of the Irish House of

165

Commons, at the period of these debates, was particularly adapted to convey to the people an impression of dignity and of splendour in their legislative assembly. The interior of the Commons' House was a rotunda of great architectural magnificence; an immense gallery, supported by Tuscan pillars, surrounded the inner base of a grand and lofty dome. In that gallery, on every important debate, nearly 700 auditors heard the sentiments and learned the characters of their Irish representatives; the gallery was never cleared on a division; the rising generation acquired a love of eloquence and of liberty; the principles of a just and proud

AN IRISH VOLUNTEER, 1780.

ambition; the details of public business; and the rudiments of constitutional legislation. The front rows of this gallery were generally occupied by females of the highest rank and fashion, whose presence gave an animating and brilliant splendour to the entire scene; and, in a nation such as Ireland then was, from which the gallant principles of chivalry had not been altogether banished, contributed not a little to the preservation of that decorum so indispensable to the dignity and weight of deliberative assemblies. . . .

After the speech of Mr. Hutchinson, which, in fact, decided nothing, a low confidential whisper ran through the house, and every Member seemed to court the sentiments of his neighbour, without venturing to express his own; the anxious spectators, inquisitively leaning forward, awaited with palpitating expectation the development of some measure likely to decide the fate of their country, themselves, and their posterity; no middle course could be possibly adopted; immediate conciliation or tranquility, or revolt and revolution, was the dilemma which floated on every thinking mind—a solemn pause ensued—at length Mr. Grattan, slowly rising from his seat, commenced the most luminous, brilliant and effective oration ever delivered in the Irish Parliament.

" I am now," said he, "to address a free people : ages have passed away, and this is the first moment in which you could be distinguished by that appellation.—I found Ireland on her knees, I watched over her with an eternal solicitude ; I have traced her progress from injuries to arms, and from arms to liberty. Spirit of Swift! spirit of Molyneux! your genius has prevailed! Ireland is now a nation! in that new character I hail her! and, bowing to her august presence, I say, *Esto perpetua*."—*Rise and Fall of the Irish Nation*.

* * * * * *

*T*HE *Irish Volunteers originated in* 1778, *during the American War of Independence, when the British Government was unable to defend the coasts of Ireland against a French invasion. The Volunteers, though controlled by the Anglo-Irish ascendancy, became increasingly nationalist in their martial parades and in the temper of their declarations and resolutions. Their armed strength made it possible for Henry Grattan to win for Ireland the repeal of Poynings' Law, liberty of external trade (called " Free Trade "), legislative independence, and the passage of an Act in British Parliament, renouncing all claim to make laws for Ireland.*

The bright prospect which appeared to be opening for Ireland in 1782–3 *is thus summarised by William Lecky : " Ireland from the slave of England had now risen to the dignity of independence. She participated at last in all that was best in the English Constitution. Her religious animosities were rapidly fading beneath the strong national sentiment which had arisen, assisted by the intellectual tendencies of an eminently tolerant age. She had regained her freedom both of commerce and manufacture, and might reasonably hope with returning peace to attain some measure of returning prosperity. After a long winter of oppression and misery, the sunlight of* hope shone brightly upon her, and a new spirit of patriotism and self-reliance had begun to animate her people."—(History of Ireland in the Eighteenth Century, vol. II, 317). The first of the following passages is from a description of the parade of the Volunteers in Dublin, 4 November, 1779; the second from the resolutions of the famous convention at Dungannon, 15 February, 1782.

* * * * *

SIR JONAH BARRINGTON (1779)

At ten o'clock in the forenoon, the different bodies of Volunteers of this city and county, consisting of the cavalry commanded by their own officers; the corps of the city and Liberty, to the right of the county, commanded by his grace, the Duke of Leinster; and the county of Dublin corps, commanded by captain Gardiner; assembled at St. Stephen's green, and having made a proper disposition, with drums beating and colours flying, they marched in files, through York-street, Aungier-street, Bishop-street, Bride-street, Werburgh-street, Castle-street, Cork-hill, and Dame-street, till they arrived at College-green. . . .

At the discharge of a rocket, and taking the word of command from his grace the Duke of Leinster, they fired grand discharges; beginning

Irish Volunteers exercising before Leinster House, Dublin, in 1779. "Leinster House," said Malton (1794), "the town residence of his Grace the Duke of Leinster, is the most stately private house in the city." Richard Castle or Cassells, the architect, designed many other fine mansions in Dublin. Leinster House is now the seat of the National Parliament (Oireachtas) of Eire. To the left are the National Library and the National College of Art, and to the right is the National Museum.

168

with the Dublin Volunteers on the north side, and followed by the county
Volunteers on the south, taking the word of command from captain
Gardiner. So much order and regularity were seldom observed, even
among veterans, nor was the uniform precision of their firing, perhaps,
to be surpassed by any troops in Europe. After this there was a discharge
of small cannon, which was placed in the centre; and the whole body
of Volunteers then separated. . . . The number of spectators on this
occasion were almost incredible. Every avenue that leads into College
green, was so crowded that all free intercourse subsided until the whole
was over. At every discharge of the musketry, repeated huzzas were
given by the surrounding multitude; and everything seemed to breathe
that noble spirit of liberty and enthusiastic patriotism which first gave
rise to those guardians of our freedom.

The firing of twenty-one cannon announced the first movement of
the delegates from the royal Exchange to the Rotunda; a troop of the
Rathdown cavalry, commanded by colonel Edwards, of Old-court,
county of Wicklow, commenced the procession; the Liberty brigade
of artillery, commanded by Napper Tandy, with a band, succeeded.
A company of the barristers' grenadiers, headed by colonel Pedder,

with a national standard for Ireland, borne by a captain of grenadiers, and surrounded by a company of the finest men of the regiment came after, their muskets slung, and bright battle-axes borne on their shoulders. A battalion of infantry, with a band, followed, and then the delegates, two and two, with side arms, carrying banners with motto and in their respective uniforms—broad green ribands were worn across their shoulders. Another band followed playing the special national air alluded to. The chaplains of the different regiments, in their cassocks, marched each with his respective corps, giving solemnity to the procession, and as invoking the blessing of heaven on the surrounding multitude. Several standards and colours were borne by the different corps of horse and foot ; and another brigade of artillery, commanded by councillor Calbeck, with labels on the cannons' mouths, was escorted by the barristers' corps in scarlet and gold (the full dress uniform of the kings' guards) ; the motto on their buttons being ' Vox populi suprema lex est.')

The procession itself was interesting, but the surrounding scene was still more affecting. Their line of march, from the Exchange to the Rotunda, was through the most spacious streets and quays of the city, open on both sides to the river . . . an immense body of spectators, crowding every window and house-top ; . . . every countenance spoke zeal, every eye expressed solicitude, and every action proclaimed triumph : green ribands and handkerchiefs were waved from every window by the enthusiasm of its fair occupants ; crowds seemed to move on the house-tops ; ribands were flung on the delegates as they passed. . . . Those who did not see or who did not recollect that splendid day, must have the mortification of reflecting, that (under all its circumstances) no man did before, and no man ever will, ' behold its like again.'—*Rise and Fall of the Irish Nation.*

* * * * * *

THE DUNGANNON CONVENTION (1782)

At a meeting of the representatives of 143 Corps of Volunteers of the Province of Ulster held at Dungannon, 15th February, 1782.

Resolved unanimously, That a claim of any body of men other than the King, Lords, and Commons of Ireland to make laws to bind this Kingdom, is unconstitutional, illegal, and a grievance.

Resolved unanimously, That the ports of this country, are by right open to all foreign countries not at war with the King, and that any burden thereupon or obstruction thereto, save only by the Parliament of Ireland, are unconstitutional, illegal and a grievance.

Resolved (with two dissenting voices only to this and the following resolution) that we hold the right of private judgment in matters of Religion, to be equally sacred in others as in ourselves.

Resolved therefore, That as men, and as Irishmen, as Christians, and as Protestants, we rejoice in the relaxation of the Penal Laws against our Roman Catholic fellow-subjects, and that we conceive the measure to be fraught with the happiest consequences to the union and prosperity of the inhabitants of Ireland.—*Resolutions.*

The

POST-CHAISE COMPANION:

OR,

Travellers Directory;

through

IRELAND.

Containing a new and Accurate Description of the direct and principal Cross Roads, with particulars of the Noblemen and Gentlemen's Seats, Cities, Towns, Parks, Natural Curiosities, Antiquities, Castles, Ruins, Manufactures, Loughs, Glens, Harbours, &c. &c.

—— Forming ——

An Historical & descriptive Account of the Kingdom.

To which is added,

a *DICTIONARY*, or

Alphabetical Tables.

Shewing the distance of all the Principal Cities, Boroughs, Market and Sea port Towns, in Ireland from each other.

Darling scrip.ᵗ   **Dublin**   J. Duff sculp.ᵗ

Printed for the Author, Nᵒ 6, Dame Street.

CHAPTER X.

Ireland Overseas

LET no one asperse the character of the Irish because they fought so often under foreign colours. Exiled, persecuted, and loyal, they lent their value to the States which supported their dethroned kings, their outlawed religion, their denationalised country, their vow of vengeance, or their hopes of freedom. Viewed carelessly at a distance, their varied services seem evidence of an unprincipled prætorian race ; examined in detail, with references to the creed, politics, and foreign relations of Ireland at each period, they only prove an amount of patriotism, piety, and valour which, concentrated at home to national service, would have made Ireland all we could wish her.—MATHEW O'CONOR : *Military History of the Irish Nation* (1855).

*　　*　　*　　*　　*　　*

ıs ᴀn ᵬꞃᴀınᵹc

ıs ᴀn ᵬꞃᴀınᵹc ım' ᴅúıseᴀċꞇ ᴅᴀṁ,
ı nÉıꞃınn Cuınn ım' ċoᴅlᴀᴅ;
ᵬeᴀᵹ ᴀꞃ nᵹꞃᴀᴅ uᴀıᴅ ᴅo'n ꝼᴀıꞃe,
'Ꝺo ċál suᴀm áꞃ síoꞃ-ꝼᴀıꞃe.

(In France I am when awake,
In Ireland when asleep ;
Little, therefore, do I love to wake,
For in sleep I am awake always).
—FATHER PATRICK HACKET, O.P. [1600–54].

*　　*　　*　　*　　*　　*

ⱞo ꞇꞃeıᵹıᴅ! mo ꞇuᵬᴀısꞇ! mo ꞇuꞃꞃᴀınn! mo ᵬꞃón! mo ᴠıꞇ!
ᴀn soıllseᴀċ muıꞃneᴀċ mıoċᴀıꞃ-ᵹeᴀl ᵬeol-ꞇᴀıs cᴀoın,
ᴀᵹ ᴀᴅᴀꞃcᴀċ ꝼuıꞃıonn-ᴅuᵬ mıoꞃcᴀıseᴀċ cóıꞃneᴀċ buıᴅe;
'S ᵹᴀn leıᵹeᴀs.'nᴀ ᵹoıꞃe ᵹo ᵬꝼıllıᴅ nᴀ leoᵹᴀınn ꞇᴀꞃ ꞇúınn.

(O my sickness, my misfortune, my fall, my sorrow, my loss !
My bright, loving, kind, soft-lipped gentle girl
In the grip of a hornéd, wicked, malicious, yellow scoundrel with his black band,
And without prospect of relief till our heroes come back over the Sea.)
—EGAN O'RAHILLY [1690–1726].

*T*HE following is a list—by no means complete—of Irish Colleges established on the Continent of Europe in the late sixteenth and during
the seventeenth century, when the education of Irishmen professing
the Catholic faith had been made impossible at home. The dates of foundation
in some instances are approximate :

Douai 1577	Louvain (Franciscan) .. 1606	
Alcala 1590	Seville (Amalgamated with	
Salamanca 1592	Salamanca 1769) .. 1612	
Lisbon 1593	Lille.. 1610	
Bordeaux 1605	Rome (St. Isidore's) .. 1625	
Paris 1605	Rome 1627	
Santiago 1605	Madrid 1629	
(Amalgamated with Sala-	Antwerp 1629	
manca 1769)	Toulouse 1640	
	Poitiers 1674	
	Nantes 1680	

*Brief impressions are given in the following pages of the most famous of
the Irish colleges—those at Salamanca, Louvain, and Rome—all still in
existence (1947). We add the moving tribute paid by a modern Irish poet,
Padraic Colum, to the old Irish College, Paris, at which more than half of the
Irish Catholic secular clergy were educated during the eighteenth century :*

    ★   ★   ★   ★   ★   ★

SALAMANCA : THE KING (1592)

*T*HE University of Salamanca was the greatest in Europe in the sixteenth
century, with its twenty-five colleges, which included " El Real
Colegio de Nobles Yrlandeses " (The College of the Irish Nobles).
This college was established by Philip II. Writing to the Rector, Chancellor
and Faculty of the University, the King says :

" As the Irish youths, who had been living in a kind of communi.y
in this city, have resolved to go to yours, to avail of the opportunities it
affords for advancement in letters and languages, a house having been
prepared for them, in which they intend to live under the direction of
the Fathers of the Society of Jesus ; besides allowing them a good annual
stipend, I desired to give them this letter to charge you, as I hereby do,
to regard them as highly recommended ; so as not to allow them to be
molested in any way, but to favour and aid them as far as you can, that as
they have left their own country, and all they possessed in it, in the service
of God, our Lord, and for the preservation of the Catholic faith, and mak?
profession of returning to preach in it, and suffer martyrdom if necessary,
they may get in that University the reception they seek."—VALLODOLID,
2nd August, 1592. *Yo El Rey.*

173

Almost all the students educated in this seminary have complied with their obligations—the exceptions indeed are very few—of going to the Mission in Ireland, and have supplied their own island and even England and Scotland, with eminent prelates, missionaries, and martyrs, as is well known to the natives of this kingdom, to the number of 510. . . .

At present there are only two priests prepared to go to Ireland in May. They will probably go from Bilbao in some Spanish or Irish vessel, or from some of the ports of France, from which there are more frequent sailings to the North. I intend to advise them to disguise themselves as sailors, that they may be able to leave the ship and get into the country, which is the most usual and the best means of effecting that object. If they receive their viaticum, they shall be more able to induce the captain with whom they sail to favour their landing disguised as I have described. —FATHER JOSEPH DELAMAR, Rector of the College, to the King of Spain.

★   ★   ★   ★   ★   ★

LOUVAIN : DR. JOHN LYNCH (1662)

*T*HE *Franciscan Convent of St. Anthony at Louvain, which became the centre of Irish life in the Spanish Netherlands in the early seventeenth century, " was established by Father Florence Conry, the Irish scholar and patriot, afterwards Bishop of Tuam, his purpose being to set up a noviceship and a house of studies for the Irish Franciscan friars lately driven from Donegal, their last regular house of studies at home."*—(FATHER BRENDAN JENNINGS, O.F.M. : *The Irish Franciscan College of St. Anthony at Louvain.) Philip III of Spain endowed the college with an annual grant, and Irish soldiers in the Spanish service helped with subscriptions. Among the Irish books printed at Louvain was Father O'Hussey's Catechism, the first Catholic book to be printed in Irish. From Louvain Brother Michael O'Clerigh was sent by his superior to collect materials in Ireland for the Annals of the Four Masters. (See page 53.)*

The labours of the Reverend Fathers of the Order of St. Francis, in the College of Louvain, will, we hope, once more revive the Irish language. . . . . In this undertaking, the indefatigable zeal of the Very Reverend John Colgan, professor emeritus of Theology, stands nobly pre-eminent among all the writers on the history of our country. We have already seen many books printed in the Irish type, at the press of the College, and we are expecting soon from the same source a copious Irish dictionary, which some of the fathers are said to be compiling.

Thus, if the English must thank their monks of Tavistock, for the preservation of the Saxon, the Irish are similarly obliged to the Louvain fathers, for the preservation and refinement of the Irish. Perhaps, of the two, the benefit conferred on Ireland is the greater, since those fathers stood forward when she was reduced to the greatest distress, nay, threatened with certain destruction, and vowed that the memory of the glorious deeds of their ancestors, should not be consigned to the same earth that covered the bodies of her children. May the wisdom of God be ever praised and adored, for inspiring those fathers with the resolve, that the ancient glory of Ireland should not be entombed by the same convulsion which deprived the Irish of the lands of their fathers and of all their property.—*Cambrensis Eversus*, Vol. II (1662).

Dr. John Lynch [1599–1673] *was Archdeacon of Tuam. He escaped to France after the capture of Galway by the Cromwellians* (1652). " *Cambrensis Eversus,*" (*published in St. Malo ?*) *is a long and able vindication of the Irish people and a reply to the anti-Irish tirades of Giraldus Cambrensis.*

*　　*　　*　　*　　*　　*

ROME : CARDINAL MORAN (1861)

THE Irish College for the secular clergy in Rome, as most of the other Irish Continental institutions, dates its origin from the time of persecution. Gregory XIII (1572–85) had more than once contemplated the establishment of such an asylum for our nation, but the demands for arms and supplies made on him by the Irish princes then combating for their lives and religion, consumed the various sums set aside by him for this purpose. The bishops of Ireland, however, were persevering in their solicitations and in a *Relatio status* of the Irish Church presented to Rome in 1625, the foundation of an Irish College is insisted on. . . .

Notwithstanding the repeated solicitations of the Irish bishops, it was only in the year 1627 that the College was at length established through the munificence of Cardinal Ludovisi, nephew of Gregory XV, and through the untiring exertions of the illustrious ornament of the Franciscan Order in the seventeenth century, Father Luke Wadding. This wonderful man, having already founded the convent of St. Isidore for the members of his own order, earnestly laboured to have a similar institution opened for the secular clergy. An occasion soon presented itself and, indeed, a truly propitious one. Urban VIII had, on his accession to the Papal throne, nominated Cardinal Ludovisi Protector of Ireland. . . . It was this Cardinal's desire, in which he was confirmed by his most intimate friend, Luke Wadding, to render to the Irish Church some important service calculated to perpetuate the memory of his protectorate. " It was not a difficult matter," says the simple narrative from which we learn these particulars, " to convince his Eminence that no other work was more worthy of his munificence, or could render more lasting service to the Irish Church, than the foundation of a missionary college for the youth of that nation."—*Memoirs of Blessed Oliver Plunket* (1861).

Father Luke Wadding (1588–1657), *a native of the city of Waterford, was educated at Kilkenny, Coimbra, and Lisbon. He was President of the Irish College at Salamanca* 1617–18, *and spent the rest of his life in Rome.* " *To write the full story of Wadding's life in Rome,*" *Father Gregory Clery justly says,* " *is to write the history of the Church in Ireland during a large and important part of the seventeenth century.* . . . *Wadding's greatest literary achievement was the ' Annales Ordinorum Minorum,' a history of the Franciscan Order from its foundation. This great work, which critics never ceased to extol, places its author in the foremost rank of ecclesiastical historians.*" *During the Confederation of Kilkenny the Irish people looked to Wadding's influence* "*for the provision of the foreign monetary and military necessaries essential for the success of the war of liberation in which they had engaged.*"

ROSC CATA NA MUMAN.

D'aitnigeas féin gan bréag ar fuact,
'S ar anfad Tétis taob le cuan,
Ar canad na n-éan go séiseac suairc,
Go gcaspad mo Séasar glé gan gruaim.
    Measaim gur subac do'n Mumain an fuaim,
    'S d'á maireann go dubac de crú na mbuad,
    Torann na dtonn le sleasaib na long
    Ag tarraing go teann 'n-ár gceann ar cuaird.

Tá lasad 'san gréin gac lae go neoin,
Ni taise do'n ré, ni téideann fé neoil,
Tá barra na gcraob ag déanam sceoil
Nac fada beid Gaedil i ngéibeann bróm.
    Measaim gur subac do'n Mumain an ceol,
    'S d'á maireann go dubac de crú na dtreon,
    Torann na dtonn le sleasaib na long
    Ag tarraing go teann 'n-ár gceann fé seol. . . .

Gac duine dfuil Milead bán na gcréact,
Curaide na dtraoi mear láidir éact,
Do millead le dlige 's do crádad le claon,
Cuiread gan moill an báire i sém.
    Measaim gur subac do'n Mumain i gcém,
    'S d'á maireann go dubac de crú na dtréan,
    Torann na dtonn le sleasaib na long,
    Ag tarraing go teann 'n-ár gceann le faobar.

—PIARAS MAC GEARAILT (1745?)

MANY of the leading personages in the Jacobite movement were Irish, and innumerable songs in the Irish language show how much the people hoped for the return to the throne of the exiled House of Stuart. Of the " Seven Men of Moidart," who landed with Prince Charles Edward in Scotland in 1745, four were Irishmen. The poem which is often called Rosc Cata na Muman—Munster War Song—was written by Pierce FitzGerald, probably in 1745. It calls on Munster to rejoice and rise up to greet the coming of the Prince. In contrast to most of the Gaelic Jacobite poetry, the tone is one of exultation : " The song," says Róis Ní Ógáin, " is full of joy of light, the singing of birds, the music of wind among trees, and the swish of the waves through which the French ships are coming under full sail to Ireland."

★ ★ ★ ★ ★ ★

176

THE OLD COLLEGE OF THE IRISH, PARIS.

The Lombards having gone back to their land,
We, who might never flock to native land
Except like birds that fly like fugitives,
Desperately, in a wind across the sea,
We drew our brood to their forsaken nest.
The Lombards' halls became the Irelanders',
And charity was craved for us—'twas given
In names of Almantza and Namur,
Cremona, Barcelona, Charleroi—
Fields that our soldiers bled on for a cause
Not ours, under command not ours.

Our order broken, they who were our brood
Knew not themselves the heirs of noted masters,
Of Columbanus and Erigena :
We strove towards no high road of speculation,
Towards no delivery of gestated dogma,
No resolution of age-long disputes.
Only to have a priest beside the hedges,
Baptising, marrying,
Offering Mass within some clod-built chapel,
And to the dying the last sacrament
Conveying, no more we strove to do—
We, all bare exiles, soldiers, scholars, priests.

—PADRAIC COLUM.

*   *   *   *   *   *

SIR JOHN GILBERT (1904)

WE now turn to . . . publications of Irish authors, and in connexion with Ireland, printed on the Continent in the seventeenth century. Most of these were in Latin, but some were in Irish, English, French, Italian, or German.

The places at which these works chiefly appeared were as follows :—Antwerp, Bologna, Bolsano in the Tyrol, Boulogne, Brussels, Cologne, Douai, Dunkirk, Frankfort, Innsbruck, Lille, Lisbon, Louvain, Lucca, Lyons, Madrid, Mentz, Milan, Mons, Naples, Paris, Passau, Prague, Rome, Rouen, Spira, St. Malo, St. Omer, Sultzbach, Trient, Vienna, Wurtzburg. The books published in these places varied in size from the folio to the octodecimo. In point of extent the greatest of them was the collection of the works of Duns Scotus in fifteen folio volumes, edited entirely by expatriated Irishmen, and published at Lyons in 1639.

Somewhat later in date were the folio volumes in which other exiled Irish scholars—Colgan and Fleming—transmitted to posterity surviving remnants of the ancient Gaelic literature of Ireland. It may be added

177

that few European publications of their age are now sought for with greater avidity or rank higher in money value than some books published abroad by Irish editors of the seventeenth century.

The Irish authors who wrote in Latin usually added to their names on the title-pages the word " Hibernus." In some cases they mentioned the part of Ireland to which they belonged, as in the case of Dr. John O'Dwyer of Cashel, who styled himself " Casseliensis," on the title-page of his treatise *Querela Medica*, published at Mons in 1686. The books in the Irish language, printed within this period, were published at Brussels, Louvain and Rome.—*Irish Bibliography*.

✱   ✱   ✱   ✱   ✱   ✱

ABBE MACGEOGHEGAN, CHAPLAIN (1758).

EUROPE, towards the end of the last century, was surprised to see your fathers abandon the delights of a fertile country, renounce the advantages which an illustrious birth had given them in their native land, and tear themselves from their possessions, from kindred, friends, and from all that nature and fortune had made dear to them : she was astonished to behold them deaf to the proposals of a liberal usurper, and, following the fortunes of a fugitive king, to seek with him in foreign climes, fatigues and danger, content with their misfortune, as the seal of their fidelity to unhappy masters.

France . . . gladly opened to them a generous bosom, being persuaded that men so devoted to their princes, would not be less so to their bene-factors ; and felt a pleasure in seeing them march under her banners. Your ancestors have not disappointed her hopes. Nervinde, Marseilles, Barcelona, Cremona, Luzara, Spire, Castiglione, Almanza, Villa Viciosa, and many other places, witnesses of their immortal valour, consecrated their devotedness for the new country which had adopted them. France applauded their zeal, and the greatest of monarchs raised their praise to the highest pitch by honouring them with the flattering title of " his brave Irishmen."

The example of their chiefs animated their courage : the Viscounts Mountcashel and Clare, the Count of Lucan, the Dillons, Lees, Rothes, O'Donnels, Fitzgeralds, Nugents, and Galmoys, opened to them on the borders of the Meuse, the Rhine, and the Po, the career of glory, whilst the O'Mahonys, MacDonnels, Lawlesses, the Lacys, the Burkes, O'Carrolls, Croftons, Comerfords, Gardners, and O'Connors, crowned themselves with laurels on the shores of the Tagus.

The neighbouring powers wished to have in their service the children of those great men : Spain retained some of you near her throne. Naples invited you to her fertile country ; Germany called you to the defence of her eagles. The Taffs, the Hamiltons, O'Dwyers, Browns, Wallaces and O'Neills, supported the majesty of the Empire, and were entrusted with its most important posts. The ashes of Mareschal Brown are every day watered with the tears of the soldiers, to whom he was so dear, whilst the O'Donnels, Maguires, Lacys, and others, endeavoured to form them selves after the example of that great man.

Russia, that vast and powerful empire, an empire which has passed suddenly from obscurity to so much glory, wished to learn the military discipline from your corps. Peter the Great, that penetrating genius and hero, the creator of a nation which is now triumphant, thought he could not do better than confide that essential part of the art of war to the Field Mareschal de Lacy and the worthy daughter of that great emperor, always entrusted to that warrior, the principal defence of the august throne which she filled with so much glory. Finally, the Viscount Fermoy, general officer in the service of Sardinia, has merited all the confidence of that crown

But why recall those times that are so long past? Why do I seek your heroes in those distant regions? Permit me, Gentlemen, to bring to your recollection that great day, for ever memorable in the annals of France; let me remind you of the plains of Fontenoy, so precious to your glory; those plains where in concert with chosen French troops, the valiant Count of Thomord being at your head, you charged, with so much valour, an enemy so formidable: animated by the presence of the august sovereign who rules over you, you contributed with so much success, to the gaining of a victory, which, till then, appeared doubtful. Lawfeld beheld you,

Ornamental Heading from the Dedication in Abbé MacGeoghegan's " Histoire de Tirlande ancienne et moderne," Vol. I (Paris, 1758).

two years afterwards, in concert with one of the most illustrious corps of France, force entrenchments which appeared to be impregnable. Menin, Ypres, Tournay, saw you crown yourselves with glory under their walls, whilst your countrymen, under the standards of Spain, performed prodigies of valour at Campo Sancto and at Veletri.

But whilst I am addressing you, a part of your corps is flying to the defence of the allies of Louis, another is sailing over the seas to seek amidst the waves another hemisphere, the eternal enemies of his empire.

According to calculations and researches that have been made at the War Office, it has been discovered that, from the arrival of the Irish troops in France, in 1691 to 1745, the year of the Battle of Fontenoy, more than 400,000 Irishmen died in the service of France.

*　　*　　*　　*　　*　　*

W. E. H. LECKY (1880)

THE Austrian army was crowded with Irish soldiers and officers, and there was scarcely a siege or a battle between the Revolution and the Peace of Aix-la-Chapelle in which Irish troops did not take part. At Fontenoy they formed a large part of the column whose final charge broke the ranks of the English. When Cremona was surprised by Eugene, the Irish troops first arrested the progress of the Imperialists, and to their stubborn resistance the salvation of the town was mainly due. When the Germans had surprised the Spaniards at Melazzo in Sicily, the Irish troops in the Spanish service turned the scale of victory in favour of their side. In the great battle of Almanza the denationalising influence of religious persecution was strangely shown. . . .

Sarsfield, having taken part in the glories of Steinkirk, closed his heroic career in the arms of victory at Landen. Irish troops shared the disasters of the French at Blenheim, Ramillies, Oudenarde and Malplaquet. They fought with Vendome at Luzzara, Cassano, Calcinato, at Friedlingen and Spires, in the campaign of Catinat in Piedmont, in the campaigns of Berwick in Flanders and in Spain.

It is in these quarters that the real history of the Irish Catholics during the first half of the eighteenth century must be traced. At home they had sunk into torpid and degraded pariahs. Abroad there was hardly a Catholic country where Irish exiles or their children might not be found in posts of dignity and power. Lord Clare became Marshal of France. Browne, who was one of the very ablest Austrian generals, and who took a leading part in the first period of the Seven Years' War, was the son of Irish parents ; and Maguire, Lacy, Nugent, and O'Donnell were all prominent generals in the Austrian service during the same war. Another Browne, a cousin of the Austrian commander, was Field-Marshal in the Russian service and Governor of Riga.

Peter Lacy, who also became a Russian Field-Marshal, and who earned the reputation of one of the first soldiers of his time, was of Irish birth. He enlisted as a mere boy in the army of James, left Ireland at the time of the Treaty of Limerick, was compelled to quit the French army on the reduction of the forces which followed the Peace of Ryswick, and

CHARLES O'BRIEN, VISCOUNT CLARE, EARL OF THOMOND, MARSHAL OF FRANCE
(1691–1761)

Lord Clare commanded the Irish Brigade at the battle of Fontenoy (1745). His uncle, the fourth Viscount, was killed at the battle of Marsaglia (1693) and his father, the fifth Viscount, was mortally wounded at Ramillies (1706). The third Viscount first raised and commanded " Clare's Dragoons," " the flower of King James's army," which were cut to pieces at the battle of Lisnaskea. Charles O'Brien refused an offer from King George I to restore to him the family title and estates—over 80,000 acres— on condition that he should change his religion and allegiance.

181

having entered the service of Russia, he took a leading part in organising the army of Peter the Great, and served with brilliant distinction for the space of half a century in every Russian campaign against the Swedes, the Poles, and the Turks. He sprang from an Irish family which had the rare fortune of counting generals in the services both of Austria, Russia and Spain. . . .

Among Spanish generals the names of O'Mahony, O'Donnell, O'Gara, O'Reilly, and O'Neil sufficiently attest their nationality, and an Irish Jacobite named Cammock was conspicuous among the admirals of Alberoni. Wall, who directed the government of Spain with singular ability from 1754 to 1763, was an Irishman, if not by birth at least by parentage. MacGeoghegan, the first considerable historian of Ireland, was chaplain of the Irish Brigade in the service of France. . . . Tyrconnel was French Ambassador at the Court of Berlin. Wall, before he became chief minister of Spain, had represented that country at the Court of London. Lacy was Spanish Ambassador at Stockholm, and O'Mahony at Vienna.

SPANISH SOLDIERS—18TH CENTURY

These examples might easily be increased, but they are quite sufficient to show how large a proportion of the energy and ability of Ireland was employed in foreign lands, and how ruinous must have been the consequences at home. If, as there appears much reason to believe, there is such a thing as an hereditary transmission of moral and intellectual qualities, the removal from a nation of tens of thousands of the ablest and most energetic of its citizens must inevitably, by a mere physical law, result in the degradation of the race.—*A History of Ireland in the Eighteenth Century*, Vol. I.

CHARLES FORMAN · (1754)

I CANNOT expect that any gallant, worthy Briton will either turn pale or grow splenetick at any praises justly bestow'd upon an Irishman, or think the worse of his Bravery because his fellow-subject has Courage. King William heard of the Business of Cremona a few Days before his Death, and the only alleviating Circumstance the generous Hero found in that unfortunate Affair, was the gallant Behaviour of the Irish : because, tho' they were his Enemies, they were nevertheless his Subjects, and the glory they acquired by their Courage in that Action, on which the fate of France and Spain depended, receiv'd still a greater Lustre by the Honour his Majesty thought it did to his British Dominions. That great Prince knew that the Irish had an Aversion to him ; he had nevertheless an Esteem and Friendship for them.

Louis XIV. not only trusted them in Flanders ; but also in Alsaace, Italy, Piedmont, Catalonia, and in every Place where the War was hottest. Wherever they served . . . it may be said to their eternal Honour, that from the Time they enter'd into the Service of France, to this Hour, they have never made the least false Step, or have had the least Blot in their Scutcheon. . . . In the Siege of Barcelona, in the year 1697, the great Vendome was so charmed with their Courage, and so amazed at the Intrepidity of their Behaviour, that the particular Esteem and Notice with which he distinguish'd them, even to the Day of his Death, is yet very well remembered in France. If what I say here is not literally true, there are Frenchmen enough still living to contradict me. Nor was the Behaviour of Clare's Regiment commanded by the Lord Clare in Person, less remarkable at Blenheim, where they cut a Dutch or German Regiment to Pieces, consisting of 1,500 Men, and commanded by Colonel Goore. . . .

At Ramillies, we see Clare's Regiment shining with Trophies, and covered with Laurels again, even in the midst of a discomfited routed Army . . . and their Courage precipitated them so far in Pursuit of their Enemy, that they found themselves engaged at last in the Throng of our Army, where they braved their Fate with incredible Resolution, till an Italian Regiment, in the Service of France, and a Regiment vulgarly called the Cravats, generously pushed up to their Relief, and as bravely favour'd their Retreat. I could be much more particular in relating this Action, but some Reasons oblige me, in Prudence, to say no more of it. However, if you are desirous to know what Regiment it was they engaged that Day, the Colours in the Cloister of the Irish Nuns at Ypres, which I thought had been taken by another Irish Regiment, will satisfy your Curiosity. The brave Lord Clare himself, who was noted in the French Army for his Intrepidity in Action, was mortally wounded in this Battle, and died a few days after in Brussels. . . .

In the Battle of Blaregnies or Malplaquet, where Lee's, O'Brian's (which was Clare's, and is now Clare's again), Dorrington's, now Roth's, called the Royal Irish, Galmoy's and O'Donnel's Regiments of Foot and also Nugent's Regiment of Horse, of whose Bravery against the Germans at Spireback, I have given an Account in my Letter to Sir

THE IRISH COLLEGE, SALAMANCA

(" EL REAL COLEGIO DE NOBLES YRLANDESES ")

*The College was founded by King Philip II of Spain in
when Spain and the Spanish Netherlands were the chief refuges
students, soldiers, clergy, and merchants, exiled for faith and fat
The building has been described as one of the most beautiful in S*

Robert. . . . As I grow quite tired with relating Facts known to so many Thousands of living Witnesses, and indeed to almost everybody but the candid, undesigning, good-natured *Free Briton*, I shall not enter into any particular Detail of the Behaviour of the Irish at Cremona, because it has been many Years in Print in more Forms than one. . . .

To their Valour in a great Measure France owes, not only most of what Trophies she gain'd in the late War, but even her own preservation. At Spireback, Nugent's Regiment of Horse, by a brave Charge upon two Regiments of Cuirassiers, brought a compleat Victory to an Army, upon which Fortune was just turning her Back. At Toulon, Lieutenant-General Dillon distinguish'd himself, and chiefly contributed to the Preservation of that important Place. To the Irish Regiments also, under the conduct of that intrepid and experienced Officer, Count Medavi himself very generously attributed his Victory over the Imperialists in Italy : and the poor Catalans will for ever have reason to remember the name of Dillon, for the great share he had in the famous Siege of Barcelona, so fatal to their Nation. . . . In short the Irish Troops did the Allies the most considerable Damage which they received in the last War.—*A Defence of the Courage, Honour and Loyalty of the Irish Nation* (1754).

★   ★   ★   ★   ★   ★

JAMES GRANT (1880)

The deeds of the Irish regiments in the Spanish service would fill volumes. . . . Owen Roe O'Neil, of Ulster, rose to high rank in the Spanish Imperial service and held an important post in Catalonia. He defended Arras against Louis XIII. in 1640, and when forced to surrender, he did so, says Carte, " upon honourable terms ; yet his conduct in the defence was such as gave him great reputation, and procured him extraordinary respect even from the enemy " ; and the brave O'Sullivan Bearra of Dunboy, who fled in the days of James I., became Governor of Corunna under Philip IV.

Lieutenant-General Don Carlos Felix O'Neile (son of the celebrated Sir Neil O'Neile of Ulster, slain at the battle of the Boyne), was Governor of Havannah and favourite of Charles III. of Spain ; he died at Madrid in 1791, after attaining the great age of one hundred and ten years.

In 1780, Colonel O'Moore commanded the Royal Walloon Guards of Charles III. In 1799, Field-Marshal Arthur O'Neil was Governor-General of Yucatan under the same monarch, and commanded the flotilla of thirty-one vessels which made an unsuccessful attack on the British settlements in the Bay of Honduras. In the same year, Don Gonzalo O'Farrel was the Spanish ambassador at the Court of Berlin, and in 1808 he was Minister of War for Spain. In 1797, O'Higgins was Viceroy of Peru, under Charles IV., one of whose best generals was the famous Alexander Count O'Reilly.

Don Pedro O'Daly was Governor of Rosas when it was besieged by Gouvion St. Cyr in 1809 ; and General John O'Donoghue was chief of Cuesta's staff, and one of the few able officers about the person of that indolent and obstinate old hidalgo, whose incapacity nearly caused the ruin of the Spanish affairs at the commencement of the Peninsular War. He died Viceroy of Mexico in 1816.

DEFENCE

OF THE

Courage, Honour, and Loyalty

OF THE

IRISH-NATION.

IN

Answer to the Scandalous Reflections in the FREE-BRITON and Others.

WITH

Some extraordinary *Particulars* relating to the Battles of the *Boyne* and *Aghrim*, and the two Sieges of *Limerick*, not to be met with in the Histories of those Times.

Also of the *Bravery* of the *Irish* at *Benburb*, *Cremona*, *Spires*, *Dettingen*, *Fontenay*, &c.

By *CHARLES FORMAN*, Esq;

DUBLIN:

Printed and sold by EBENEZER RIDER in *George's lane*, near *Chequer-lane*.
M DCC LIV.

O'Higgins was Viceroy of Peru under Ferdinand VI. and the third and fourth Charles of Spain. He signalized himself with great bravery in the wars with the Araucanos, a nation on the coast of Chili, who were ultimately subdued by him and subjected to the Spanish rule. . . . In 1765, he marched against the Araucanos with a battalion of Chilian infantry and fifteen hundred horse named Maulinians. He was thrice brought to the ground by having three horses killed under him; but the Araucanos were routed, and the Spanish rule extended over all Peru, of which he died Viceroy in the beginning of the present century, after fighting the battles of Rancagua and Talchuana, which secured the independence of Chili.

Few names bear a more prominent place in Spanish history than those of Blake, the Captain-General of the Coronilla, and O'Reilly, a soldier of fortune, who saved the life of Charles III. during the revolt at Madrid, and who reformed and disciplined anew the once noble army of Spain.

Alexander Count O'Reilly was born in Ireland about 1735, of Roman Catholic parents, and when young entered the Spanish service as a sub-lieutenant in the Irish regiment with which he served in Italy during the war of the Spanish Succession, and received a wound from which he was rendered lame for the rest of his life. In 1751 he went to serve in Austria, and made two campaigns against the Prussians, under the orders of Marshal Count Lacy, his countryman. Then in 1759 he passed into the service of Louis XV. under whose colours was still that celebrated Irish Brigade whose native bravery so mainly contributed to win for France the glory of Fontenoy.

*　　*　　◂　　⁂　　*　　*

SIR CHARLES OMAN (1918)

The continuous history of the Spanish-Irish regiments may be started on 1st November, 1709 ; but Irishmen not only served under the Spanish colours, but had formed whole units in the Spanish army for short periods in the preceding century. . . . Not only O'Donnell and Tyrone, but thousands of other Irish rebels made their way, some to Spain and some to the Spanish Netherlands. . . . There was a similar development in the reign of Charles I., when, from the moment of the sending of Strafford to govern Ireland in 1633 down to the extinction of the Irish rebellion by Cromwell in 1652, there was an enormous emigration of fighting men of the Catholic party from the island. Those of them who drifted to Spanish soil were welcomed, and embodied in the ephemeral regiments of O'Reilly, O'Brien, Gage, Murphy, Coghlan, Dugan and Dempsey. . . . The first Irish regiments taken into the Spanish service were those of the Marquis of Castlebar and Dermot MacAuliffe, both of which received their patent of creation from the King of Spain at Saragossa on 1st November, 1709 . . . . When the Spanish War Office (long years before our own made the same reform) resolved to give every unit a permanent title, Castlebar received the name of Hibernia ; MacAuliffe that of Ultonia [Ulster] ; Vendome that of Limerick ; Comerford that of Waterford ; Waucope that of Irlanda. But this sensible change was only made by a

188

royal decree signed at Barcelona on 15th May, 1718, long after all the regiments had been some time in the Spanish service.—*Journal of Royal United Services Institute.*

* * * * * *

THOMAS CARLYLE (1858)

A GERMAN-IRISH gentleman, this General (ultimately Field Marshal) Graf von Browne; one of those sad exiled Irish Jacobites, or sons of Jacobites, who are fighting in foreign armies; able and notable men several of them, and this Browne considerably the most so. We shall meet him repeatedly within the next eight years. Maximilian-Ulysses Graf von Browne: I said he was born German; Basel his birthplace (23rd October, 1705), Father also a soldier: he must not be confounded with a contemporary Cousin of his, who is also 'Fieldmarshal Browne,' but serves in Russia, Governor of Riga for a long time in the coming years. This Austrian General, Fieldmarshal Browne, will by and by concern us somewhat; and the reader may take note of him.

Who the Irish Brothers Browne, the Fathers of these Marshals Browne, were? I have looked in what Irish Peerages and printed Records there were, but without the least result. One big dropsical book, of languid quality, called *King James's Irish Army-List*, has multitudes of Brownes and others, in an indistinct form; but the one Browne wanted, the one Lacy, almost the one Lally, like the part of *Hamlet*, are moitted. There are so many Irish in the like case with these Brownes. A Lacy we once slightly saw or heard of; busy in the Polish-Election time,—besieging Dantzig (investing Dantzig, that Munnich might besiege it); that Lacy, 'Governor of Riga,' whom the *Russian* Browne will succeed, is also Irish; a conspicuous Russian man; and will have a Son Lacy, conspicuous among the Austrians. Maguires, Ogilvies (of the Irish stock), Lieutenants 'Fitzgeral'; very many Irish; and there is not the least distinct account to be had of any of them.—*History of Frederick the Great of Prussia.*

* * * * * *

THE ANNUAL REGISTER (LONDON), 1767

O N the 17th of this month [March] his Excellency, Count Mahony, Ambassador from Spain to the Court of Vienna, gave a grand entertainment in honour of St. Patrick, to which were invited all persons of condition, that were of Irish descent; being himself a descendant of an illustrious family of that kingdom. Among many others were present Count Lacy, President of the Council of War, the Generals O'Donnel, McGuire, O'Kelly, Browne, Plunket, and McEligot, 4 Chiefs of the Grand Cross, 2 Governors, several Knights Military, 6 staff officers, 4 Privy Councillors, with the principal officers of state; who, to shew their respect to the Irish nation, wore crosses in honour of the day, as did the whole Court.—*The Annual Register.*

Index

	PAGE
ABBOTT, W. C. (*Preface to Cromwell's Speeches*) ..	67–9
ADVERTISEMENTS OF IRELAND ..	11
AHERLOW, GLEN OF	9
ANNALS OF THE KINGDOM OF IRELAND (*Four Masters*)	
" ⱥnoċⱅ ıs uⱥıꝼneⱥċ éıꝛe " (" *To-Night Ireland*	30, 52 , 20–9
AUGHRIM, BATTLE OF, THE ..	95–6
BANNER OF IRELAND, THE ..	148
BARRINGTON, SIR JONAH ..	123, 163–7
BELFAST ..	48, 49, 131
BELMORE, EARL OF	45–6, 126–7
BENBURB, BATTLE OF ..	64–6
BERKELEY, GEORGE, BISHOP OF CLOYNE	109–11
BOYNE, BATTLE OF THE	VIII—IX
BUSH, JOHN ..	125
CAMPBELL, REV. T. ..	101, 128–32, 147
CASTLEHAVEN, EARL OF	56–8
CATHOLICKS OF IRELAND, STATEMENT	55–6
céıⱅınn, seⱥċꝛún (*Geoffrey Keating*)	8–10
CHART, D. A. ..	147
CHICHESTER, SIR A., LORD DEPUTY	30–5, 42–3
" cıll ċⱥıs " (*Kilcash*) ..	26–7
CLARE, CHARLES, 6TH VISCOUNT	181
CLONMEL, SIEGE OF ..	73–5
COLLEGES, IRISH, ABROAD ..	173–5, 177–8, 184–5
COLUM, PADRAIC	177
CONFEDERATION OF KILKENNY	54–66, 154–6
CONNAUGHT ..	24–5, 103
CORK ..	12, 130, 136–7, 147
CROMWELLIAN SETTLEMENT, THE	67–77
cúıꝼı̇ò nⱥ h-éıꝛeⱥnn	101
CUSTOM HOUSE, DUBLIN, THE	128
DAVIES, SIR JOHN ..	30–1, 42
DAVIS, THOMAS ..	158
DE ROCHEFORT, A JOUVIN DE	16–17, 135–6
DERRY, SIEGE OF, THE	78, 83–6
DINELY, THOMAS ..	20–2
DROGHEDA, STORM OF, THE ..	69–70
DUBLIN ..	5, 16–17, 128–9
DUNGANNON CONVENTION, THE	170–1
" eⱥmon ⱥn ċnuıc " (" *Ned of the Hill* ")	111
FERGUSON, SIR SAMUEL	38–9
FLIGHT OF THE EARLS, THE ..	28–337